METHUEN LIBRARY REPRINTS

BRITISH ANTIQUITY

BRITISH ANTIQUITY

by

T. D. KENDRICK

Keeper of British Antiquities
in the British Museum

with 16 plates
and 4 text illustrations

BARNES & NOBLE, Inc.
New York
METHUEN & CO. Ltd
London

First published, 1950

This edition reprinted, 1970
by Barnes & Noble, Inc.
and Methuen & Co. Ltd.

Barnes & Noble ISBN 389 04050 9

Methuen ISBN 416 17360 8

Printed in the United States of America

Ad Jo. Piperum necnon et Jo. Betjehominem,
Lelandi discipulos

Preface

THIS book is based on the notes I have made under the heading "Britain" while studying some general varieties of antiquarian thought in Europe. It seemed to me that the British chapter covering the period from the late fifteenth century to the early seventeenth century was interesting enough to stand as a story by itself, for not only does it introduce us to great men like Leland and Camden, but its strictly antiquarian content has the importance of being closely linked to both the history and the literature of Tudor and early Stuart times. I have added a preliminary section dealing briefly with the Middle Ages and our two fifteenth century antiquaries, Rous and Worcester; but the book is in the main concerned with sixteenth century England, and the transition from medieval to modern antiquarian thought.[1]

I should like to thank the Trustees of the British Museum, the Chapter of the College of Arms, and the Master and Fellows of Corpus Christi College, Cambridge, for permission to take photographs of manuscripts and books in their respective collections, and for permission to reproduce them. I thank, especially, my colleague, Bertram Schofield, for his photograph (Pl. V) from Corpus, Cambridge, MS. 210, brilliantly replacing one of my failures. I likewise acknowledge gratefully, help received from Martin Holmes F.S.A., Hugh London F.S.A., Dr. W. Douglas Simpson F.S.A., Anthony Wagner F.S.A., Richmond Herald, and from my colleagues T. C. Skeat and Francis Wormald. For permission to reproduce photographs supplied to me I am indebted to the Trustees of the British Museum and to the National Buildings Record, and I also desire to thank the Royal Numismatic Society for allowing me to reproduce the medal of Richard White (Pl. VI, a).

T. D. KENDRICK

British Museum, 1949

---

[1] Because it is thus parochial in scope and intention, I have not attempted here to define the terms 'antiquarian thought' and 'antiquary', a difficult task that will be more conveniently performed in a work on a larger scale. I hope, however, the omission will not cause confusion in this circumscribed study.

Contents

		PAGE
	PREFACE	vii
I	THE BRITISH HISTORY IN THE MIDDLE AGES	I
II	JOHN ROUS AND WILLIAM OF WORCESTER	18
III	THE TUDOR CULT OF THE BRITISH HISTORY	34
IV	JOHN LELAND	45
V	THE MEDIEVAL TRADITION	65
VI	THE BATTLE OVER THE BRITISH HISTORY	78
VII	THE ECLIPSE OF THE BRITISH HISTORY	99
VIII	BRITANNIA	134
	INDEX	169

Plates

Between pages 20–21

I   *a.* Brutus sacrificing to Diana: Matthew Paris, 13th Century
Corpus, Cambridge, MS. 26, p. 7
    b. Brutus sacrificing to Diana: Fabyan's *Chronicle*, 1516

II   *a.* John Rous, self-portrait
    b. The youthful Edward III, drawing by John Rous
both from Rous Roll, College of Arms

III   *a.* Caradoc; *b.* Rohand; *c.* Wolgeat
Rous Roll, College of Arms

IV   *a.* Thurkill; *b.* John de Plessitis; *c.* Thomas Beauchamp
Rous Roll, College of Arms

V   Page from William of Worcester's notes
Corpus, Cambridge, MS. 210, p. 129. Photo by B. Scholfield

VI   *a.* Richard White of Basingstoke: medal by Ludovico Leoni,
1568   *Numismatic Chronicle 4S. IX (1909), Pl. XXI*
    b. William Camden: bust in Westminster Abbey
Photo by National Buildings Record

VII   Stonehenge, an engraving signed R.F. 1575. *British Museum*

VIII   Illustrations in Camden's *Britannia*, edition of 1600

Between pages 116–117

IX   Illustrations from Norden's *Cornwall*, MS. of *c.* 1610
    a. Doniert Stone; *b.* Dunheved Castle
British Museum, Harley 6252, pp. 85, 93

X   Drawings of tombs by Robert Cooke, Clarenceux. 1569
    a. Edward, Lord Despenser. Tewkesbury
    b. Robert, Duke of Normandy. Gloucester
College of Arms MS. CN. 1659

XI   *a.* Brutus: from Godet's *Chronicle*, *c.* 1562
    b. Royal Arms of Queen Elizabeth: from Norden's *Hertford-shire*, 1598

XII   Drawings by John White, *c.* 1585
    a. A Red Indian; *b.* A native of Britain   *British Museum*

XIII *a* A Pict: drawing by John White, *c.* 1585   *British Museum*
    b. Ancient Britons: drawing by Lucas de Heere, *c.* 1575
                    British Museum Add. MSS. 28,330, f. 8b

XIV Engravings by Theodore de Bry, 1590
    a. Male neighbour unto the Picts;
    b. Woman neighbour unto the Picts

XV Illustrations of Ancient Britons: from Speed's *Historie,* 1611

XVI Title-page of Speed's *Theatre,* 1611

Text Illustrations

FIG.   PAGE

1 Lead cross found in King Arthur's grave. Camden, 1607   98

2 Medieval inscription, St. John's-sub-Castro, Lewes.
    Camden, 1586   151

3 Carew's illustration of the Doniert stone, 1602   162

4 Camden's illustration of the Doniert stone, 1607   163

The British History in the Middle Ages

THE medieval antiquary in Britain—who in the context of this chapter is the chronicler writing on the subject of his country's early inhabitants—knew little and cared little about the sympathetic understanding of prehistoric man that had been achieved by the educated Roman. In pagan Latin literature, among grimmer references to the beastlike barbarism of the first men, there are frequent reflections upon the simplicity and happy innocence of the life of the ancient folk—*quam bene Saturno vivebant rege*—and to the Roman poets had been given a vision of the actual state in which an early food-gathering or simple agricultural community lived. Lucretius (Book V) thought in terms of a Stone Age, Bronze Age, and Iron Age, and speculated about the first use of fire and the origin of language and navigation and farming and weaving. Varro and Ovid were prehistorians. The Romans could picture their city vanished, and in the unspoilt countryside where it had stood they imagined the Stone Age shepherd with his flocks; they could picture the Tiber desolate except for the primitive fishing-boats; they guessed what life must have been like in the poor little hut with its rough furniture; they wrote of the wooden platter and the simple food of fruit and herbs. Where in their day stood the temple and the imposing stone statue, they could imagine the original tiny clearing and the rough-hewn figure of the wooden god.

The medieval chronicler had no interest in this archæologically plausible vision. The remote history of Rome was in his view more properly represented by fables about heroic founders. Livy, for instance, though he did not believe in such stories as that of Romulus and Remus, had nevertheless expounded the grand story of the Aeneid, and that was precisely the right kind of plausible and splendid past for a great people. The medieval antiquary believed his own nation's history should start in a similar manner, and he was in no way prepared to think of these origins in anything but the familiar terms of his own later annals; he wanted to find a long succession of early dynasties and full lists of their kings with regnal years; he wanted to trace them back to Japhet or Aeneas; he wanted his heroes of the distant past to be adventurous princes, with armed followers, who founded empires and built towns. In other words he was searching not for an unexplored prehistory, but for more history of a familiar and favourable kind. That his antiquarian enquiry was conducted with almost no sense of historical propriety and an equally small regard for truth is in the main due to two causes.

In the first place our chronicler was a man who had lost touch not only with Roman antiquarian sensibility, with which indeed he was not professionally concerned, but with the methods of chronological research that had produced the intelligently controlled antiquarian studies of the Early Christian scholars, particularly of the third and fourth century A.D. He was, it is true, acquainted with the principal results obtained by these writers of the Early Church, but he knew nothing of the pains and discipline that the preparation of their works demanded, and he could turn to no medieval school of history for instruction in the duty of criticism or even for just a modest standard of accuracy. A medieval chronicler with the challenging powers of an Abelard or a John of Salisbury might have thought it worth while to break through the crust of traditional racial nonsense so solemnly and so often repeated in the opening pages of every chronicle that began with a "first inhabitants" chapter; there were indeed, as we shall see, a few writers who did express some surprise at the statements they read in other chronicles and were expected to pass on as proven history; but for the most part the chronicler-antiquary was not more than an ordinary scholar of the monastic scriptorium, an uncritical servant of his age. Secondly, not only had he lost touch with Late Antique historiography, but he was to so great an extent influenced by the theology of the medieval Church that he was disposed to regard the business of the antiquary as something that was in its main aspect irrelevant; for he knew that the past, whether discovered or undiscovered, was as God had ordained, and that human history, once corporate pride had been satisfied, did not really matter. What did matter was God's direction of human history, and in comparison with the providential story of the human race on its short journey from the Garden of Eden to the Gates of Heaven— with its incessant demand for a theodicy and its overwhelming

apprehension of an apocalypse—the antiquary's little preface to a
history-book seemed an insignificant trifle of almost unnecessary
information. It is, indeed, this sense of a lack of ultimate significance in a sequence of merely human activities that must be the
source of the nonchalance and irresponsible equanimity with
which historical fables were so often repeated—"he that will
trow it, trow it; he that will nowt, lefe."

The chronicler-antiquary may have been uncritical and easily
gullible, but the story he told about his own country's remote
past was not an innocent fairy-tale. In our own land, even though
"Abraham be ignorant of us, and Israel acknowledge us not",
it was his purpose to establish that the British, like the ad-
mittedly senior nations of the Mediterranean and the Near
East, did come into remote history, and were not barbarians,
deservedly left out of the main story of the ancient world. He
contended that the founder of the British people was descended
from Noah through Aeneas. It was a matter of pedigrees, and it
was everybody's game. In Western Europe it may have been the
Germans who first claimed membership of the family of the
truly venerable nations. They had begun with an ordinary origin-
myth of a primitive people, declaring themselves sprung from an
earth-god; but those of them who became the Merovingian
Franks and, after Clovis's triumph in the early sixth century, a
great nation, felt it necessary to tell a correspondingly grander
tale. One seventh century legend stated outright that the Franks
were dispossessed Trojans, of whom a party under a King Francio
had settled on the Rhine; another story named four brothers
Francus, Romanus, Britto, and Albanus, who in due course
founded the united people of Merovingian Gaul, that is to say
the Franks, the Gallo-Romans, the Bretons, and the Alamanni;
and then it was shown that these brothers were descended from
Japhet, the first proprietor of Europe after the Flood. Gregory of
Tours (d. 594), the great historian of the Franks, had done nothing to advance or support these claims, but by the reign of
Charlemagne the second story was accepted history, and the
British chronicler Nennius repeated the legend in the ninth century; needless to say the British had concluded that Britto had
founded not the Bretons but the Britons.

They found it easy to improve on this story. Consulting the

encyclopædic synopses of early history such as the Eusebius—
Jerome *Chronicon*, they found there were *reges Albanorùm*, surely
the kings of Albion, descended from Aeneas, through his son
Silvius, and a Brutus who conquered Spain *usque ad Oceanum*; he
was assumed to be Britto, and to put him far enough back[1] in
time he was at first said to be a brother of Romulus and Remus,[2]
and, later, the son of Silvius and grandson of Aeneas. After all the
Italians had accepted a saga of Trojan origin; the Franks had one;
let Britain do the same and begin its history with the splendid
figure of Brutus, the prince of Trojan blood.[3]

It was, be it noted, the British chroniclers, not those of the
Saxons, who thus claimed a Trojan ancestry. The Saxons were
comparatively recent settlers, and their historians knew it.
Neither the Venerable Bede in the eighth century nor the
chronicler Ethelwerd in the tenth century referred to the story of
Brutus; but the Britons, who were the dispossessed inhabitants of
a Roman province, took great pleasure in the legend, for it
showed them to be a people of high antiquity whose ancestors
were connected with a major event in world-history, the fall of
Troy. No doubt boasts of their Trojan origin and references to
Brutus occurred often in the recitals of the *fili*, the British poet-
antiquaries, during the Viking Period; but the times were not
propitious for the composition of a long romantic history, and
there is no early sign of a detailed story about Brutus; it was not,
in fact, until about seventy years after the Norman Conquest
that a complete saga of Brutus was given to the world, and when
it came, it was a stirring narrative complete with copious detail
and much exciting action and many grandiloquent speeches.
This is the brilliant book, the *Historia Regum Britanniae* of Geoffrey of Monmouth, that became one of the principal successes of
European secular literature in the Middle Ages.

The famous " British History" was written *c.* 1135, probably at
Oxford, by a Welsh cleric, believed to be of Breton birth, who at
the end of his life became Bishop of St. Asaph. Unlike the usual
medieval histories here and on the Continent, chronicles continuing to the writer's own times, Geoffrey of Monmouth's book
was exclusively a study of the remote past, and it contained in-

[1] D. Junius Brutus Gallaecus was Consul in 138 B.C.
[2] The first Consul, L. Junius Brutus, of the time of the Tarquins is a link.
[3] See in general Nennius, Chartres text, ed. Mommsen, M.G.H. Auct. Ant. xiii, p. 149,
n. 1 and p. 150. Cf. Eusebius-Jerome, a. ab. Abr. 878 and 1875.

formation that the author regarded as his own very special contribution to antiquarian studies. It was, Geoffrey claimed, a scoop, the triumphant publication of a most important discovery, a complete account of the British kings between Brutus the Trojan and Cadwallader, the last of the ancient rulers and a known historical personage. Henry of Huntingdon (d. 1135), for the purposes of his own history, had been inquiring about these kings, and, finding nothing, had had to begin with the Roman occupation; Henry made no secret of his delight in Geoffrey's remarkable find, and Geoffrey himself strongly advised his contemporary historians to keep off the subject of the early kings of Britain until they had heard what he had to say. He maintained that his good fortune was due to a *vetustissimus liber*, a book in the British tongue brought from Brittany[1] by a learned and important friend, Walter, Archdeacon of Oxford; this Geoffrey said he had translated into Latin, and he described it as a continuous narrative written in a very elegant style; but he explained he had made a digest of it rather than a literal translation, and had interpolated a number of passages of his own.[2]

There has since been much controversy about this *vetustissimus liber*, and even to-day it is not finally decided whether Geoffrey was an outright liar or was telling what might be generously described as a quarter-truth. There was no traditional knowledge that such a long and detailed chronicle about the British kings had been written before Geoffrey's time—the surprise of his contemporaries is proof of this—and there is no allusion to such a work in any surviving historical manuscript known then or thereafter; and, of course, the *vetustissimus liber* itself has disappeared. It is immediately certain to give just one example of the doubts that arise on reading the *Historia*, that a truly ancient source would not have contained references, as does Geoffrey's book, to Iceland by that name, and there is, in fact, plenty of internal evidence to show that Geoffrey could not have been translating an earlier chronicle that bore any close relation to his own work. Therefore the *Historia Regum Britanniae* rests under the suspicion of having been an imaginative historical novel written by Geoffrey, and if this be indeed the case, we should note not only that the author told lies about his source, but also that he

---

[1] "From Wales" is a possible reading.
[2] Cf. *Hist. Reg. Brit.* I, 1; xi, 1; xii, xx.

was an antiquary of remarkably wide reading and of very great ingenuity.[1]

It was probably not true, however, that the *Historia* is a complete invention from start to finish. Geoffrey was certainly a man of immense imaginative powers, but it seems likely that he did have a collection of fragmentary sources of a derived and inferior kind, perhaps traditional material transmitted orally in the form of short tales about King Arthur and the Trojan origin of the British, and possibly a Celtic text of the Viking period that added something to the meagre information given by Nennius. His jubilant references to Archdeacon Walter's mysterious volume are much more emphatic than the usual "old book" story, and there are signs that he did in fact compose his *Historia* under some kind of guidance and restraint. The failure of such a supposedly mischievous author to make his Celtic romance a little more plausible by a sensible use of the Roman histories has often been noticed; but it is not so much the omissions as the actual matter that suggests Geoffrey was at least under some control from previously written records. Thus it is improbable that to a few lines, a mere skeleton entry, about Malgo (Maelgwn Gwynedd), described as a sodomite, Geoffrey would of his own accord expand Gildas's brief reference to Malgo's conquests into a statement that this unpleasant king made himself master of the Viking empire (Ireland, the Orkneys, Iceland, Norway, Sweden, and Denmark), an achievement that with much greater solemnity is later said to be one of the principal glories of Geoffrey's King Arthur.

This controversy about the *vetustissimus liber* must not, however, delay us. Even if Geoffrey did occasionally incorporate some information obtained from a quite recent document written during the Viking dominion in Western Europe, the *Historia Regum Britanniae* may safely be regarded as in general a twelfth-century invention, and our present study of antiquarian thought in England begins with the publication of this famous work, which, in accordance with later custom, we shall henceforward call the British History or, occasionally and for variety, the Brut, as Geoffrey's *Historia* in various condensed and strangely embroi-

[1] Geoffrey's learning will be best appreciated by those who have read Arthur E. Hutson's *British Personal Names in the Historia Regum Britanniae*, University of California, English publns. 5, No. 1 (1940).

dered forms is the invariable opening of the great English chronicle known as the Common Brut. What we have to note now is that however much Geoffrey may have cheated, even if he were nothing more than a romantic novelist with an antiquarian taste, he was the author of the most significant book in the history of British antiquities. Within fifteen years of its publication not to have read it was a matter of reproach; it became a respected text-book of the Middle Ages; it was incorporated in chronicle after chronicle; it was turned into poetry; it swept away opposition with the ruthless force of a great epic; its precedents were quoted in Parliament; two kings of England cited it in support of their claim to dominion over Scotland; it was even used to justify the expenditure of the royal household; it became the subject of a noisy battle between modernist and medievalist scholars in the sixteenth and seventeenth centuries; even in the eighteenth century there were antiquaries who believed it to be truthful history, and it is still the subject of study and argument. Though in very brief summary, we must therefore remind ourselves of the contents of the British History.

The story is this. Brutus the Trojan arrived in Britain at the time when Eli was High Priest [*c.* 1170 B.C.]; he conquered the Giants whom he found in possession of the island, and he built London, which was called Trinovantum or New Troy. After his death his eldest son ruled England, his second son Scotland, and his third son Wales, but the King of Scotland, Albanact, was killed and the whole realm reverted to the line of Brutus's eldest son, in other words to the kings of England.

In direct descent from Brutus and about a century later there was a great king Ebrancus who built many towns and conquered Gaul and Germany; and later kings were Bladud, who built Bath [*c.* 900 B.C.] and his son Lear, the father of Goneril, Regan and Cordelia; but the dynasty afterwards changed with the usurping king of Cornish origin, Dunwallo Molmutius, a famous law-maker; his sons Belinus, the builder of Billingsgate, and Brennus conquered Gaul, and afterwards captured Rome, at a date Geoffrey probably imagined to be about 500 B.C.[1] A son of Belinus then subdued Denmark. There follows a succession of about fifty kings of the Molmutian dynasty, and then we come to Cassibellanus, brother of King Lud, who had given his name

[1] He confused the sack of Rome by Brennus (390 B.C.) with that by Porsenna.

to London, and this is the period of the invasion of Julius Caesar
who is twice defeated by the British and glad to be allowed to
make peace and get back to Italy. At length Arviragus, King of
the Britons, submitted to Claudius; but the British king married
the daughter of the Roman Emperor, and eventually revolted, at
which point Vespasian was sent to Britain with the result that a
chastened Arviragus was forced to rule in an orderly manner in
friendship with Rome. Thereafter comes the period of the great
King Lucius who was buried in Gloucester Cathedral in the year
A.D. 156 after a reign during which Britain was first converted to
Christianity. The dynasty is interrupted by Carausius, a man of
humble birth, but he is succeeded by a king from the Cornish
nobility, Asclepiodotus, who freed his country of the Romans
after a campaign that ended in the massacre of Walbrook, where a
whole legion was wiped out by decapitation.[1] The next notable
figure is King Coel of Colchester who was succeeded on the
throne of Britain by Constantius, a Roman senator who married
Coel's daughter Helen, the British mother of the Emperor Constantine the Great.

After the Romans depart we have the story of Vortegirn and
the coming of the Saxons, and the prophecies of the great seer
Merlin that foreshadow much of the history of England from the
sixth to twelfth century. The hero, Aurelius Ambrosius, a man
of British and Roman birth is victorious over the Saxons, and it
is he who at the suggestion of Merlin moves Stonehenge from
Ireland to Wiltshire. His brother Uther Pendragon succeeds him,
and then comes King Arthur, Uther's son, who, aided by the
Bretons, completes the triumph of the British over the Saxons,
renders the Picts and Scots harmless, and conquers Ireland, Iceland, Sweden, the Orkneys, Norway and Denmark, and then
Gaul. A Roman Procurator, Lucius Hiberius, invites the kings of
the East to ward off this danger from the Britons, but Arthur
defeats these armies in a battle in which Lucius is killed, and many
of the Romans surrender in order to become slaves of the Britons.
Arthur, who was preparing to march on Rome, then hears news
that recalls him to Britain, and after a civil war is borne away
wounded to the Isle of Avalon. A Cornish Constantine succeeds

---

[1] Thought to be a real contribution to history because of the discovery of numerous
skulls in the bed of the Walbrook, see A. Griscom, *Hist. Reg. Brit.* London, 1929,
pp. 212–14.

him, and he and his house continue the wars with the Saxons, but in the end the land is overrun by hordes of Saxons and Africans, with the result that the Britons lose their kingdom and retire to Wales and Cornwall. A group of British leaders enjoy one last triumph, driving the Saxons out of the south and midlands, but after Cadwallader had come to the throne, famine and plague drive the miserable Britons to leave the country altogether and to take refuge in Brittany. Cadwallader died in Rome, and though his sons for a time revived the fortunes of the British, they could not save the country; so the British became the Welsh and never recovered the monarchy, the Saxons possessing their former territories in England. In the closing chapters of the book once more we are reminded of the background of prophecies against which the story is told, and an angelic voice tells Cadwallader of the eventual return of the Britons and their recovery of the kingdom they had lost.

We wonder now why Geoffrey wrote this extraordinary book; he was an ambitious man, and its purpose cannot have been merely to console a few educated Celts in the west of Britain; yet though it was addressed to the English court, there are no concessions to the fashionable Anglophil tendencies; by the title of the book Geoffrey cut the English right out, and he ended his story before the Saxons became a great people. A more plausible explanation is that Geoffrey, who was well aware of court opinion, knew a book that raised no Anglo-Norman issues and contained new and gratifying information about the Anglo-Norman territory, would be popular. Normans and Saxons were alike newcomers, but their kings called themselves Kings of England, and they would certainly be pleased to know that the first King of England had become by right the master of the whole island; and they might also be expected to hear with interest and a thoughtful regard to the future that the Britons under their own great world-conquering hero, King Arthur, had been masters of a huge North Sea empire, had held Gaul in subjection, and had resisted with victorious arms a Rome jealous of Arthurian power. The Frenchmen of Geoffrey's own day were fostering the cult of Charlemagne; here was the record of an achievement as magnificent and as significant as that of the Franks, the creation by the British of an empire in the glory of which not only the British, but the Bretons, and the Normans, and indeed the English, might justly share. If it be added that Henry I might have thought the unity of his own dominions here and in France would itself be strengthened by this vision of the forgotten empire, the political[1] theory of the origin of Geoffrey's book sounds probable enough. Moreover, it is quite certain that in composing Merlin's prophecies Geoffrey predicted many happenings that his readers were intended to recognise as allusions to the history of their own times. Yet, though Geoffrey may indeed have been aware of the general attractiveness of his revelation of a united Britain and an enormous British Empire, there is really no sign that his book was deliberately charged with political significance for his own times, except in so far as Merlin's prophecies can be reasonably connected with the affairs of the twelfth century. To go to the root of the matter, the conception of the great King Arthur and his European conquests, we find that the picture Geoffrey drew does not in reality resemble that of a Charlemagne and a Western Empire. Arthur was not crowned at Rome; he was not a law-giver or a reformer or the noble-minded architect of an era of peace; in fact in a career of storm and violence his single recorded act of merit was the rebuilding of the churches of York, and, this apart, he was a warrior-king who fought with a bloody-minded zest every nation he could find time to attack, a barbarian who could not be restrained, even though he had a Roman wife, from a violent attack on the Romans themselves. Geoffrey does not exalt Arthur's conquests as the achievement of an empire; on the contrary, he admits that they were short-lived and unsubstantial.

There may, indeed, be an explanation on a more modest level of Geoffrey's purpose. He may after all have been doing no more than write a book of antiquarian interest for fellow-antiquaries, and his astonishing success may have been due to the fact that the story he told was—in its detail—thrillingly new, personally important to his readers, and exceedingly well told. George Gordon rightly clarified the matter of the fame of the *Historia Regum Britanniae* by insisting that the first point to make about it is that it was an irresistibly good book in an age when

---

[1] See G. H. Gerould. *King Arthur and Politics, Speculum* II (1927), p. 33; for further references and discussion, ib. p. 317, and F. P. Magoun, *E L H*, Sept. 1947, p. 178.

such works were very rare.[1] Geoffrey's fellow historians had heard about Brutus; they were already inquiring about the British kings of the Trojan line; King Arthur was an important and rather mysterious Celtic hero long before Geoffrey wrote;[2] there was, in short, a background of antiquarian expectancy, and, more than that, of antiquarian sentimentality, for the romantic contemplation of the prowess and adventures of the heroes of the past was already influencing literary thought in England in the first half of the twelfth century. To this waiting public Geoffrey gave a wholly admirable volume, full of fact, ablaze with victories and the pageants of great kings, sombre with murders and bloody defeats, enlivened with tales like that of Lear and his daughters, and not without an occasional sting for the luckless contemporary writers to whom this great parade of British history was unknown. The *Historia Regum Britanniae* really could not fail, and the truth may be that it is important politically not because of its purpose, but because of its potential inflammatory effect upon a too ardent and too ambitious British section of the people.

Geoffrey did not triumph without some opposition. Medieval chroniclers could carry credulity almost to the point at which the critical faculties were no longer used; but Geoffrey had been deliberately jubilant and provoking, and it was not long before some of his readers began to voice their surprise. Within fifteen years of the publication of the *Historia Regum Britanniae* one chronicler was already asking the uncomfortable question that was to vex Geoffrey's supporters for the next five hundred years. Why does no historian of the world outside Britain mention these wonderful British kings, and in particular and above all, if near the middle of the sixth century A.D. Arthur fought the Romans in France in a war of almost global magnitude, the whole strength of the Arthurian empire of Britain, Scandinavia, and Gaul pitted

---

[1] *The Trojans in Britain*. This fine essay, first published in 1924 (*Essays and Studies, English Assoc.* 9), is reprinted in Gordon's *Discipline of Letters*. Oxford, 1946.

[2] As early as 1113 Bretons used to fight Frenchmen about King Arthur, and Cornishmen of the same period, who could boast of an "Arthur's Seat" and an "Arthur's Oven" in their county, believed that Arthur was still alive (Herman of Tournai, Migne *P.L.* 156, 983). The grave of Gawain had been discovered in Pembrokeshire before Geoffrey was born, and William of Malmesbury, who mentions this (*Gesta Reg. Ang.* 111, §287, Rolls ed. 90, 11), also comments on the wild tales told by the British about Arthur (ib 1, §8). For other evidence of the pre-Galfridian Arthur legend see R. S. Loomis's summary (*Speculum* xiii, 1938, pp. 229–31).

against the Mediterranean and Eastern world, why is it that not a
single Roman or Frankish or Greek or Oriental writer refers to
him and his achievements? These questions were first voiced
rather apologetically by Alfred of Beverley[1] in a popular history
book, the early part of which is a detailed résumé of the whole of
Geoffrey's narrative; he believed in the British History, and he
wanted it to become known to all those who had not come across
it; but he did wonder why there was no external corroboration
of the main narrative. Another critic was a distinguished Welshman of the next generation, Giraldus Cambrensis (1146–1220);
he likewise believed in Brutus and his Trojans, and in Camber and
in Merlin and King Arthur; for the benefit of the Pope he
quoted Geoffrey's text of the Merlin prophecies;[2] he even copied a
bit about the gilded roofs of Caerleon from Geoffrey's book, and
put them in his own *Itinerary*, as though he had himself seen them;
he did not challenge any single part of Geoffrey's story; and his
only quibble was about the derivation of the name Wales; yet he
treated the British History with contempt, making it ridiculous
by telling the tale of the devils who vanished when the Gospel of
St. John was placed on the bosom of their familiar, but returned
in greater numbers than ever when the lying *Historia Regum
Britanniae* was substituted. No doubt Giraldus, who was twice
elected Bishop of St. David's, disliked Geoffrey's insistence on the
ecclesiastical seniority of Caerleon; but it seems obvious from the
way he talks that his own studies had convinced him that, apart
from an agreed outline of traditional Welsh history, Geoffrey
had made up most of the British History out of his own head.

Geoffrey's critic who was most to be feared was Giraldus's
contemporary, William of Newburgh, a Yorkshireman, for he
had no need of Geoffrey's material in his own *Historia Rerum
Anglicarum* (1066–1198), yet he felt it his duty as a conscientious
and scholarly historian, which indeed he was, to protest in a
strongly-worded preface against the growing tendency to accept
the *Historia Regum Britanniae* as honest history. He denounced
Geoffrey of Monmouth as the author of an historically valueless
collection of Celtic fairy-tales. He said it was nonsense to describe
Arthur's wonderful triumph over the giant on St. Michael's
Mount in Brittany, because there were no giants in Arthur's

---

[1] *Aluredi Beverlacensis Annales*, ed. Hearne, Oxford, 1716, p. 76.
[2] *De Jure et Statu Menevensis ecclesiae.* Rolls 21, III, p. 171; cf. *Hist. Reg. Brit.* viii, iii.

day; there had not been any since the time of King David. William pointed out that Geoffrey's account of the noble and virtuous Britons was palpably distorted in their favour, as anybody could discover who took the trouble to read Gildas, and he insisted that the description of Arthur's deeds could not be expected to survive critical investigation. A man who had conquered all Gaul in one short campaign, a task that had taken Julius Caesar ten years! A man who is made out to be a veritable Alexander the Great, and yet is unknown to contemporary historians abroad! William showed that it was hopeless to try to fit the Galfridian sixth century Arthur with his absurd world-conquests into the established frame of Saxon history.[1] What about Bede's history, and the known facts of the Saxon settlement and the rise of Jutish Kent! What was the good of talking about the three Archbishops of London, Caerleon, and York, being present at Arthur's Pentecost feast, when there was no Archbishop in England before St. Augustine! William of Newburgh was delivering a major attack. His preface was a short one, but it was a thunderclap of courageous and devastating criticism, and though most succeeding medieval chroniclers stopped their ears, its echoes went rumbling loudly down the ages and even disturbed antiquaries of the seventeenth and eighteenth centuries.

It was over a century and a half later, however, before criticism was heard again, and thereafter Geoffrey's tale triumphed unchallenged until Whethamstede and Thomas Rudborne in the fifteenth century, and John Major and Polydore Vergil and John Twyne in the sixteenth century expressed the doubts of a new age. The fourteenth century English chronicler who, like William of Newburgh, distrusted the marvellous stories about King Arthur and Merlin in the British History was the Chester monk, Ralph Higden, for the scheme of his laborious *Polychronicon* once again revealed the weakness that Alfred of Beverley had found; Higden did believe in Brutus and the fabulous British kings, and, with certain reservations, Geoffrey's alleged source; but he could not accept names like "Frollo" as that of a Roman governor of France, and the even more suspicious "Lucius Hiberius"; and he

---

[1] William of Newburgh, however, forgot Geoffrey's date (542) for the passing of Arthur, and using a dead reckoning on the basis of descents from Vortigern and Hengist, he calculated that Arthur was the contemporary of K. Ethelbert of Kent and St. Augustine.

challenged Geoffrey's chronology. Higden's doubts were mildly expressed; but they were of a kind that, as we shall see, most of all madden the Arthurian enthusiast. One of the first people to be so offended was Higden's own translator, John Trevisa, a Cornishman, who pointedly interrupts his English version (1387) of the *Polychronicon* in order to protest against this unexpected folly of its author. He insisted above all things that the argument *ex silentio* was plainly ridiculous. "Seint John in his gospel telleth meny thinges and doynges that Mark, Luk, and Matheu speketh nougt of in there gospelles, ergo, John is noyut trowynge in his gospel? He were of false byleve that trowede that that argument were worth a bene."[1]

Thus did the trusting medieval mind shut doubts and scruples away. The chroniclers continued writing in all seriousness about Brutus and King Arthur,[2] and no one, not even William of Newburgh, attempted to dispute the Trojan origin of the British; this was medieval dogma, and it was not doubted until the appearance of the first English humanists in the middle of the fifteenth century. The British History rode majestically forward, brushing quibblers and doubters aside. No English grumblers could hurt King Arthur, and even before the twelfth century was over the hero of the Britons had emerged from the shadowy world of mythology and become an unchallengable historical personage. In 1187, King Henry II's grandson, a possible heir to the whole Angevin dominion, was called Arthur, at the request of the people of Brittany, who believed that King Arthur had promised to return to them, and thought that the providential baby of an English prince and Constantia,[3] daughter of their own Duke, was the fulfilment of their hopes,[4] a predestined instrument of the revival of the Arthurian glories related in the British History. King Arthur was now as real as Alfred the Great or William the Con-

---

[1] Higden, *Polychronicon*. Rolls ed. 41, 5, p. 337.

[2] Gervase of Canterbury (died *c.* 1210), writing about the same time as William of Newburgh, gives a précis of the *Historia* in his *Gesta Regum*, John de Cella, Abbot of St. Albans, 1195–1214, another contemporary, uses Geoffrey's work freely in the early portion of the *Chronica Majora*, and Matthew Paris (d. 1259), re-editing this, accepted everything copied from the *Historia*. For subsequent writers see Laura Keeler, *Geoffrey of Monmouth and the late Latin Chroniclers* 1300–1500. University of California, English publns., Vol. 17 (1946). The fame of the *Historia* was further increased by the metrical versions in contemporary English by Robert of Gloucester (*c.* 1300) and Robert Mannyng (1338).

[3] This name is not necessarily to be connected with the Arthurian tradition; it is to be found in the eleventh and twelfth century royal houses of France and Spain, and was the name of one of William the Conqueror's daughters.

[4] William of Newburgh. *Hist. Rerum Ang.* iii, viii.

queror, and three or four years after the christening of the Prince
the bodies of the great king himself and of Guinevere were discovered at Glastonbury. At about the same time (1191) Arthur's
renowned sword Excalibur was presented by Richard I to Tan-
cred of Sicily.

The extraordinary importance of the British History is further
emphasized by the fact that it remained throughout the Middle
Ages a growing concern, not a static system of antiquarian belief
liable to drastic pruning and revision, but a thriving garden of
spurious history in which any transitory nonsense about the remote past might take root and flourish. Thus in the fourteenth
century a Malmesbury historian, presumably on the grounds that
the syllables *Malm* and *Molm* were very much alike, claimed that
the great British king Dunwallo Molmutius, author of the Molmutine Laws, was the founder of the *civitates* and castles of
Malmesbury, Tetbury, and Lacock.[1] In the fifteenth century the
liberties taken with the British History sometimes lacked even this
miserable minimum of reason, and we shall find, too, that in the
sixteenth century many antiquaries were still as recklessly in-
ventive as their medieval forerunners. Some of these Tudor
fancies will have to be mentioned later; but for the present it will
suffice as a further illustration of medieval antiquarian thought if
we consider only one of the extraneous oddments, each with its
independent tangle of legends, that in the course of the Middle
Ages stuck themselves like burrs upon the accommodating body
of the British History.

The legend of St. Joseph of Arimathea was a Glastonbury pro-
duction, like the bones of King Arthur, and had in origin nothing
whatever to do with Geoffrey of Monmouth. After the fire of
1184 the monks produced for the glorification of their abbey not
only the bodies of Arthur and Guinevere to accompany the remains of St. Patrick, Gildas, and St. Dunstan, but they also made
a very important contribution to the history of Britain by discovering that St. Joseph of Arimathea came to this country in
A.D. 63 and built the first church at Glastonbury, where he was
eventually buried. This story was not known to William of
Malmesbury when he wrote a history of Glastonbury about fifty
years before the fire; it belongs therefore, like the discovery of

---

[1] *Eulogium Hist.*: ed. Rolls, 9, II, 236.

Arthur to the rebuilding period, and naturally it was carefully inserted in subsequent editions of William of Malmesbury's book. Glastonbury could henceforth proudly call herself Roma Secunda; for the St. Joseph legend, which included the conversion by him and his disciples of the whole country, not only gave the monastery precedence in antiquity of foundation over all other religious houses in Britain, but also, when the date of arrival had been pushed back to A.D. 31, it made the British Church more ancient than the Churches of France and Spain. The Glastonbury story did in fact cause considerable argument in the fifteenth century Councils of the Church.

The development of the St. Joseph legend gives us some idea of the tortuous processes behind the achieved creed of the medieval antiquary. It was believed on the Continent, at least as far back as the seventh century, that St. Philip had preached to the Gauls and had converted to Christianity barbarous peoples dwelling on the borders of the Ocean; there was also a British legend, at least as old as the tenth century, that the first Christian missionaries to this country found at Glastonbury a church already built for them by Divine agency. It was assumed at Glastonbury that these missionaries were St. Philip's disciples, and about 1125 William of Malmesbury in his history of the Monastery said he thought it quite probable that they were. In the meantime more was being told about St. Joseph of Arimathea than the story, in his apocryphal acts, of his miraculous release from prison and his adoption as a disciple of St. Philip; European romance had further exalted him by telling how the Risen Christ had given him the Holy Grail, and this early Grail legend connected Joseph with the evangelization of distant countries far to the west; and in Robert de Boron's *Joseph*, written before the twelfth century was over, one of the missionaries is made to declare that he would go as far as the "Vale of Averon". We do not know whether he meant the Arthurian Avalon, but it is obvious that an ingenious Glastonbury antiquary had now all the necessary material. The first missionaries to Glastonbury were described as the twelve disciples of St. Philip and St. James under the leadership of St. Joseph of Arimathea; they built the first church at the bidding of the Archangel Gabriel, and received a grant of land from the British king Arviragus; they were buried at Glastonbury, and in St. Joseph's tomb there were two cruets containing the Blood and

Sweat of Our Lord. That was the Glastonbury legend of the thirteenth and fourteenth centuries.[1]

It is to be observed that Glastonbury did not claim that the Grail had been brought to the Abbey. The medieval Church in England, in spite of its passion for relics and its unfathomable credulity, would not countenance the Grail of lay romance; but what Glastonbury did do in order to win the maximum permissible glory in the three domains of sanctity, history, and romance, was to claim that King Arthur was descended from Joseph of Arimathea. The monks in the fourteenth century said that this was through his mother, Igerne of Cornwall, first the mistress and then the wife of Uther Pendragon, and it was later explained that Igerne's ancestry could be traced back to the marriage between St. Joseph of Arimathea and a daughter of Longinus, the spearman of the Crucifixion, who was said to be the natural son of Julius Caesar.

---

[1] On this whole subject of King Arthur and St. Joseph at Glastonbury see J. Armitage Robinson, *Two Glastonbury Legends*, Cambridge, 1926.

II

John Rous and William of Worcester

THE British History with its natural accretions and supplementary material was in truth a formidable deadweight of antiquarian opinion. Even honest and conscientious chroniclers, struggling with their Chapter I, found it easier to accept the whole rigmarole and hand on a conveniently potted version of it than to attempt to probe this amorphous coagulation of vanities and fairy-tales in the hope of isolating one or two morsels of credible fact. It is obvious, however, that belief or disbelief in the British History is not the total content of our antiquarian thought in the Middle Ages, and there is in fact occasional record of ordinary antiquarian duties performed to a past that was not shadowy and remote, but attainable through the intelligent use of archives and visible monuments. No doubt the study of archives, and, where necessary, the deliberate manufacture of them, must be regarded as the most important of these activities; but there had been spasmodic work of another kind. Matthew Paris's fine illustrated catalogue, complete with weights, of the rings and gems in the St. Albans treasury is an example;[1] there had been casual references to antiquities in the field;[2] there had been instances of an antiquarian regard for long out-moded fashions;[3] and there had even been excavations.[4]

[1] B.M. MS. *Nero D.I.* ff. 146, 146b; reproduced *Rolls* 57, *VI*, frontispiece, and *Walpole Society* XIV (1926), Pl. XXV, and p. 23.

[2] E.g. speculation about a Roman inscription at Carlisle by William of Malmesbury, *Gest. Pont.*, *Rolls* 52, 209 and cf. Higden, *Rolls* 41, II, 70; also the reference to Caerleon by Giraldus Cambrensis, *It.*, *Rolls* 21, VI, 55 and his description of St. Cynod's gold torc, ib., p. 25. Note also the picturesque references to discoveries of Roman Chester in Ralph Higden's *Polychronicon*.

[3] Two effigies of Saxon bishops at Wells, carved *c.* 1230, have antique low mitres possibly copied from the original effigies, *Archæologia*, 65, p. 109. For effigies of Saxon bishops at Hereford carved *c.* 1300, see R.C.H.M. *Hereford* I S.E., 110.

[4] The best-known is the excavation of Verulamium by two Saxon abbots in the early eleventh century, Walsingham, *Gest. Abb.*, *Rolls* 28, *I*, pp. 24, 27; they noted the inscriptions and pottery and glass that they found, but their real purpose was to level the ruins and obtain building material for the Abbey. The numerous medieval excavations were usually treasure-hunts or searches for the bones of saints, cf. the discovery of St. Amphibalus in a Saxon barrow near St. Albans, *Archæologia* 33, 263.

Taken all together, however, it does not add up to any very impressive story, and the truth is that no person emerges as a practising antiquary of general importance and with a real interest in the tangible relics of the past until we come to John Rous (1411–91), and William of Worcester (1415–82), both of them antiquaries who lived and worked in, so to speak, the comfortable shadow of the British History, believing in it and, as far as we know, content with every word of it.

John Rous was a Warwickshire man, born about 1411 and educated at Oxford. About 1445, he became one of the two chaplains of the Guy's Cliff chantrey, close to Warwick, that had been founded by Richard Beauchamp, Earl of Warwick, some twenty years earlier, and he lived for the rest of his life here under the patronage of the Beauchamps and Nevilles; and he was buried in St. Mary's Church, Warwick. He did some travelling, in Wales and as far south as London and Winchester, and he collected a large library, which, after his death was installed in a specially built room over the porch of St. Mary's, together with his own writings and illuminated rolls. The great antiquary, Leland, in the sixteenth century, saw all these books and made some notes of Rous's works, but by the middle of the seventeenth century they had all been stolen and lost, though Sir William Dugdale and Sir Simon Archer tried very hard to recover them. Two of the vanished works are losses that seriously injure the history of English books, for Rous's *History of the Town of Warwick*, and his *Antiquity of Guy's Cliff*, in whatever form they were drafted and however full they may have been—as they probably were—of historical nonsense, would be regarded now as landmarks in British topographical studies. What remain to-day of Rous's works are the two *Warwick Rolls* and the *Historia Regum Angliae*.

Some knowledge of Rous and his life is to be gained from these works. The *Historia* contains long digressions on agrarian misery, and violent tirades directed against the rich and greedy sheepfarmers who were depopulating and ruining the Warwickshire villages Rous knew and loved. He gives a list of the places in his own neighbourhood that had suffered, and he angrily denounces afforestation and park-enclosure. He had in vain petitioned the Coventry parliament of 1459 on behalf of the dispossessed villeins, and the document he drew up at that time has overflowed into the pages of the *Historia*,[1] wherein he makes his appeal to the new King, Henry VII.[2] He preached also in moving terms a Christian socialism, pleading, with the aid of a jumble of aphorisms from Socrates, Plato, Aristotle and St. Augustine, the need for peace, for unity among men of all stations and, above all, for charity to one's neighbour; we are all members of one body, he says, and the rich spoilers of the countryside have sinned against the corporate life of the community. All these things he felt most deeply. *Torrens eloquentia*, said Leland, was Rous's fault,[3] but Leland was almost the last of men likely to have sympathy for this voluble heart-cry from the miserable Midlands at the end of the Wars of the Roses.

Rous's relations to York and Lancaster also form part of his personal story, and are revealed in the Warwick Rolls. These, one in English and one in Latin[4] are pictorial catalogues of the founders of Warwick and of the Earls of Warwick from the town's legendary beginnings to the late fifteenth century; they are Rous's tributes to the families of the Beauchamps and the Nevilles, his patrons, and they were to a great extent influenced by the fifteenth century history of Warwick Castle. Rous witnessed an astonishing pageant of events, the equal of anything in the old chronicles he studied, for he was a favoured member of the household of a man who was for a time the most powerful nobleman of the age, Richard Neville, Earl of Warwick, the Kingmaker, and the Wars of the Roses dragged out their wearisome and spiteful course under the chantrey priest's close observation. The Castle was a Yorkist stronghold during Rous's first twenty years at Guy's Cliff, and though in the closing years of Warwick's life, the Kingmaker took up arms against Edward IV, the Lancastrian episode was only shortlived, ending in 1471, when the Earl was killed, and Edward of Westminster, the son of Henry VI, who was married to Anne Neville, the Kingmaker's younger daughter, died at Tewkesbury. For

---

[1] *Historia Regum Angliae*, ed. Hearne, Oxford, 1745, pp. 120–1; cf. also pp. 28–44, 80–96, 113 ff.

[2] Ib. pp. 135–7.

[3] *Commentarii*, (see p. 56 above), DLXXXV.

[4] The Latin Roll, measuring 24½ feet in length and 11 inches in width, is in the College of Arms, *Cat.* 39, Pls. XXV, XXVI, and *Burlington Magazine* XXX, 1917, p. 23: the English Roll is Add. MS. 48976 in the B.M. See *B.M.Q.* XX (1956), pp. 71–81. A copy, made *c.* 1845, was published by William Courthope, *Rows Rol,* 1859.

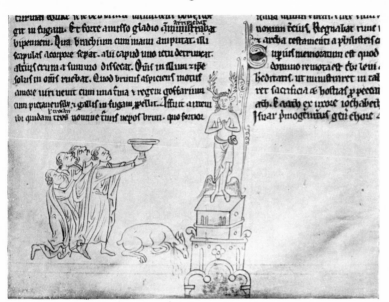

a   BRUTUS SACRIFICING TO DIANA :
Matthew Paris, 13th Cent.
Corpus, Cambridge, MS. 26, p. 7

b   BRUTUS SACRIFICING TO DIANA
Fabyan's *Chronicle*, 1516

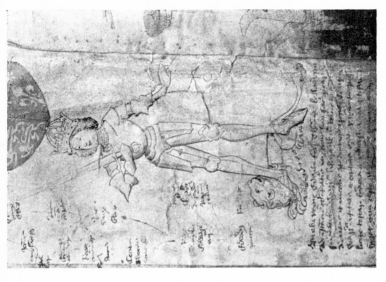

a   JOHN ROUS, SELF-PORTRAIT

b   THE YOUTHFUL EDWARD III
Drawing by John Rous

Both from the Rous Roll, College of Arms

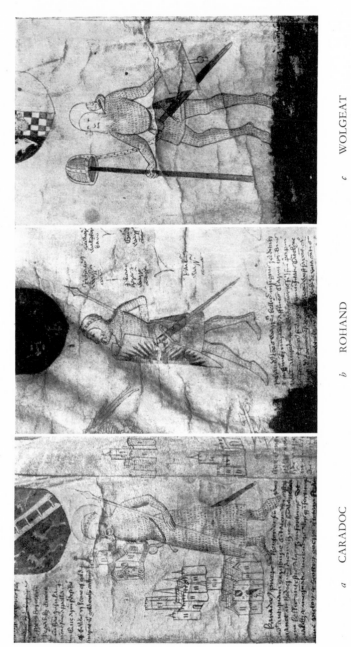

a CARADOC   *b* ROHAND   *c* WOLGEAT

Rous Roll, College of Arms

IV

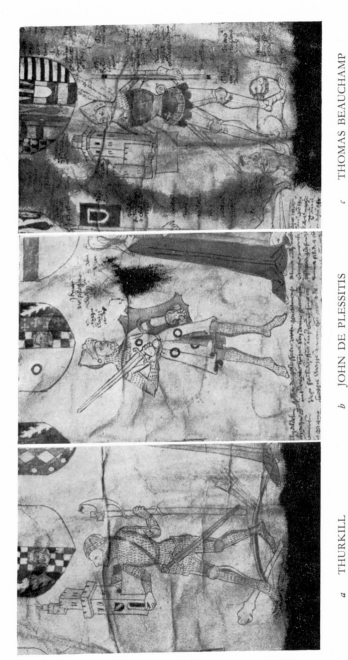

a THURKILL   *b* JOHN DE PLESSITIS   *c* THOMAS BEAUCHAMP

Rous Roll, College of Arms

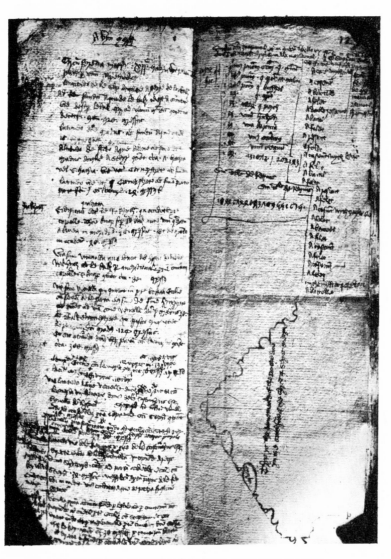

V

PAGE FROM WILLIAM OF WORCESTER'S NOTES

Corpus, Cambridge, MS. 210, p. 129

a RICHARD WHITE OF BASINGSTOKE
Medal by Ludovico Leoni, 1568

b WILLIAM CAMDEN
Bust in Westminster Abbey

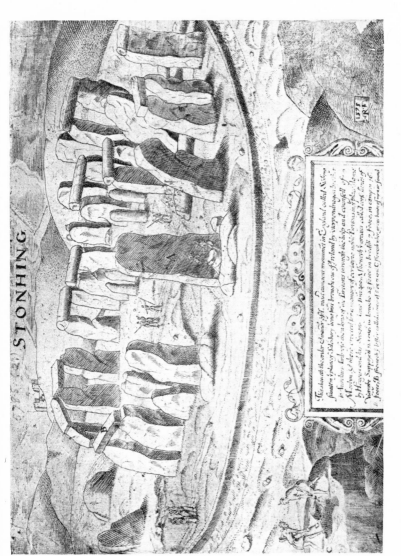

STONEHENGE, AN ENGRAVING SIGNED R.F. 1575

British Museum

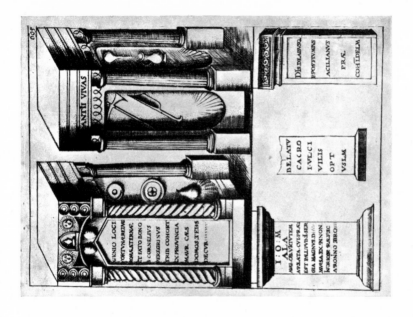

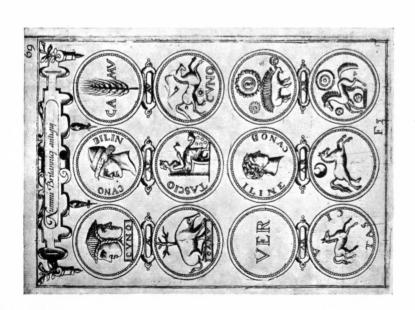

ILLUSTRATIONS FROM CAMDEN'S *BRITANNIA*, EDITION OF 1600

fourteen years to come the closest ties united Warwick Castle to the throne itself. In 1472 Anne, Prince Edward's young widow, married the Duke of Gloucester, the future Richard III, and two years later Edward IV's nephew, Edward, son of George, Duke of Clarence, and Isabella, the Kingmaker's eldest daughter, was born as heir to the Earldom of Warwick. Rous must then have felt that Neville fortunes and the Castle's future depended entirely on Yorkist favour. In 1483, the King, Richard III, with his Warwickshire Queen, made a state visit to the Castle, and it was about that time—certainly not more than a few months later—that Rous completed his first Warwick Roll.[1]

This is the "English" Roll, and it is also called the "Yorkist" Roll, because it is consistently loyal to the Yorkist cause and extols in bold and high-sounding words the virtues of the mighty Princes, Edward IV and Richard III, who are both introduced as benefactors of the town of Warwick. After it was completed, however, came the Yorkist downfall. In 1485, Queen Anne died, and Richard fell at Bosworth. Henry Tudor became King of England, and the young Earl of Warwick, now Yorkist heir to the throne, was shut up in the Tower, where he remained until his execution fourteen years later. The glories of the Nevilles were ended, and though the Kingmaker's widow recovered her rights in 1487, it was only to convey the Warwick estates to the Crown, and for many years there was no Earl of Warwick at the Castle. Rous was a man of seventy-four at the time of the Battle of Bosworth. He saw in Henry VII, as so many thankful and excited Englishmen did at that time, the beginning of a new age of peace, and he realized that Henry's Lancastrian background must now be duly honoured. The English Roll was apparently no longer in his possession, but he had still the second or "Latin" Roll, and this he cut up and re-edited by removing the Yorkist figures of Richard III and Edward IV, and inserting in their place a youthful Edward III (Pl. II, b), who had granted Warwick a charter; he also inserted a figure of Edward of Westminster, the late Queen Anne's first husband, son of Henry VI, and honoured him with the title of Prince of Wales. His new enthusiasm for the Tudor King is revealed not only in the Latin Roll; he dedicated his *Historia Regum Angliae* in most fulsome terms

[1] Edward, Prince of Wales, d. 1484, was still alive when the Roll was completed.

to Henry VII, and therein permitted himself to say some very unpleasant things about Richard III; that he remained two years in his mother's womb and came forth at last with teeth and with hair on his shoulders; that he poisoned his wife, imprisoned his mother-in-law, put his nephew to death and murdered Henry VI, perhaps with his own hands.[1] This is the talk that caused Horace Walpole to jeer at Rous as a despicable and lying author, "a vehement Lancastrian";[2] but the old chantry-priest had done no more than report the current gossip that circulated after Richard's fall; indeed, he also courageously stated what he knew could be said in favour of Anne Neville's unfortunate husband. Richard III, he wrote, was responsible for some fine buildings and generous endowments; he had refused money-gifts from his people, desiring rather to possess their hearts; "he was a noble knight, and defended himself to the last breath with eminent valour".

We shall speak of Rous first as the traditional medieval antiquary and begin with his favourite subject of "founders". The *Historia Regum Angliae* is based on notes made for one of Rous's Oxford friends, John Seymour, master of the works begun by Edward IV at Windsor, who had asked for particulars of kings and princes who had founded churches and towns, in order that statues of them might be put in St. George's Chapel, which was then being rebuilt.[3] Rous began this catalogue about 1480, but he did not finish it, and the *Historia* is a subsequent attempt to turn it into a narrative history of England. At this late date in the fifteenth century, Rous was able to consult such fanciful versions of the British History as that at the beginning of John Hardyng's *Chronicle*—wherein eponymous founders are particularly plentiful, for instance, King Westmer of Westmorland and King Grandobodian (Geoffrey of Monmouth's Gorbonius) founder of Grantham and Cambridge, and Rous contributed generously to this ever-growing list. His own town, Warwick, is mentioned on only one occasion by Geoffrey as the residence of an Arthurian

---

[1] *Hist. Reg. Ang.*, p. 215 ff.

[2] *Historic Doubts*, in *Works*, ed. 1798, II. p. 167.

[3] *Hist. Reg. Ang.*, p. 120. Rous's detailed suggestions were not used in the Windsor sculptures, but it is probable he was responsible for the iconography of the west window, the key to which may, I think, be found at the end of the Latin Roll. Rous had long been familiar with the custom of depicting founders and ancestors; close at hand, for instance, were the historical figures, now lost, in the stained glass (*c.* 1450) of the Beauchamp chapel, and at Guy's Cliff itself the great stone carving of Guy of Warwick.

knight, but Rous had no difficulty in discovering that it was a city originally called Caerleon-in-Loegria, that is to say, the English Caerleon, and this information he got from Gildas, whom he describes as the principal chaplain of King Arthur. The first founder, in the fourth century B.C., was King Guithelinus (hence the name, Caer-Gutheleon, Caerleon), but there was rebuilding at the beginning of the Christian era by King Guiderius, Cymbeline's son, and later restorations by St. Caradoc, who built a palace and the church of St. John the Baptist, formerly standing in the market-place, and by King Constantine the Breton, grandfather of King Arthur, and by a Welsh prince Gwayr, the hero of the combat with the ragged staff and a cousin of King Arthur. Rous then recorded that St. Dubritius, afterwards Archbishop of the Welsh Caerleon, chose Warwick as his episcopal seat, and it was here that he consecrated St. Samson of Dol. Warwick, Rous explains, had been called Caerumbre by Constantine and Caergwayr by Gwayr, and it got its present name from the Saxon King Wermund.[1]

In the case of Guy of Warwick, Rous followed the tradition of the Beauchamps. They had identified Guy's Cliff—up to at least 1335 an ordinary hermitage called Kibbecliva or Gibbeclyve —as the retreat of the famous Saxon giant-killer, their ancestor through the Newboroughs and the D'Oylies, and Earl Richard had founded the chantry here in 1422; the chapel provided for in his will was built in the years 1450–9, after Rous's appointment as a chantrey-priest, and it is obvious that he would have no difficulty in supporting the family legend, for the nine feet high statue of Guy was daily before him, and in Warwick Castle he often saw Guy's sword and hauberk among the Beauchamp heirlooms. Another ancestor of the Beauchamps seemed to him a similarly real person, and that was Sir Enyas, the Knight of the Swan. He was the equivalent of the German Lohengrin, and was one of the seven children who had been turned into swans each with a chain round the neck; according to the legend a cup that plays an important part in the story had been made of these chains,

---

[1] This is from the St. Albans *Lives of the Offas*, but Rous's history of Warwick is a *locus desperatus*. He presumably made use of hints in Welsh chronicles and the occurrence of names like Cair Guiragon in the Nennius list of British cities. St. Caradoc is presumably the sixth century St. Cadoc, and Gwayr may be Gawain (Gwalchmer, son of Gwyar). For Rous's Welsh sources see *Hist. Reg. Ang.*, pp. 12, 45; *Rows Rol*, 2; Leland, *Commentarii* DLXXXIII, p. 464.

and the Beauchamps possessed this cup.[1] It was of gold, and Rous had examined it in Warwick Castle, and had drunk very good wine out of it in the company of the Kingmaker's wife, the Countess Anne. "I have dronke of the same," he said, "I dar the better wrighten it." He also drew a picture of it, a rich jewelled vessel with the sacred monogram on the print.

Rous wrote a book on giants, and had much to say about them also in his *Historia*; no one doubted the former existence of these creatures; there was abundant Biblical proof, and Sir John Mandeville had actually seen the forty feet long rib of one of them at Jaffa;[2] giants' bones had also been found in England, and Rous knew of life-size hill-figures of Gogmagog and Corinius that were kept scoured even in his own time. Here, however, he comes to a difficulty that reveals the medieval mind struggling to believe all that it was told and accepting none of the responsibility of a critical historian. The British History had reported giants in this country before the arrival of Brutus; to account for their existence and also to explain the island's alternative name Albion, chroniclers of the fourteenth and fifteenth centuries related that the daughters of Danaus, after being exiled for murdering their husbands, headed by the eldest, Albina, had arrived in this island, which was in consequence named Albion, and had there consorted with devils and bred a race of giants. The story had become much confused; in some accounts the father of Albina was "Dioclisianus, King of Syria", and it was uncertain how many sisters there had been, some said fifty and some said thirty, and some said thirty-four. Rous, like Hardyng before him, explained the various inconsistences; he was thankful that,

---

[1] Rous also said that both the Beauchamps and the Staffords, whose families had been united by a marriage in the fourteenth century, claimed Sir Enyas as an ancestor, and the Cup of the Swan was divided between them, the Beauchamps having the bowl, and the Staffords the cover, *Rows Rol*, No. 18, description. He knew that Sir Enyas was connected with Godfrey de Bouillon and the crusades, and as both families had crusading ancestors and a swan crest, there was nearly as good a case for this ancestor as for Guy of Warwick.

[2] *Voyages and Travels*, ed. Warner, Roxburghe Club, 1889, p. 16, and note p. 166. Mandeville was making a muddled reference to the story of Andromeda and her chains on the rock at Joppa, and of the forty feet bones of the monster found there; the monster's rib bone, that he attributed to the giant Andromodes, is shown hanging on the city walls in Pl. XXIV of this work (early fifteenth century illumination). Rous admitted that Mandeville's tales were not believed by everybody, but he said a Mappa Mundi, or the life of Alexander the Great, of the adventures of Ludolph von Sudheim and of Marco Polo, were often just as difficult to believe as Mandeville's narrative. He pointed out that in 1483, John de Solius and Bernard de Breydenbach, Dean of Mainz, confirmed the story of "Andromadus" and his rib. (*Peregrinatio in terram sanctam*, 1st ed. 1486).

at any rate, the rival names for the father began with D; but he could not decide what the correct story was. *Hanc ambiguitatem*, he said, *non determino, totum relinquens Deo*.[1] Whatever had happened was God's will, and one could leave it at that.

No subject studied and developed in the light of the British History flourished more successfully than the vexed question of the antiquity of the universities of Oxford and Cambridge. Rous had written a book stating the medieval case for each university as it was known to him, and though this work is lost, we know what he had to say.[2] His views are important, not only as an illustration of what we may call the British History mind, but also because they were discussed with all the heated unintelligibility of a schoolman's wrangle right into the seventeenth century, long after Rous was dead. His version of the Oxford story was that the city dated back to the time, a century after the arrival of Brutus, when King Mempricius[3] built "Beaumont", just outside the present walls; but the *University* did not come into being until later when the Greek scholars, who had come to England with Brutus and had hitherto lived at Cricklade (Greeklade), migrated to Beaumont sometime not very long before the settlement of the Saxons. This Cricklade establishment, however, was a mere school or academy. The great man who really created the present university was King Alfred. He did this in 873 in collaboration with St. Neot, and he made St. Grimbald the first Chancellor. The new university had three Halls, one of which was University College, and Alfred sent one of his own sons to Oxford, which speedily eclipsed all the educational establishments that had previously existed in this country. *Velut Lucifer in aurora prima Anglorum Universitas in Anglia effulsit*.[4]

Rous told his story of the foundation of Cambridge *ut scribunt Cantabrigienses*, and their tale was that the town had been founded in the year Anno Mundi 4317—in some versions A.M. 4321—by

[1] *Hist. Reg. Ang.*, p. 14.

[2] In addition to the material in the *Historia Regum Angliae*, Leland, who had read Rous's book, quotes it on seven occasions, *Commentarii, passim*.

[3] A treacherous, tyrannical, homosexual murderer; Rous may have chosen him because he was finally devoured by wolves, and thus presumably died at Wolvercote, but he does not himself offer this explanation; it is to be found in a sixteenth century annotation to a transcript of the *Historia*, C.C.C. Cambridge, M.S. 110, and is quoted with approval by Hearne in the eighteenth century. *Valeant Oxoniensia argumenta quantum valere possunt*, he remarks, in introducing the subject.

[4] *Hist. Reg. Ang.*, p. 77. For the legendary history of Oxford and Cambridge, see James Parker, *Early History of Oxford*. Oxford Hist. Soc. 1885.

Cantaber the Spaniard, one of the Iberian exiles who, so the British History said, had been found sailing in Scottish waters by King Gurguntius Brabtruc. This prince became Gurguntius's son-in-law, and he built his town on a river called after him the Cant, which was eventually bridged by his son, Grantinus, thus explaining such names as Cantbridge, Caergrant and Grant-chester. Cantaber, who was a patron of learning, gathered scholars in his newly-established town, and their arrival was the beginning of Cambridge University. Rous, however, mentioned Bede's reference to schools in East Anglia founded by the seventh century king, Sighebert, and this indubitably real person naturally increased in popularity as the founder of Cambridge when Cantaber became less and less a convincing person in honest history; but medieval Cambridge took Cantaber as seriously as did Rous, and though he was himself apparently not aware of it, Prior Nicholas Cantelupe of the Carmelites (d. 1441) had very considerably enriched the simple story outlined above.[1] This ingenious antiquary related that astronomers and philosophers from Athens were brought to Cambridge, and that Anaximander and Anaxagoras were among these early visitors; that Cambridge doctors played a leading part in the conversion of King Lucius to Christianity; that St. Swithin and St. Dubricius were Cambridge men; that King Arthur gave the university a charter in 531; that St. Augustine instructed the Cambridge professors of his day; that Theodore of Tarsus and Hadrian and Aldhelm and Aidan and Bede were at Cambridge, and that King Cadwallader granted a second charter (681).[2] It is possible that Rous might have accepted these claims; but he could hardly have failed to comment with a vociferous indignation that would still ring in our ears if he had been aware of the challenge to the Oxford legend contained in the further claim that King Alfred's foundation of Oxford University was achieved by his settling there the descendants of a band of Cambridge scholars who had migrated to Cricklade in the days of Penda. *Suam itidem vim habeant Cantabrigiensium ratiocinia,* said Hearne.

[1] Cantelupe's *historiola* is printed by Hearne, *De Antiquitate et Origine . . . Univ. Cantebrigiae* in T. *Sprotti Chronica.* ed. 1719, p. 262, from an Oxford MS. that agrees closely with the copy dated 1464 in Gonville and Caius library (*M.S.* 249, f. 191, ff) for copies existing in 1719 see Hearne, *op. cit.*, p. 246. Mr. P. Grierson, F.S.A., tells me of another fifteenth century version of the Cambridge *historiola* at Dublin (T.C.D. *MS.* 64.).

[2] 685 in Caius *MS.* above.

It is with a sense of refreshment and thanksgiving that we turn from Rous's medieval vision of his country's ancient history to his work as a practical antiquary. There is not, to be candid, very much to be said, but Rous had formed some sort of picture of past events in which people behaved with other manners and wore other clothes, and small though the advance actually was, the importance of the step forward was very great indeed. His principal achievement was his history of armour as sketched in the Warwick Rolls, but in the *Historia* also he refers to matters that have a genuine archæological flavour. He quotes references to the dress and arms and dwellings of the Saxons and the Normans;[1] later when his history has reached the end of the fourteenth century, he denounces the exaggerated pointed shoe of the period, repeating the contemporary story that in the more preposterous forms the curling shoe-tips had to be supported by gold and silver chains attached to the knee;[2] he notes also the then fashionable horned head-dress of the women, and their gowns with long trains, and their new habit of riding side-saddle, a custom that has been introduced, he said, by Anne of Bohemia.[3] Another interest of Rous's was seals. He recorded that Henry I was the first to seal in wax,[4] that is to say to substitute the seal for the sign-manual, and this is within half a century a correct estimate;[5] he also observes, rightly, that in the early thirteenth century, the seals of the barons began to have an armed equestrian figure on the obverse, and on the reverse an armorial shield, and he notes that this was the time canopies first appeared over the heads of the figures, which is again an approximately accurate observation.[6]

Rous could draw very well, and he believed in the usefulness of drawings, and many years before Breydenbach took an artist out to the Holy Land, Rous had tried to persuade John Tiptoft, Earl of Worcester, then on a visit to Warwick Castle, to do the same.[7] The nicest drawing he has left us is the picture of himself (Pl. II, a) on the back of the Latin Roll, a drawing about seven inches high in a soft blurred line, showing a lovable and rather dumpy old gentleman at work on a long roll that is spread over

---

[1] *Hist. Reg. Ang.*, p. 106, cf. p. 86.
[2] Ib., p. 205, cf. *Eulogium Historiarum, Rolls*, 9, III, p. 231.
[3] Ib., p. 205.
[4] *Hist. Reg. Ang.*, p. 138.
[5] Cf. R. Lane Poole, *Studies in Chronology and History*. Oxford, 1934, p. 106.
[6] *Hist. Reg. Ang.*, p. 198.
[7] Ib., p. 5.

his desk; he has a close-fitting brown cap and brown hair, a light
purple gown with hood and white-bordered cap, and dark blue
cassock with white cuffs and a rumpled white collar. The quality
of the drawings in this Roll vary considerably, but a few are
admirable sketches of a most attractive and gentle daintiness, the
young Edward III (Pl. II, b), for instance, or St. Caradoc (Pl.
III, a), a figure in mail shaded light blue, and having a crimson
sword-belt and scabbard.[1] The main interest, however, of Rous's
drawings in the Warwick Rolls is that in them the artist had a
problem that his antiquarian taste, his knowledge of manuscripts,
effigies and armour, and his opportunities in Warwick Castle
itself, encouraged him to try to solve; for he had to depict the
legendary founders of Warwick, and the Saxon Earls, and the
Norman Newburghs, and the thirteenth and fourteenth century
Beauchamps, and the Kingmaker, and the contemporary Yorkist
royal family. Rous gave serious thought to this task, and he
studied the changing fashions in armour in order to make remote
ancestors look as though they belonged to ages far past. He was
not consistent in this endeavour. He took no care about the
chronology of female fashions, though he copied outmoded
styles with great accuracy, and Aelfleda, daughter of Alfred the
Great, is in fourteenth century dress in the style of the costume
on the effigy of the Countess Katherine in St. Mary's Church,
Warwick. His ancient kings are people in conventional late
Gothic robes, who wear hooped crowns of the period of Edward
IV, and his Edward the Confessor is a fourteenth century figure in
a slit robe revealing a leg in blue hose; the men's swords are
fifteenth century throughout. But when it came to suits of armour
there are changes of style that follow a carefully considered system, and this is so interesting and so well done that Sir James
Mann, noting this first outstanding survey of the development of
medieval armour, has suggested that the early armour of the
Earls of Warwick was still in the Castle when Rous was at work
on the Rolls.[2] The series starts quaintly with Arthurian and Saxon
earls completely clad in very long mail hauberks reaching almost

---

[1] The attribution of the Warwick Pageant (B.M. MS., *Julius E. IV*) to Rous cannot
be supported as the writing thereon is certainly not Rous's. On this matter see *Burlington
Magazine*, I, p. 159; ib., XXX, 1917, p. 23, and Viscount Dillon and W. H. St. J. Hope,
Pageant . . . of Richard Beauchamp, 1914. Note that the attribution was supported by Sir
Simon Archer in the seventeenth century (Archer's copy of the Rolls is in the possession
of the Earl of Plymouth and now deposited in the Birthplace, Stratford-on-Avon).
[2] *Arch. Journ.* 89 (1932), p. 254.

to their ankles, and carrying big heater-shaped shields. The short hauberks, ending just below the knees, begin with the Late Saxon earls. Most of the Conquest period earls have a simple hemispherical ribbed helm attached by a chain to the sword-pommel, a misinterpretation of the sword chained to the hauberk that Rous had seen on Beauchamp medieval seals; one earl, Wolgeat (Pl. III, c), wears the leather cap over which the helm fitted. The latest of the Saxon earls have knee-caps and elbow-caps and a short shield; with the first of the Newburghs (d. 1123), the helm is no longer chained and has ear-pieces, and later, thirteenth century, members of the family have armorial surcoats; the first visored bascinet is that of Earl Thomas de Newburgh (d. 1242), which is about half a century too early. William Maudit and the early Beauchamps wear mixed mail and plate, and Guy Beauchamp (d. 1315) has cuisses and grieves, palettes and gauntlets; Rous is now alluding to armour of the kind on the D'Abernon brass (*c.* 1325) and the Black Prince effigy (*c.* 1345), and has obviously a very clear idea of the actual styles of the fourteenth century. The suit of Thomas Beauchamp (d. 1369) may well have been drawn from the armour on his effigy (Pl. IV, c) if not from the armour itself, and the picture of the great Richard Beauchamp suggests that Rous was imagining the old Countess's father in the beautiful full-plate armour in which, though of a fashion fifty years after his day, he is represented on his effigy in the Beauchamp Chapel.

Rous's achievement was not brilliant, but he had got his development of armour in its main principles correct, and a modern antiquary's heart warms to him as the great Warwick Roll unfolds. With no less affection we now cherish the memory of his contemporary, William of Worcester or William Botoner as he sometimes called himself, our first practising antiquary who was a layman. He was born in Bristol, went to Oxford in 1431, and five years later he became Sir John Fastolf's secretary. He served him until the knight's death in 1459, spending some of his time in Fastolf's manor at Castlecombe in Wiltshire, at Fastolf's house in Southwark, and, after 1454, at Caister Castle. Fastolf trusted Worcester, and Worcester loved Sir John. When Fastolf died, his secretary's professional life ended, and he said he

would "never have oder master butt his old master".[1] In the
knight's service he married and had children, and he claims that
Fastolf had made him a grant of land for the support of his
family, but Fastolf, who had underpaid him while he was alive,
did not provide for him in his will, so that eventually the loyal
Worcester became a man with a grievance, and quarrelled with
the Pastons when Fastolf's will was disputed. In the settlement
he was awarded property in Norwich and Southwark, and he
also had a house in his native Bristol.

At Oxford, Worcester studied medicine and astronomy; later he
learned French and had Greek lessons under William Sellyng at
Canterbury. The notes he has left behind him contain passages
in Greek and Hebrew, and mathematical and astronomical figures,
and it is recorded that he wrote on Ovid and translated Cicero
from the French.[2] He possessed a good library, and was able to
make what was for Norfolk of 1460 impressive classical allusions,
in his letters;[3] but he was never a scholar of great attainments
and there is no hint that there was any Renaissance incredulity
in his mind on the subject of the British History; on the contrary,
his memoranda suggest he was entirely content with the story of
Brutus, though he did not himself make any contribution to the
rigmarole of the Brut. We may pass, therefore, at once to the
practical work for which he is remembered.

He is the first antiquary now known for his "itinerary", though
he was not in fact either the first or a particularly notable traveller
in the cause of learning,[4] and he made no comprehensive tour of
Britain. His work was based on his homes in Bristol and Norfolk,
and his principal antiquarian adventure was a journey made in

---

[1] *Paston Letters*, ed. Gairdner, III, letter 391. For William of Worcester see the Paston
Letters *passim*; F. A. Gasquet, *The Old English Bible and Other Essays*, London, 1908, p. 247
ff.; James Dallaway, *Antiquities of Bristow*, 1834.
[2] This work was intended for Fastolf and was eventually (1473) presented to William
Wykeham—"sed nullum regardum recepi de episcopo", (It. p., 368).
[3] Cf. *Paston Letters*, ib., letter 401.
[4] In the second half of the eleventh century the Frenchman, Goscelin, had shown in
his English studies the importance of travelling, and John of Tynemouth (died *c.* 1350),
the hagiographer, was also a traveller. The most important of the itinerant scholars was
the fifteenth century John Boston of Bury St. Edmunds, the librarian of the Abbey, who
set himself the colossal task of making an index of all the religious works in the libraries of
Britain; and, though he doubtless used existing catalogues, he did examine many, and
perhaps most, of the 200 libraries in England, Wales and Scotland, that are tabulated in his
lists. For his lists (now imperfect), see Tanner, ed. Wilkins, *Bib. Brit. Hib.*, 1748, p. XXIV,
and for Boston see M. R. James, *Abbey of St. Edmund at Bury*, Cambridge, 1895, p. 40, and
Eng. Hist. Review, XLI, 1926, p. 252.

1478 from Norwich to St. Michael's Mount in Cornwall;[1] he has left a day-to-day diary of this trip, and it is now part of the collection of topographical and historical notes on long narrow slips of paper, bound up in no very clear order with some half-sheets and letters, in the library of Corpus Christi College, Cambridge. This volume is the *Itinerary* edited by James Nasmith in 1778.[2]

Worcester wrote a chronicle of recent history,[3] and also seems to have been collecting for a description of Britain, the material he gathered for this second purpose being partly historical and partly geographical; he noted, for example, inter-town distances, the courses of rivers, lists of bridges, and he made various extracts from chronicles and calendars. He had no antiquarian prejudice; the size of Caister Castle, and the names and tonnage of the ships built by Cannyng at Bristol, were as important to him as the dimensions of an ancient cathedral. His work has to us two main interests, the first being his passion for extracting information from talkative strangers. Many such characters appear in his notes; a lawyer of Tavistock who was an authority on West Country Saints; a sailor who knew Scotland and Ireland; an Avon ferryman who knew the Bristol Channel mileages, a porter of Bristol Castle; a man doing the leadwork on the roof of St. Mary Redcliffe; the masons building St. Stephen's Church, Bristol (see p. 32); a Shropshire man who knew the upper Severn; a merchant of Dublin who could tell him about Ireland and the Isle of Man, and a chance acquaintance who knew Scandinavia; he was in fact insatiably curious, and he took careful notes of all he was told. The second interest of his work is that he measured and described buildings, and even towns, in a way that no antiquary had done before. A plan of medieval Bristol has been reconstructed from his notes.

His measurements are generally the rough jottings of a visitor content with a very simple record of size. Generally, he paced

---

[1] Notes relating to what was apparently a single trip occur in two places in the "Itinerary", C.C.C. Cambridge *MS.* 210, f. 13 and f. 60.

[2] *Itinerarium sive Liber Rerum Memorabilium* in *Itineraria Symonis Simeonis et Willelmi de Worcestre.* Cambridge, 1778. An admirable modern edition has been edited by Mr. John Harvey, *William Worcestre Itineraries* (Oxford, 1969).

[3] See his *Annales Rerum Anglicarum, 1324–1491* and 'Ανέκδοτα *quaedam alia historica* in *Liber Niger Scaccarii,* 11, 1771, pp. 424 and 522.

the distances and set them down as so many of his steps, which varied on his own admission from a foot and a half to just over two feet; he also used a "bracchium" of two yards for heights, and for small distances the span of his hand. His measurements of buildings destroyed do not provide us with a satisfactory plan, and were not intended to be surveys of that kind of thoroughness; for instance, the lay-out of the vanished church of Holm St. Benet on the River Bure in Norfolk, which he knew well, cannot properly be determined from his numerous notes, though he tells us the length and breadth of the nave, of the cross, of the choir, and the size of Fastolf's south choir aisle, and also the dimensions of its arcade, and also the number of the windows therein and the number of their lights, and the length of the altar at the end of it, and the length of the high Altar. Worcester was making only an intelligent layman's notes, but there can be no doubt of his genuine interest in architecture. Twice he lists the technical terms for mouldings, and on one occasion he made a sectional drawing (Pl. V)[1] of a jamb of a door in St. Stephen's Bristol, a work on which no doubt he actually saw the masons engaged.

Worcester's great achievement was his survey of Bristol, the most painstaking and detailed piece of topographical fieldwork undertaken before the great topographers and cartographers of the next century began systematic work. We do not really know how serious his intentions were with regard to any larger task in the nature of a *Britannia*, but he is indisputably the first British antiquary who addressed himself with enthusiasm and intelligence to that task in the performance of which Leland and Camden are regarded as the most famous pioneers. Until Nasmith printed the notes Worcester left, he remained unhonoured, and the Tudor antiquaries seem to have had no knowledge of his work. Fifty years were to pass before Leland's journies carried forward the kind of practical topographical survey that Worcester had so meretoriously begun, and it would not suit our purpose to make a continuous story of this single antiquarian endeavour —what we may call the *Britannia* theme of this book—by turning at once to his celebrated itineraries. Leland, we shall find, was a very complex person whose varying interests and oddly differing performances will demand our attention in several chapters. If

[1] C.C.C. Cambridge, *MS.* 210, f. 129 (Nasmith, p. 220).

we are to understand him and the antiquaries of his age, we must for the moment set topography aside and first of all allow the progress and fortunes of the British History to guide us into the Tudor period and to prepare us for the major conflict in Tudor antiquarian thought.

III

The Tudor Cult of the British History

JOHN ROUS was a thorough-going medievalist in his attitude to the British History; he believed in every word of it, and added to it, as we have seen, a group of wonderful personages of his own invention; but even when he was still a young man British scholars who were in touch with the new thought of the fifteenth century must have begun to regard the familiar story with suspicion and disfavour. For the first time since the story took shape in the twelfth century men had begun to doubt whether Brutus the Trojan had ever existed, and we can feel fairly certain that when Abbot John Whethamstede of St. Albans, writing in his *Granarium* somewhere about 1435 gave four[1] reasons for not believing in Brutus, he was probably expressing the opinion of all members of the small group of English humanists to which he belonged. Humphrey, Duke of Gloucester, may well have been the first English royalty who did not believe that the kings of England were ultimately of Trojan descent, and it can be taken for granted that visiting Italian scholars like Poggio and Frulovisi would have emphatically expressed their approval of the scepticism in Humphrey's circle.

Whethamstede did not denounce the whole British History, and only a few pages away from his short article in which he expressed his doubts about Brutus, he described the exploits of Belinus, basing his account largely on Geoffrey of Monmouth's story, and informing us that he was the son of the law-giver Dunwallo Molmutius, that he and his brother Brennus sacked Rome, that he founded the four sacred main roads of Britain, and that he gave his name to Billingsgate; but the reason that Whethamstede admitted Belinus into the *Granarium* was because he thought he was the Belgius mentioned by Justinus,[2] and he took no interest in British kings not sponsored by Continental

---

[1] British Museum MS. *Nero C. VI*, f. 33; the passage as quoted by Camden in the *Britannia*, and repeated in all editions, is curtailed.
[2] *Hist. Phil.*: XXIV, V, 1.

historians; he did not even think King Arthur was worth mention. Thomas Rudborne briefly summarized the Brut in one chronicle, but sharply denounced the fabulous Arthur in another,[1] and John Capgrave, who was of Duke Humphrey's world, wrote coldly of both Brutus and Arthur. At this point, and thereafter in the presence of such prominent humanists as William Sellyng or William Grocin, or John Colet and Thomas Linacre, the famous story must have been in serious danger of extinction, for antiquaries like John Rous, and the other believers of his day such as John Hardyng, would be powerless as defenders of medieval antiquarian thought as soon as the overwhelming weight of Renaissance learning was directed against their treasured fables; but the surprising fact is that at the end of Rous's life the British History was, so to speak, reprieved, and allowed to flourish with —in many quarters—its original medieval popularity, and at least another century of vigorous life before it. This revival was in a large measure due to the outbursts of patriotic enthusiasm that follow the accession in 1485 of the Welshman, Henry Tudor, to the throne. The prophecy made to Cadwallader, last king of the Britons, that his people would once again possess the land of their fathers seemed to be fulfilled when, after a dramatic dynastic upheaval, a man whom Wales could call her son became King of England. The British History, in other words, had suddenly proved to be true, and we find that it was not considered inappropriate to include in fanciful designs for Tudor Royal Arms the quarterings Brutus, Belinus, and King Arthur.

These curious arms have the interest that in themselves they demonstrate the sustained and developing strength of the British History in the sixteenth century. Henry VII had a coat quartering England, France, Brutus, Belinus, Arthur, Swain, Edward the Confessor, and William the Conqueror,[2] but an even more remarkable design was made for Elizabeth in which the whole history of the country from Brutus onwards was set forth in blazon. John Norden published this in the printed version of his survey of Hertfordshire in 1598 (Pl. XI, b); and it is also displayed as the official royal arms in the church of Preston, Suffolk; copies of it are to be found in many collections of arms dating

---

[1] Wharton, *Anglia Sacra*, I, 188; cf. British Museum MS. *Nero A. XVII.*
[2] B.M. *Add. MSS.* 46,354. Wriothesley Heraldic Collns., p. 144. I am grateful to my friend Mr. H. Stanford, London, F.S.A. for this reference.

from the end of Queen Elizabeth's reign and later, and several of
these tricks are accompanied by explanations of the principal
quarterings, though there is, as can be expected in the case of
fictitious coats, some obvious confusion in matter of details; the
first quarter is England, and the second the Saxon kings—
Edward the Confessor, St. Edmund, (?) King Egbert, King
Edward the Elder, with an escutcheon of the Danes in pretence
over all; the third quarter represents the Romano-British kings
and the fourth the British kings, Brutus, Belinus, Arthur, and
Arviragus;[1] in the base point is Ireland, and over all in pretence
the "princes of Wales conquered by the Saxons".

The most important figure in the Brut was King Arthur, the
mightiest of all the British heroes, the man before whom the
whole continent had trembled, who had vanquished the might of
Rome and was still the darling of his people—a king about whom
there had grown a cherished legend that he was not dead, but
would return. When a Welshman sat on the throne of England,
the memory of King Arthur acquired a new and lovely importance in the hearts of the Welsh and of all who passionately
supported the Tudors, and, no doubt with the deliberate intention
of endorsing the antiquarian significance of his accession, in 1486
the new King of England named his first-born son, Arthur. The
verses and pageantry that celebrated the main events of this
young prince's short life prove that Court and people alike enjoyed the stirring notion that the infant Tudor was destined to
renew the fame of the illustrious ancestor whose name he bore.[2]
When the young prince visited Coventry in 1499 he was greeted
by players representing King Arthur and the rest of the Nine
Worthies, and the actor-king addressed the thirteen-year-old
son as one whom Providence had chosen to be equal to himself
in might, who should spread again the fame of his name, and to
whom all enemies should kneel:

[1]The arms of St George were held to have been conferred on the Christian British
kings by St. Joseph of Arimathea, and the third and fourth quarterings might also be read
Uther Pendragon and Arthur, or Arthur and Lucius, or Arthur and Arviragus. The usual
fourth quarter in this shield is Cadwallader (azure a cross patty fitchy or).

[2] Cf. *Memorials K. Henry VII*. ed. Gairdner. Rolls 10, pp. 41–6; for the pageants see
especially E. Greenlaw. *Studies in Spenser's Historical Allegory*. Baltimore, John Hopkins.
1932, p. 172 ff. Note also the poem by the Latin Secretary, Peter Carmelianus, British
Museum, *Add. MSS*. 33736 f. 10 b.

Thurgh the fere of Pallas that favoreth your lynage
And all outward enmyes laboreth to subdue
To make them to do to yewe as to me dyd homage.[1]

The boy, in short, was reminded that he was descended from
Aeneas, and, more ominously, of the conquests that had made
King Arthur the master of Europe. Half a century later, after
poor Arthur was dead, there were still writers glad to insist that
the glory of King Arthur had returned and that the ancient hero
had reawakened in the heart of Henry VII. John Twyne, the
Canterbury schoolmaster who did not believe in Brutus and was
one of the most sagacious antiquaries of his day, writing about
1540, applauded the wisdom of Henry in reintroducing Arthur's
name as a splendid token of his Arthurian heritage;[2] and in 1542
the chronicler Edward Hall said that at the christening of Prince
Arthur "Englishemen no more rejoysed than outwards nacions
and foreyne prynces trymbled and quaked, so much was that
name to all nacions terrible and formidable".[3]

Even over a century after the event, when enthusiasm was
notably cooling, Francis Bacon recorded that the infant prince
was called Arthur "in honour of the British race, of which himself (Henry VII) was . . . according to that ancient worthy
king of the Britaines, in whose acts there is truth enough to
make him famous, beside that which is fabulous.[4]

There is, indeed, no doubt about the nation-wide reverence
felt for the memory of King Arthur in the Tudor period;[5] many
people saw nothing at all preposterous in Geoffrey's fantastic
account of his exploits. Dr. John Dee, for instance, in his notes
on his map of the northern hemisphere, dated 1580, extended
Arthur's conquests "even unto the North Pole (in manner)" and
made him lord of Greenland and all the northern isles "cum-
passing unto Russia"; and he was of the opinion that Arthur had
sent colonies to these remote places.[6] In fact, pride in King Arthur
manifested itself in a popular cult of the British hero, and as an
example of the more extreme evidences of this fervour, there is

---

[1] Thomas Sharp, *Pageants . . . at Coventry.* Coventry 1825, p. 155.
[2] Thomas Twyne. *De Rebus Albionicis.* London. 1590, p. 161. See p. 105 *infra*.
[3] *Hall's Chronicle*, ed. 1809, p. 428.
[4] *Hist. Reigne K. Henry VII.* London, 1622, p. 18.
[5] The subject has been fully treated by Professor Charles Bowle Millican, *Spenser and the Table Round*, Cambridge, Harvard University Press, 1932.
[6] British Museum *MS. Aug. I*, Vol. I, 1.

the foundation in 1543 of a Society of Archers consisting of "knights" with Arthurian titles and Arthurian coats of arms, that yearly celebrated "the renowened memorie of the magnificent King Arthur".[1] There were antiquaries and historians, English and Welsh, who shared this popular feeling, as we shall presently see, and it was the Arthur-cult that was the real cause of the extraordinary battle about the British History in which a small group of learned writers argued and raged and abused each other in a roaring and turbulent dispute that lasted for over a hundred years. The Arthurians saw the danger clearly enough, and it was on behalf of the darling hero of the Tudors that the whole British History was solemnly studied and restudied at a time when continental nations no longer thought it worth while to hold such passionate views about their fabulous origins; for, plainly, if Trojan Brutus were abandoned as a fictitious person, the all-conquering Arthur would run the risk of being destroyed by the same arguments that swept Brutus out of real history; for Arthur, the conqueror of Rome, was unknown to contemporary or nearly contemporary chroniclers of the Empire. How sensitive the true believers were is illustrated by the anger with which the historian Polydore Vergil was assailed, for the Italian's cruel little paragraph in his *Anglica Historia*—taking the place of the pages of glorious narrative that Tudor patriots expected—a few lines about a mysterious man of romance and legend, a kind of British Roland who was subsequently very magnificently entombed in a monastery that had not even been founded in his day, this, from above all people a foreigner, was an almost insupportable insult, and in it lay the real challenge that the outraged romantic scholars of Britain were determined to withstand.

There were other reasons for the continued popularity of the British History. For Welsh readers it was the paramount charter of their country's greatness; Englishmen, who were often extremely unwilling to acknowledge the barbaric Saxons as their ancestors, saw in the heroes and conquests of the Brut an obvious source of their country's present pride and valiant heart; the antiquaries of Oxford and Cambridge could trace their universities back into the most remote past by means of the Trojan chronicle; moreover, the British History was an ancient and

---

[1] Richard Robinson, *Auncient Order, Societie, and Unitie Laudable of Prince Arthure.* London, 1583. On this subject see Millican, *op. cit*, p. 54.

familiar thing; it was, so to speak, a standard work, and one that was, so far as the pre-Roman books were concerned, unchallenged by any attractive and interesting competitor.

It is also important to remember that the British History had now become accessible in print. Caxton's *Chronicles of England* first published in 1480 stands at the head of a long series of printed editions of the common Brut that thereupon acquired the status of an up-to-date official history of England. Higden's *Polychronicon* was another Caxton publication, and throughout the sixteenth century most of the compilers of the English histories intended for general reading began their narrative with an uncritical account of Brutus and the Trojans.[1] Some well-known names occur to us here. Fabyan (1516), Hardyng edited by Grafton (1543), and Grafton (1568), all helped to popularize the British History, and so, of course, did Raphael Holinshed and his collaborator, William Harrison (1577), and so also did John Stow in the various editions of his Chronicles and Annales.[2] We must remember too that one of the results of this repeated telling of the stories of the Trojans in Britain and of the great King Arthur was that the British History became a cherished source of material for poets and playwrights, and at the end of the sixteenth century and in the reign of James I this gave the famous story a new and increased measure of popularity. *The Tragedy of Gordubuc* by Sackville and Norton was one of the early dramatizations of a story from the Brut, and it was performed before Queen Elizabeth in 1562. There were also many plays for the popular theatre, and we know that *The Misfortunes of Arthur* (1587), *Locrine* (1595), *Uter Pendragon, Molmutius Dunwallow, Brute Greenshield*, and the *Conquest of Brute*, were produced on the Elizabethan stage before the turn of the century.

The dramatist, however, used the stories from the British History without any personal comment on their antiquarian validity; some poets on the other hand adopted the legends of the Brut with a partisan enthusiasm for a neglected chapter of the annals of Britain. Arthur Kelton of Shrewsbury, a great cham-

---

[1] In contrast to these popular English versions, note also that the Latin text of the *Historia Regum Britanniae* was now in print, having been published by the Ascensius Press in Paris with the title *Britannie utriusque Regum et Principum Origo et Gesta Insignia* 1508, 2nd ed. 1517. The editor was a Celtic student, Ivo Cavellatus, who found that Geoffrey's famous book had for a long time been completely neglected by scholars in Paris University.

[2] For Edmund Howes's editions of Stow's Annals, see p. 100.

pion of the Welsh people, published in 1547 his rhyming *Chronycle with a genealogie*, and this leaves us in no doubt whatever of his passionate sympathy with the cause of the British History and of his opinion of Polydore Vergil. The ghostly lamentations of Albanact, Humber, Locrinus, Mempricius, and Bladud, were inserted in the 1574 edition of the *Mirror for Magistrates* because the editor, John Higgins, objected to the reluctance of certain chroniclers to "fetch out our histories from the beginning". William Warner, whose *Albion's England* (1586) fetched our history so far back that he did not come to the story of the Trojans in Britain till the third book of the poem, set forth the whole British History in the elaborate frame of a very long poem, and he did so with every sign of seriousness:

> Now, of the conquerour this isle
> Had Brutaine unto name,
> And with his Trojans Brute began
> Manurage of the same.

A year later (1587) the second versifying champion of the Welsh from Shrewsbury, Thomas Churchyard, sung the praises of King Arthur—and the shame of Polydore Vergil—in his descriptive poem, *The Worthines of Wales*.

> And though we count, but Robin Hood a Jest,
> And old wives tales, as tatling toyes appeare:
> Yet Arthurs raigne, the world cannot denye,
> Such proofe there is, the troth thereof to trye:
> That who so speakes, against so grave a thing,
> Shall blush to blot, the fame of such a King.

Churchyard was, like others of his age, a diehard Arthurian.

We need not ask for further proof of the existence of a Tudor cult of King Arthur and of the renewed affection for the British History in the first half of the sixteenth century. They were real enough, and of such pervasive significance that they cannot be ignored in a history of antiquarian thought; but it must also be noted that they were founded either on popular emotion or on a fanatical patriotism, and they are expressed largely in verse or in the most violently worded passages of the most emotionally loyal historians and antiquaries such as Leland. They have little to do with cool thinking, and they certainly do not reflect the most intelligent antiquarian opinion of the day.

We shall discuss later on (p. 104) the scholarly opinion of a sceptical kind, but let us note here that there is evidence of it among British writers at an early date. Even before Polydore Vergil first published his history in 1534, Robert Fabyan, who was prepared to believe most of the British History, revolted from the traditional account of Arthur's victories in France,[1] and the wise John Rastell, who brought to the problems of the Trojans and King Arthur, the trained mind of a legal antiquary, was obviously distrustful not only of Arthur's fabled exploits, but of the whole British History,[2] just as he was also extremely doubtful of the genuineness of Arthur's seal in Westminster Abbey (p. 96). Leland's contemporary, John Twyne, the Canterbury schoolmaster, most clearly stated that he did not believe in Brutus: his schoolfellow, George Lily, son of the first High Master of St. Paul's and chaplain to Cardinal Pole, a student of Renaissance scholarship and a man well aware of the best contemporary Italian thought, was completely unaffected by the sentimental patriotism that coloured Leland's antiquarian life, and into the opening twenty-five lines of his short *Chronicon*[3] published in 1548, he compressed the most withering dismissal of the Trojan origin of the British that had yet appeared. He offered no arguments. He made it quite clear that the story of Brutus was nonsense and must be omitted, and in so doing, of course, he reveals the probable views on this subject of the humanists of the earlier generation, such as Colet, and his own father, and Sir Thomas More. A year later, in 1549, appeared the first edition of the chronicle begun by Thomas Lanquet (d. 1549) and continued by the future Bishop of Winchester, Thomas Cooper. In this popular work, subsequently known as "Cooper's Chronicle", Lanquet said that though he could not ignore the British History and must summarize its contents, yet in his view it was "full of errours, and hath in it no manifest apparance of truthe, as beyng written neither of no ancient tyme, nor yet by no credible hystorian", and as for King Arthur, of him "be

---

[1] *Cronycles.* Pynson, 1516. Quinta Pars Arthuri, cap. VI, f. XLIII.

[2] *The Pastyme of People,* 1529. After expressing his doubts Rastell gives a summary of the British History for the sake of the moral precepts to be deduced therefrom.

[3] For this see Bp. Paolo Giovio, *Descriptio Britanniae,* Venice, 1548.

written many thinges in the englyshe cronicle of small credence and farre discordant from other wryters."[1]

It is probable that educated opinion at court, if it had been forced to declare itself, would have supported Lily and Lanquet rather than a passionately over-loyal antiquary like Leland. We can do little more than guess here, but we note, for instance, that the British History is not named in his tutor's list of the school-books that young Prince Arthur read. There is, in fact, nothing to show that the worldly-wise Tudor sovereigns thought that they were really and truly descended from a line of Trojan kings, or believed that King Arthur had been master of Western Europe. No doubt they regarded him as an ancestor and an authentic historical personage, and were prepared to take every possible advantage of their descent from him; no doubt Henry VII genuinely thought that Arthur had founded the Order of the Garter;[2] no doubt he and his successors would take seriously the considerable placename and archæological evidence to which we shall presently refer (p. 95); no doubt the Tudor monarchs willingly permitted Arthur's conquest of Europe to supply some sort of historical authority for their own territorial ambitions;[3] but it is to be observed that neither Henry VIII nor Elizabeth took offence when the Brut and the historicity of Arthur were attacked. Henry VIII, whose personal background at the field of the Cloth of Gold was made magnificent with impressive Arthurian figure-paintings,[4] allowed Polydore Vergil, unreproved by royal rebuke, to publish and republish a book in which King Arthur was treated with an unpleasantly critical historical candour, and the scholar-diplomat, Sir Thomas Elyot, did not think it imprudent to declare in the 1545 edition of his dictionary that he doubted the Trojan ancestry of the British and thought that King Arthur had done no more than vanquish the Saxons and subdue Scotland and

[1] *An Epitome of Cronicles*, 1549 (printed MDLXIX), p. 32, p. 144b, and cf. p. 147.
[2] *Calendar of State Papers*. Venetian I. 1202–1509, No. 790, p. 281.
[3] For instance in 1531 the Duke of Norfolk showed the French and Spanish ambassadors a copy of the legend on King Arthur's seal (p. 95), presumably in connection with Henry VIII's aggressive foreign policy; but he knew so little about Arthur that he thought it was the inscription on the tomb, and the Spanish ambassador wrote down the name as that of the constellation Arturus, and admitted he did not know to whom the Duke was referring. Chapuys remarked that this wonderful all-conquering Arthur had forgotten to call himself Imperator Asie, and he referred to the Norman Conquest as an example of the tide flowing in an opposite direction.
[4] *Calendar of State Papers, Venetian*, II. 1520–6, No. 50, p. 33. For a flattering reference to Henry as the noblest and most famous prince since King Arthur, see *Letters and Papers Henry VIII*, VI. No. 1263, p. 515.

Ireland. Elyot said that Arthur's household had been so magnificent that the French and the Spanish had invented incredible fables about him; "yet of them which wrote histories about this tyme, he was unremembered".[1] So, too, in Elizabeth's reign the Queen's godson, John Harington, was permitted to refer to Arthur as though it were an open question whether this hero had ever existed.[2] She and the sceptical Burghley, however kind they may have seemed to the ingenious Dr. John Dee, were very careful to take no action when in 1580 he presented his argument, based on Arthur's conquests, that the English crown had rights to Iceland and a North Sea empire,[3] and a very plain indication that in spite of Kenilworth pageants and the fulsome Arthurian flattery of the poets, Elizabeth herself thought little of her Arthurian ancestry is to be found in Churchyard's *Worthines of Wales*, published in 1587, for, burning with Welsh pride in King Arthur's fame, the writer there revealed what is likely to have been one of the principal causes of the soreness felt by the patriot-antiquaries of a fundamentalist persuasion. Not only was the historicity of Arthur attacked by foreigners, but Arthur's glory was not really being taken as seriously in court circles as his Tudor propagandists hoped—he says:

> King Arthur's reign (though true it weare)
> Is now of small account

and, recalling the Arthurian splendours of Caerleon, and the ancient renown of Arthur's name, he continued:

> Would God the brute thereof were knowne,
> In countrey, court, and towne,
> And she that sits in reagall throne,
> With septer, sword, and crowne
>
> Who came from Arthur's rase and lyne
> Would mark these matters throwe
> And strewe thereon her gracious eyne
> To help Caerleon now.

[1] Bibliotheca, s. v. *Arthurus and Britannia* (the entries are not in the *Dictionary* of 1538).
[2] *Orlando Furioso in English*. London, 1591, p. 29.
[3] B.M. MSS. *Vitellius c. VII*, ff. 249 b–265 f; this episode is well described by Professor Millican, op. cit., pp. 42–3. The argument depends on the remarks of Lambarde in his ’Αρχαιονομια (1568), which include the statement that King Arthur persuaded the Pope to consent to Norway being for ever annexed to the British Crown; all this was repeated at some length by Richard Hakluyt, *Principell Navigations*, 1589, p. 243.

A year before, Warner in *Albion's England* had written of Arthur:

> His Scottish, Irish, Almaine, French,
> And Saxon battelles got,
> Yeild fame sufficient: these seem true,
> The rest I credit not.

and those who have considered the antiquarian thought of the period in its larger aspect will know that it was not a very surprising thing that in 1574 the twenty-year old Sir Philip Sidney, newly down from Oxford, where some of his elders were still talking about Brutus's Greeks at Cricklade, should have laughed over the British pretensions in Humphrey Lhuyd's *Breviary of Britaine*, a particularly vigorous outcry on the part of the fundamentalists that we shall presently examine.[1]

But here is a point, now that we are acquainted with the principal antiquarian conflict of his age, that we can change our topic and come to Leland himself.

---

[1] *Works* III. Cambridge, 1923, p. 85.

IV

John Leland

WE have seen that as the Middle Ages draw to a close, two
men, Rous and Worcester, emerge as identifiable antiquaries whose writings made it possible for us to discover in
some measure what sort of men they were like and how they
worked. Now that we have come to Tudor England, it is again
possible to give an account of one man and his work, a man whom
we expect to represent the Renaissance with its wider learning
and sharper critical sense. This is John Leland, who is important
to us in this book chiefly for his topographical work and for his
rigidly medieval attitude to the British History; but the first
thing to say about him is that on a larger stage he is also important as a man of many other antiquarian activities. This
is why we have to interrupt our sequence of chapters devoted to the aspect of antiquarian thought concerned with the
propagation or discrediting of the British History in order to
obtain a general portrait of a great man who in the first half of
the sixteenth century publicly described himself as *Antiquarius*.
We shall not, nevertheless, finish with Leland here and now; his
defence of the historicity of Brutus and King Arthur will be
mentioned with more detail later (Chapter VI), and his celebrated itineraries discussed again when we return to the subject
(Chapter VIII) of the British topographers of the Tudor Period.

John Leland was born in London about 1503.[1] He was an
orphan, and a man called Thomas Myles adopted him, and sent
him to the newly founded St. Paul's School during the years
when William Lily was still High Master (1512-22). There the
little boy became a member of what was perhaps the most remarkable company that an ordinary lad of his day could join.
The High Master was one of the great scholars of the age; he had

---

[1] The reference books say *c.* 1506. If this date be accepted Leland graduated B.A. at
Cambridge age fifteen or sixteen and would be only five or six years older than his little
pupil when, on leaving Cambridge, he became tutor in the Norfolk household. For the
life of Leland see Miss L. Toulmin Smith's edition of the *Itinerary* (London, 1907), and
the Centaur Press reprint of this (London, 1964), with foreword by myself.

been to Jerusalem; he had studied the classics in Italy; he had become famous for his learning in Greek and as a grammarian; and he was a close friend of Sir Thomas More. His pupils included several boys who became distinguished diplomats and lawyers and scholars, and Leland retained the friendship of these youths in later life when they had grown into men of dignity and high position.

When Leland left St. Paul's, Myles sent him to Christ's College, Cambridge, and he took his B.A. in 1521-2. He then entered the Lambeth household of Thomas Howard, second Duke of Norfolk, as tutor to the Duke's sixth son, Thomas, then a lad of about eleven;[1] but in 1524 the old Duke died and Leland went to Oxford.[2] He was very proud of both his English universities, and he kept a string of the most fulsomely appreciative adjectives ready for any mention of either of them in his poems; but he did not like the still dominantly scholastic mood of the teaching, and after two or three years at Oxford, he went to the University of Paris. He was able to study there not merely because of the continued benefactions of Myles, but because by this time he had obtained some kind of royal endowment and was a King's Scholar. In Paris he met more famous men, chief of them the illustrious Greek scholar and numismatist, William Budé (1467–1540), and here he found the kind of teaching he sought. It was here too that he began to devote himself seriously to the composition of Latin poetry.

When Leland came back from Paris, probably about 1529,[3] he took orders and became a royal chaplain, being appointed to the living of Pepeling, near Calais, in 1530. He presided over this cure as an absentee, and in 1533 he was allowed by papal dispensation to hold as many as four benefices, provided he were ordained a priest; but by this time he had already acquired some fame as an antiquary and an official position in the royal libraries. Later, about 1540, in his book *Antiphilarchia* he tells us that Henry VIII had established three libraries especially devoted to the collection of ancient texts and that these were housed in the

[1] The second child of his father's second marriage; his elder brother, William, was born 1509–10, and as there were five more children before the Duke died, aged eighty-one, in 1524, Thomas was probably born *c.* 1511.

[2] He is traditionally connected with All Souls (cf. *Life*, p. 4, note k), but he was not a Fellow of the College.

[3] He was in Paris before the death of Paolo Emilio in 1529, cf. *Commentarii*, ccxvii.

palaces at Westminster, Hampton Court, and Greenwich, and, though he was probably only one of a small staff of librarians[1] serving these institutions, his personal success as a court-scholar was, in fact, remarkable, for he had persuaded King Henry VIII that he should be given a royal commission to search the libraries of the country for lost or forgotten works. In Leland's own words this famous warrant of 1533 was "to peruse and diligently to serche al the libraries of monasteries and collegies of this yowre noble reaulme, to the intente that the monuments of auncient writers as welle of other nations, as of this yowr owne province mighte be brought owte of deadely darkenes to lyvely lighte."[2]

As his historical studies continued, as he moved about the country from library to library, and as his material increased for his biographies of British historians and chroniclers, he became more and more anxious to write a description of Britain, that is to say to study for its own sake this land of memorable historical happenings and the fortunate home of the Tudor state Leland so dearly loved. According to his own account it was about 1540 that his topographical studies assumed a dominating importance. In 1546, addressing his New Year's Gift to Henry VIII, he wrote thus:

". . . after that I had perpended the honest and profitable studies of these historiographes, I was totally inflamed with a love to see thoroughly all those parts of this your opulent and ample realm that I had redde of in the aforesaid writers. In so much that all my other occupations intermitted, I have so travelled in your dominions both by the sea coasts and the middle parts, sparing neither labour nor costs by the space of these 6 years past, that there is almost neither cape nor bay, haven, creak or pier, river or confluence of rivers, breeches, washes, lakes, meres, fenny waters, mountains, valleys, moors, heaths, forests, woods, cities, burroughs, castles, principal manor places, monasteries, and colleges, but I have seen them, and noted in so doing a whole world of things very memorable."

One object of this new-born British topography was quite clear in his mind:

---

[1] Cf. British Museum, *Catalogue of the Royal MSS.* Introduction, pp. XIII, XIV. There does not seem to be any evidence that he was appointed "King's Antiquary", as is often stated.

[2] From his *Laboriouse Journey*, the New Year's Gift of 1546.

"So shall your Majesty have this your world and impery of England so set forth in a quadrate table of silver, if God send me life to accomplish my beginning, that your grace shall have ready knowledge at the first sight of many right delectable, fruitful, and necessary pleasures, by contemplation thereof . . . And because that it may be more permanent, and farther known, then to have it engraved in silver or brass, I intend by the leave of God, within the space of XII months following, such a description to make of your realm in writing, that it shall be no mastery after, for the graver or painter to make the like by a perfect example."

Leland then, intended to make a map of England and Wales, and to write the first detailed topographical description of these two countries, which was to be called *De Antiquitate Britannica* or *Civilis Historia*. We must imagine him as about forty when he thus declared his purpose. He had spent a great part of the last twelve years in travelling throughout England and Wales, and he had done more to make himself properly equipped for the undertaking than any man before him. Leland was, indeed, an antiquary of a new kind, and though he had had experience of the difficulties and disappointments of a scholar's life, he was in a position to write what would have certainly been the most famous book in the history of English antiquarian studies, for he had continued to receive substantial tokens of the royal favour; he had become rector of Haseley in Oxfordshire, and had been for two years a canon of King's College (Christ Church), Oxford; and by 1550 in addition to Pepeling and Haseley, he held a prebendship at Salisbury.

He did not fulfil his high promises. Our knowledge of his prebendship comes from a melancholy document of 1550 which tells us that Leland had gone mad, and had been committed to the care of an elder brother of whom we then hear for the first time. He died in 1552 and was buried in St. Michael at Corne, a church by St. Paul's that was destroyed in the Great Fire, near which he had a house. The *Britannia* was left unwritten and the map undrawn; but he had copied out his travel notes in preparation for this work, and most of these survive; he had also completed his lives of the British writers, and he had also written several long Latin poems.

It is said that Polydore Vergil, the Italian historian at the English court, never believed that Leland would really produce the books about which he spoke so grandly; the great John Caius of Cambridge, who knew Leland very well indeed, explained that, though undeniably a very learned man,[1] he was a boaster and a bad poet and a man whose antiquarian opinion must not be too readily accepted; Bale, who genuinely admired Leland and made considerable use of his papers, said: "I much do fear it that he was vainglorious."[2] We can add after studying Leland's writings, other than the itinerary-notes and collections, that he was often angry, incoherent, and illogical in argument, that he was sometimes credulous beyond our understanding, that he had little critical appreciation of the relative values of his sources, and that his fanatical adoration of Henry VIII and Tudor England repeatedly deprived him of judgment and good humour. He flattered the king by conducting an anti-Papacy propaganda; he wrote a long controversial book *Antiphilarchia*[3] "against the ambitious empire of the Roman bishop"; he "cut and rased" a line out of a tablet in York Minster that referred to a king who "took this kingdom of the Pope by tribute to hold of the Church of Rome";[4] he claimed that one of the purposes of his learning and researches was to expel "the crafty coloured doctrine of a rout of Roman bishops".[5] Leland was, before everything, a boastful, bigoted, and extremely touchy patriot with, in spite of his Renaissance upbringing, a medieval mind.

Yet John Leland is one of our greatest English antiquaries, illustrious alike in splendour of vision and purpose, in achievement, and in the direct and enduring usefulness of his work. Moreover, probably no other antiquary of this country has been more extensively quoted; for in topographical works from the

[1] *Ant. Cantab. Acad.* London, 1548, p. 36.

[2] *Laboriouse Journey*, 1549, sig. B. IV.

[3] This book is still in manuscript (Cambridge Univ. Library, MS. Ee V. 14). It is in the form of a dialogue, taking place on the banks of the Thames, in which a reformer's views of the *Tu es Petrus* text (Matt. XVI. 18–19) are expounded with a system and clarity not always to be found in Leland's antiquarian writings. The discussion concludes with a loud burst of praise for Henry VIII and contains a few details of historical interest, for instance the account of the examination before the king of John Lambert in 1538. Leland represents Henry as initiating not merely this particular heresy-hunt, but also documentary research into Church history in defence of the Faith, and he mentions that a study of Saxon laws had shown that the Early English Church was independent of Rome. The general intention of the book is a refutation of the *Hierarchiae Ecclesiasticae Assertio* by the Dutch controversialist Albert Pigghe (Cologne, 1538).

[4] This took place in 1534, *Letters and Papers Henry VIII*, VII, App. 23, p. 637; doubtless the tablet, which gave the reigns of various kings, was not a monument of importance but a board painted with some late medieval historical propaganda.

[5] *Laboriouse Journey*, 1549, sig. C. 1.

grandest county history to the humblest little guide Leland is mentioned repeatedly as a first and most interesting source of information about the former appearance of a town or a village or a building, about monuments now vanished, and about the history of persons and places, elsewhere unrecorded. And he is no less well-known to-day as a fount of biographical knowledge; for his *Lives and Works of the British Writers* (the *Commentarii*) and his poems addressed to his contemporaries, and his references to them in his longer poems, are prime sources that are acknowledged again and again in the volumes of the *Dictionary of National Biography*; furthermore, in catalogues of manuscripts Leland's name is of frequent occurrence because of the usefulness of his notes on the contents of the medieval libraries, and his references to the whereabouts of chronicles and other books that had interested him.

Leland's inspection of the libraries was certainly thorough, and he said he had been to all the most important. There are many notes on his finds in the pages of the *Commentarii*, and he also left about a hundred rough lists of books, containing over a thousand short titles, that were made in ne libraries at the time of his visit. Broadly speaking, the main purpose of these was to record informally and for his own use works on British history and books by British authors; and the collection of books for the Royal library was similarly influenced b Leland's special interests. He had no direct orders to hunt out the chief treasures of the libraries, and to mark them for confiscation like monastic lands and plate, and the fact is that, though he said the king "had no little esteem" for the books he obtained, they were not really a very interesting series, except to Leland himself.[1] He took no great interest in bindings and illuminations,[2] and his acquisitions were mostly historical books, with a few bible commentaries and general theological works; his greatest prize, if we may believe him, was St. Patrick's Charter from Glastonbury (p. 91),

---

[1] A few Lincolnshire lists have books marked for subsequent collection, see *English Historical Review*, LIV (1939), p. 88; in general, see also British Museum *Cat. Royal MSS.* Appendix 69, and N.R. Ker, *Medieval Libraries of Great Britain*, London, 1941, p. XIII.

[2] At Warden, Bedfordshire, he noted a "codex belle pictus", and at Wells a very fine Terence; at St. Albans he saw a *Life* of the martyr painted in gold and red, and bound in silk; at Eye in Suffolk he noted the Lombardic capitals in the "Red Book". He was also much impressed by a book of Carolingian poems belonging to Richard Talbot (*Coll.* IV, p. 97), for the first and middle and last letter of each line was coloured red, and throughout each poem the letters so coloured were all the same letter. There are not many other instances of Leland as a bibliophile.

which was presumably lent him in the hopes that its extraordinary claims might be brought to the notice of Henry VIII. Leland was particularly anxious to strengthen the section of the royal collections that we should call "British Authors", for the nationality of some of the lesser known writers was in doubt, and there were unscrupulous foreign scholars to be feared. In a letter written to Thomas Cromwell in 1536 about the need for securing books by these writers, Leland said: "The Germans perceiving our desidiousness and negligence, do send daily young scholars hither, that spoileth them and cutteth them out of libraries, returning home, and putting them abroad as monuments of their own country."[1] His supreme task of exalting the British dominated every aspect of Leland's life as an antiquary.

He did not say much about the libraries themselves. He regretted, however, that so little was left of the former immense treasure of books in St. Augustine's Abbey, Canterbury, though he himself continued the depredations. Many works of famous authors have been taken away for the royal library, and I have some now in my own possession that I hope to publish shortly."[2] He describes the library at Wells as notably rich in ancient books, and another library that he sincerely admired was that of the Abbey of Glastonbury. He began his stay by resting, for he arrived tired by his studies; but when Richard Whyting, the last Abbot of Glastonbury, showed him the library, as a great privilege, Leland's enthusiasm at once returned. "It contained, I suppose, the richest collection in Britain of books on our church history; the mere sight of this incredible series of most ancient books inspired me, and for a while I stood lost in wonder on the threshold. I spent days examining the shelves."[3] This was a happy experience; but there were others of a different kind, such as his visit to the library of the Franciscans at Oxford, where he wanted to see the books left by Robert Grosseteste. He said: "I was at once obstructed by some asses who brayed about nobody being able to see the library except the Warden and the Bachelors of the college; but I persisted, and waived my royal commission in their face, and came very near to using force. Then one of the asses, grumbling a good deal, at last reluctantly

---

[1] Wood. *Athenae Oxonienses* ed. Bliss, 1813, I, p. 198.
[2] *Commentarii*, Oxford, 1709, 301. For this and the following passages the text is Latin.
[3] Ib., p. 41.

opened the doors for me. Ye Gods! What did I find there! Dust, cobwebs, moths, cockroaches, mould, and filth. I even found some books, but I wouldn't willingly have given threepence for the lot! And it is this wonderful mass of rubbish that the Oxford Franciscans guard so jealously; for, needless to say, all Grosseteste's books, once a most valuable collection, have gone, stolen by the monks themselves. This will show bishops how foolish it is to bequeath important books to friars of this sort.'[1]

Leland began his antiquarian work as an historian and a student of placenames, and he considered himself a leading authority on the general subject of British antiquities; he referred to himself as the Beatus Renan of this country,[2] and boasted that it was he who had first shown the light to the Italian historian, Polydore Vergil, who thought himself so knowledgeable in these matters.[3] The truth, however, is that as a writer and a theoretical antiquary Leland did not show himself possessed of a distinguished and original mind. We shall study later on some of his arguments in support of the British History, and we need only note now that in these impassioned essays of his instances of a healthy Renaissance scepticism, such as his refusal to believe the Glastonbury legend of Joseph of Arimathea or his contempt for Nicholas Cantilupe's fanciful account of the origins of Cambridge, are rare indeed. He would not perhaps have understood why we now count him so great an antiquary; for we should have to tell him that his supreme antiquarian merit resulted from his resolution to go to look at places of interest instead of merely reading about them. There is no evidence that he had any idea of the important contribution to antiquarian practice that his long journeys had made; he just said that he had been exceedingly anxious to see these places, and had been rewarded by the acquisition of a mass of valuable notes.

The famous itineraries, based on his programme of research in the libraries, covered all England and Wales from Berwick and Carlisle in the north to the western extremes at Caernarvon, St. David's, and Land's End. They took him nearly ten years. The various groups of journeys have been mapped, as far as is possible, by Miss L. Toulmin Smith, and there was no one better

---

[1] *Commentarii*, p. 286.
[2] *Collectanea*, ed. Hearne, 1770–74, V. p. 120.
[3] Ib., V. p. 127.

able than she to speak on Leland's plan and the way he carried it
out. Little can be added to her remarks.[1] There is no discoverable
progression in the thoroughness of Leland's records, and it is
only by examining a series of specimen entries of one kind taken
from the narratives of various itineraries that we can find out
what Leland wanted to see and know. By this method we discover first of all that he had a great love for landscape and the
countryside and country life; and he was interested in what the
country could produce and in its mineral wealth; he was also
eager to make genealogical notes and to record the history of the
land-owning families; but we get a better idea of his antiquarian
interest from a selection of town-entries, and with their aid we
can describe his topographical purpose thus. When he came to a
town, he recorded its distance from other places, and he made
notes about its wall and gates, its castle, its parish church, its
streets and markets, and its finest houses; he observed, if there was
one, the course of the river through it, and recorded the bridges;
he also mentioned the suburbs, if any, and he inquired about the
staple industry; then he asked about any archæological discoveries
that had been made, and occasionally he recorded some bit of
local folklore or speculated about the meaning of the town's
name. The notes taken for any one town are usually far less
complete, often indeed totally inadequate, and there are many
omissions and some mistakes; but on the whole Leland aimed at
a sound impersonal recording, and he made very few comments
of his own. He was impressed, for instance, by the delightful
situation of Bewdley[2] in Worcestershire, and describes the town
with an unexpected warmth; he thought the market-place and
main street of Nottingham "the most fairest without exception
of al Inglande"; other places he sometimes said were mean or
bare or poor, and one was "a very filthy town and il kept"; but
his general purpose, as revealed in the description of Denbigh
quoted later (p. 137), was to record what he was told, and to
note points on which further information was desirable. The
description of the Droitwich salt industry[3] is an example of his
omnivorous interest in current affairs, and the observation of the

[1] *The Itinerary of John Leland.* London, 1907–10. See *Introduction* to Vol. I and maps in
each volume.
[2] *Itinerary,* ed. Toulmin Smith, II, pp. 87–8. He was similarly impressed by Bury
St. Edmunds, see *Cygnea Cantio,* commentary s.v. Curia.
[3] Ib., II, pp. 92–3.

three building-periods of Lincoln[1] an instance of sensible antiquarian interest.

Leland seldom attempted to judge the age of a building for
himself, but in a dim and rudimentary way he was aware of the
changing architectural styles; thus he thought Leominster church
so ancient that it might be the pre-Conquest building; at Grey's
Court in Oxfordshire he saw there were very old towers, proving
it had once been a castle, whereas the timber and brick court
was clearly later work; and he realized that in Carlisle Cathedral
the nave was older than the choir; but such expressions of opinion
are very rare, and Leland, like William of Worcester before him,
preferred to record information about buildings derived from
chronicles, inscriptions, and from local talk; the nave of Thorn-
bury church in Gloucestershire was built within the memory of
living man; Nottingham Castle had buildings of the reign of
Edward IV, that is to say about sixty years old; Bolton Castle in
Wensleydale was finished before King Richard II died, and so
on. He took very little notice of exterior detail; Southwell
Minster he described as "of no pleasant building, but rather
strong", he admired the "costly and fair" west front of Lichfield
Cathedral, and mentioned the pillars bearing beasts and giants on
the bridge of Nottingham Castle, and the chimney flues of Bolton
Castle; interiors of secular buildings interested him even less, with
the notable exception of the study in Wressle Castle, Yorkshire,
where he found the most ingenious and convenient library furniture he had ever seen. In churches, however, he noted the
more important tombs and epitaphs, usually very briefly, but
sometimes, as at Glastonbury Abbey and in St. Mary's, Warwick,
with greater care.

Though he shared the insensitiveness of his age to the magnificent medieval sculptures and paintings and stained glass that he
must have seen in all the greater churches, he had a fondness for
one particular kind of monument, the carved standing cross. His
notes on this subject are often very interesting. At Durham on
the south side of the cathedral he saw at the head of a grave a
cross seven feet high with a long illegible inscription, and he was
told it had been brought to its present site from Lindisfarne; at
Ripon in the "chapel garth" were three crosses of the most
ancient work standing in a row; at Brackley, Northants, there

[1] *Itinerary*, I, p. 30.

were three splendid crosses, one of medieval work and carved with ladies and armed men in tabernacles; in Reculver church on entering the choir he came upon the "fairest and most ancient" cross that he had ever seen, richly carved, circular in section, and nine feet high. He described the iconography and legends, and it is believed that this was the Saxon cross now represented only by some fragments that have been published by Sir Charles Peers.[1]

Leland did not look at the antiquities of pre-Conquest Britain with more than the ordinary interest he took in everything else. A few Arthurian sites, of course, like the camp of Camelot (Cadbury) seemed to him to be of special significance, because they had a bearing on the veracity of the British History; other archæological remains he took as he found them. He visited the Roman wall and noted the existence of the turf wall; he describes Caerleon, Caerwent, Richborough, and Cirencester, and finds in many other Roman towns are recorded; he made a long and most delightful list of the Romano-British sculptures he saw at Bath; he was interested in Roman coins. He recognized Roman tiles, which he called "long Briton bricks", in masonry, that therefore seemed to him to be early. He knew Watling Street was used as a Roman highway, but he probably regarded it as of British origin, as he did the Fosseway. He recognized Offa's Dyke at several points of its course, and he visited the group of menhirs known as the Devil's Arrows near Borough Bridge in Yorkshire, which he thought to be a Roman trophy by the side of Watling Street. He took considerable interest in hill-forts, the camps "of the men of war", and realized that some of them were pre-Roman. Silbury Hill did not arouse his curiosity, and he did not mention a visit to Stonehenge, though he passed close by and knew the legend about it.[2] He recorded chance discoveries reported to him; the gold sword, sword-harness and spurs from Kyloe, Northumberland, the monks' garments dug up at Bangor-on-Dee, and the wonderful gold helmet studded with gems found at Harlaxton, Lincs. He also noted little bits of folklore, for instance the jingle about Dolbery Camp in the Mendips, "If Dolbyri dygged ware, of gold shuld be the share."

[1] *Archæologia*, LXXVII (1927), p. 241.
[2] Cf. *Commentarii*, Oxford, 1709, p. 45 ff. cap. 26.

Such were the topographical and archæological interests of the great antiquary. He was not a herald;[1] he was not specially interested in ancient castles or old churches or ruined buildings, and he would not have understood why an antiquary should be supposed to want to confine his studies to antiquities. He looked at everything and he liked or disliked everything, according to his own notions, and without the slightest prejudice in favour of antiquities, with the result that his opinions are significantly more precious to-day. The "fair new church" at Fairford was as important to him as the ancient "glorie" of Fotheringay. He was, in short, studying the topography of the Tudor England of his time, because he was in love with Tudor England, and he loved this glorious present all the more because he so loved the British past. The land where King Henry VIII reigned was for Leland the land where King Arthur had lived, and ancient Britain and modern England were not only equally dear to him, but each was for him incomplete without the other.

We turn now to Leland's extremely important biographical researches which resulted in the *Commentarii de Scriptoribus Britannicis*. This great work, still under revision in 1545,[2] was based on the long years of inquiry in the many libraries of Britain, and is a collection of short lives of British scholars, authors, poets, and patrons of learning, arranged in chronological order with lists of their works. There are in all nearly 600 entries, and the latest refer to men who died about 1500. About 470 are post-conquest personages, and about 100 are Saxon or British; there are also a score of legendary authors taken out of the British History, and there are also notes on the Druids and the Bards. Much use was made of this book while it was still in MS. by Bale, but it was not published till 1709.[3]

It was not a new kind of book in form and arrangement; there was the example of St. Jerome's *De Viris Illustribus*, written over 1150 years earlier, and in Leland's own day biographical dictionaries and bibliographies were well-known and much in

---

[1] Though Leland copied out a thirteenth century roll of arms (*Collectanea* ed. Hearne 1770–4, II, p. 610) he was not greatly interested in arms; he did, however, occasionally blazon coats for subsequent identification.

[2] Leland includes fifteen references to Gesner's *Bibliotheca Universale* and six to Lily Giraldus's *Historia Poetarum*, both published in that year. He mentions his stall at Christ Church, tells us that he had completed his *Encomia*, and 'speaks of his visits to some libraries as taking place ten or twelve years ago. Cf. *Itinerary*, ed. Hearne, 1768–9, IX, p. 73.

[3] ed. Anthony Hall, Oxford, 1709.

demand.[1] What Leland had set out to do was to declare the British achievement in scholarship; his book was to be a national record of a most impressive kind, and he was particularly desirous to recover for Britain writers who had been claimed for other countries. It was to be, so to speak, the British retort to Tritheim's *Catalogus illustrium virorum Germaniae* of 1491.

Leland's impassioned devotion to the national glory led him to include some most surprising characters in the ranks of the British men and women of distinction. There is Silvius Britto, for instance, who is otherwise only known to us as the unfortunate subject of some minor lampoons by Ausonius; Leland thought that the graceless poet betrayed by his jeering that he was in fact jealous of Silvius the Briton. *Nemo bonus Britto est*. This kind of talk always made Leland angry. *O novum acumen!* Ausonius was merely an envious Frenchman, and his fatuous epigram had neither art nor sense. There was also Martial's Claudia Rufina. According to the poet she was a woman of this country who married a Roman official and had such good manners that she might have been mistaken for an Italian. Leland lists her as *femina incomparabilis* and remarks that Aulus Pudens, her Roman husband, was a very lucky man.[2]

The most astonishing characters in the early part of the book are two birds. One was the eagle that prophesied when Shaftesbury was built. Leland did not think Geoffrey of Monmouth, whose account in Latin of the happening was his source,[3] meant just a bird when he referred to this *aquila*, and so in the *Commentarii* this creature becomes "Aquila the Prophet", the author of prophetic books to which Leland had seen references in the catalogue of the cathedral library in Canterbury.[4] The second bird was a partridge. In the abridgement by the sixteenth century Italian, Ponticus Virunnius, of the British History, the story of the rain of blood and plague of mice in the time of King Rivallo is expanded by information that a large and brilliantly feathered

[1] Leland was not, however, aware of what John Boston of Bury had already achieved in the English libraries in the early fifteenth century (p. 30, n. 4).

[2] Leland did not, as Bale did, (*SS. Bryt*, 1557, p. 21) identify this couple with the Pudens and Claudia of 2 *Timothy*, IV, 21.

[3] *Hist. Reg. Brit.* II, IX; XII, XVIII.

[4] Cf. M. R. James, *Ancient Libraries of Canterbury and Dover*. Cambridge, 1903, p. 77. Leland's interpretation was followed by Bale, Grafton, and Holinshed, and repeated in the eighteenth century by Tanner (*Bib. Brit-Hibernica*, 1748); the alternative reading *eagle*, with variant *angel*, was adopted by Wace, Hardyng, Fabyan, and Ponticus Virunnius.

partridge flew into the temple of Diana, where Rivallo was making a sacrifice, and addressed to him a prophecy that was afterwards inscribed in a very old tongue on the temple walls, and subsequently discovered and recorded by the first century British poet, Gildas Cambrius. Leland believed that "Perdix" was the pseudonym of one of the early British *vates*, so he, and of course Gildas Cambrius,[1] henceforth played their part in the history of British literature.

Naturally this sort of thing invited ridicule. By the middle of the next century the church historian Thomas Fuller, speaking of the similar books of Bale and Pitts, was making fun of these odd characters Aquila and Perdix and various others as ridiculous. He referred to them as "trash" and said, "Of these, some never were men; others, if men, never were writers; others, if writers, never left works continuing to our age"; the "manuscript-mongers", he observed, apparently thought they had read everything, and Fuller was surprised not to find the Book of Life in their lists.[2] Leland also included in the early part of his book much traditional, and now almost equally absurd, material that was commonly accepted by scholars of his day. There was the story of St. Helen, for instance, the daughter of King Coel of Colchester, and the discoverer of the Cross—how much more creditable, Leland said, was Helen of Britain to her country than Helen of Troy to hers! There was also Pope Joan, in his eyes a learned Joanna Anglica or Joannes Anglicus, not the figure of fun, the John-Joan or He-She whom Fuller omitted from the "mess of English natives" advanced to the Papacy.[3] Leland's book, however, was far too important to be harmed by a few opening indiscretions, for the great majority of the writers he described are historical personages who most certainly did exist, and it is to

---

[1] In his preface Virunnius says the Gildas poems were found in an old book that had been brought from Ireland in the second half of the fifteenth century by an Italian agent buying horses for the Duke of Ferrara. This Gildas turned out to be the author of the well-known verse in the British History *Diva potens nemorum* . . . (*Hist. Reg. Brit.* I, XI), and was not to be confused with the later Gildas Sapiens. Lily Giraldus in *De Poetarum Historia* (Opera, ed. 1696, II, 306), published in 1545, recognized Gildas Cambrius, and so did Bale (*SS. Bryt.* 1557, pp. 19, 10, 49). Leland had certain doubts (*Commentarii*, p. 55 and *Collectanea*, ed. Hearne 1770-4, V, p. 58), but he was impressed, as later was John Milton (*Hist. Brit.*, 1670, p. 12) by the argument that the *Diva potens* lines were too good to have been composed by Geoffrey of Monmouth (*Itinerary*, ed. Hearne, 1768-9, IX, p. 43; the reference is to the commentary on the *Cygnea Cantio*, s.v. Britanniae).

[2] *Worthies*, I, p. 29.

[3] Ib., I, p. 11.

Leland that we owe thanks for, in sum, a considerable share of our present knowledge about them.

Another source of biographical information is to be found in Leland's Latin poetry, principally in the *Encomia Illustrium Virorum*, a collection of over 260 epigrams, complimentary verses, and short pieces, written during the period 1523-45,[1] and published posthumously.[2] Of these about 170 are addressed to contemporaries, or near contemporaries, mostly his own country-men, and contain a variety of personal references that have been of interest to modern students of Tudor England. There are also biographical details in some of Leland's longer poems, for in-stance in the description of the English fleet at Deptford, intro-duced into the *Cygnea Cantio*, where we learn that his friend Sir Thomas Wyat, the poet, commanded a ship. All this, however, is an aspect of Leland's work into which we need not now in-quire very closely; but we cannot thus summarily dismiss Leland's prolonged struggles to be a great poet.

In this respect he took himself very seriously, and as a young man he thought it was for his verse that he was going to be re-membered:

> Mantua Vergilium genuit, Verona Catullum
> Patria Londinum est urbs generosa mihi.[3]

and it was not till 1545 that he admitted his antiquarian interests were beginning to take first place.[4] He said he wrote his little poems in the *Encomia* "tersis auribus et exquisitis nostri saeculi judiciis",[5] and we need not dispute this; for his poetry is almost indistinguishable in quality from the ordinary exercises of his day as practised by most scholars and amateurs of learning. It is only on the very few occasions when he departs from his insipid complimentary style and writes with a more natural and formal

---

[1] *Principum ac illustrium aliquot et eruditorum in Anglia virorum, Encomia, Trophaea, Genethliaca, et Epithalamia.* London, 1589. This work is also referred to by Leland and others as his *Epigrammata*. The *Encomia* was republished by Hearne, Leland's *Collectanea*, 1770-4, Vol. V, and references here are to that edition.

[2] At one end is a poem celebrating the marriage of William Cecil to Mildred Cooke in 1545; at the other end a poem to Thomas Howard, son of the Duke of Norfolk, must be earlier than his succession to the honours in 1524, and the poems celebrating the return of Pace and Lupset from the Venice mission must be dated about 1523 or 1524.

[3] *Collectanea* ed. Hearne, 1770-4, V, p. 85, cf. p. 89, 91.

[4] *Itinerary*, ed. Hearne, 1768-9, IX, p. 4.

[5] *Commentarii* Cap. XXVIII, p. 49.

warmth that his poetry can now give pleasure, as in the passage describing the boys diving for coins in the Roman baths at Bath,[1] or in the pretty verses about the capture and taming of a squirrel,[2] or in the lines in the *Genethliacon* of the infant Prince Edward spoken at the royal christening by the nurse, Mistress Jack.[3]

In this last passage the fourth Eclogue is not far away in the background, and indeed in the previous verse a Vergilian line is put into the mouth of Jane Seymour;[4] but direct borrowing from the classics and obvious allusions to well-known passages therein were both fashionable and natural in Renaissance poetry. Our present criticism of Leland's verse would be that in general his matter is dull, and his manner marred by a too frequent use of humourless and tiresomely preposterous flattery; but his work is competent[5] in style and often agreeably phrased, though in the *Encomia* there are far too many enthusiastic vocatives of a kind that even in Leland's time the best writers of Latin verse avoided. There is certainly no poetry left to-day in salutes to *facunde Georgi, Coxe diserte, Foxi, studiose Jone, candide Thoma,* and *Barkere polite.*

Leland did not write any English poetry,[6] but he was an admirer of Sir Thomas Wyat's poems, and he had studied Chaucer.[7] His opinion, however, was that the Middle Ages in England were rough and graceless, and the English language itself a barbarous tongue; he thought that Chaucer, by his style and art, had improved it as a vehicle for verse, but he believed Wyat was the first to show that the writing of English poetry was a civilized art. Chaucer, Leland thought, had lived in a hard and rude time; if he had enjoyed the happy and cultured environment of the Greeks and Romans, he might have equalled his classical forerunners in renown; therefore Leland was not prepared to take any risks with such an unsuitable medium as the English tongue, and he remained faithful to Latin verse.

---

[1] *Collectanea*, p. 90.

[2] Ib., 9, 97.

[3] For a general account of Leland's poetry quoting this see Wolfgang Mann *Lateinische Dichtung in England vom Ausgang des Frühumanismus bis zum Regierungsantritt Elisabeths.* Halle, 1939. p. 79 ff.

[4] *Incipe chare puer risu dignoscere matrem.* Note Leland's tasteless alterations, *chare* for *parve,* and *dignoscere* for *cognoscere.*

[5] Leland wrote mainly in hexameters and elegiacs, but he was also very fond of hendecasyllabic verse; a few of his short poems are in sapphic and choriambic metres.

[6] The English verse quoted by Ralph Brooke, *Second Discoverie of Certaine Errours,* 1723, p. 156 is a translation of one of the Latin poems in the *Encomia.*

[7] *Collectanea*, ed. Hearne, 1770–4, pp. 141, 152.

Leland's first poetical publication was his *Naeniae in mortem Thomae Viati* which appeared in London in 1542, the year of Wyat's death.[1] In the following year he published the *Genethliacon*[2] of the little Prince Edward, and this is one of two poems by him that have a considerable topographical interest. It was no doubt drafted in 1537, the year of Edward VI's birth, but it was subsequently revised, for Edward was Prince of Wales, Duke of Cornwall, and Earl of Chester, and Leland had visited these provinces by 1543, and had had time to reflect on their topography and placenames. He describes the joy at the birth of the infant prince and his baptism at Hampton Court; then the Muses, the Graces, the nymphs of the British rivers, woods, dells, and mountains sing songs in varying metres in honour of the event, and finally Wales, Cornwall and Cheshire pay their tributes. The 160 lines entitled *Cambria* are not much more than a list of towns, some of which have Latin names of Leland's own invention; but Cornwall makes a more interesting speech, with reference to the rejoicings of the miners and the fishermen and the traditional wrestling matches and a grand boat-race that was held at Falmouth; then the riches of the Duchy are offered to the little Duke, its foods and fruits and minerals, including gold and diamonds,[3] and its ships. In the County Palatine of Cheshire there are also enthusiastic celebrations, and in Chester a feast followed by dancing and games on the Roodee that culminate in a stirring archery contest, the principal target being the painted figure of a man.[4]

At this period in the sixteenth century no other man could have written a poem of this kind. Its novelty lay not in the fact that it contains allusions to a place or an event, but in the remarkable range of Leland's topographical knowledge that enlivens this otherwise jejune and formal work. Taking three large territories of Western Britain as his province, he introduced for each area a real picture of the country that he actually knew, not with the deliberate intention of giving his verse the documentary value we may now recognize in it, but to charge it with what seemed

---

[1] Reprinted by Hearne. *Itinerary*, 1768–9, II, p. 15.
[2] Ib., IX, p. VII.
[3] *Adamas*, possibly loadstone, but more probably the Cornish "diamond", concerning which see Richard Carew, *Survey of Cornwall*, ed. 1811, p. 24 and note t.
[4] Leland gives a detailed but somewhat obscure description of this event. *Itinerary*, op. cit., IX, p. XXIV.

to him relevant information about the geographical extent, present splendour, and noble past of selected constituent elements in the Tudor national state; indeed, to make it quite clear that he was enriching his poem with knowledge that was intended to be an impressive adornment of his theme, he added to the *Geneth-liacon*, as he also did to the next poem we shall mention, his *Cygnea Cantio*, an elaborate glossary and commentary explaining placenames and giving additional historical details. These two poems, therefore, have a factual content that was Leland's own creation; they are, though no doubt secondarily rather than primarily, expositions to the Tudor reader of topographical and antiquarian lore, and of the two their nature is perhaps better revealed by the *Cygnea Cantio*, completed in 1545.[1] The first part of this poem is a description of the Thames between Oxford and Greenwich as seen by a swan sailing down the river between these two points. There are impartial observations about some of the principal sights on the upper river, Abingdon, Dorchester, the camp on Sinodun Hill, Wallingford, and so forth; but when he reached Windsor the over-loyal bird revealed himself to be a Tudor panegyrist of such exceptional ardour that thereafter he could waste very little time on scenery or buildings that did not contribute to the Tudor glory. There are nevertheless various interesting references to buildings in London, to the beautiful gardens of Ratcliffe, and to the acrid smoke of the kilns at Limehouse, and there is a description of the fleet at Deptford; but the swan was, in fact, in a great hurry to get to Greenwich, and having succeeded in arriving there in 300 lines, the voyage is forgotten and we are entertained by a recital, nearly 400 lines long, of the history and the glories of the great palace,[2] and of the virtues and performances of its master, Henry VIII.

The last of Leland's long poems is without this topographical interest. The *Encomium Pacis* was published in 1546[3] and celebrates the end of the war with the French. Leland described the concord achieved between Henry VIII and François I as the most important event in the history of peace since the Nativity of Our

---

[1] Republished by Hearne, *Itinerary* 1768–9, IX, p. 9.

[2] Referring to Humphrey, Duke of Gloucester's *Placentia*, Leland mentions his badge, the Garden of Adonis, that can be seen on his tomb at St. Albans: see *Antiquaries Journal*, XXVI (1946), p. 118.

[3] Republished by Hearne, *Coll.* 1770–4, V., p. 69.

Lord and the angelic promise; he tells of the pagan goddess, Peace, her retreat into the skies as a constellation, the prayers offered to her, and the approval of this desire for peace by Almighty God who through the mouth of the prophets enjoined that peace be kept. Christ came to bring peace; the Apostles and St. Paul urged that peace must prevail; Euripides, Aristophanes, Ovid, Tibullus, and others are of the same mind. There is, needless to say, a considerable confusion of pagan and Christian images in the unfolding of this theme; but here Leland was following a custom established in Renaissance Latin poetry. Very considerable liberty was allowed,[1] and it is probable that no reader of his age would see any cause for offence when he thus described the people of Chester going to church:

> Templa petant cuncti, suave et fumantibus aris,
> Sancta sacerdotes fuderant verba Tonanti.[2]

At the beginning of this chapter we said of Leland that we expected him to represent the Renaissance. Now that we have described his works, we know that we can indeed say that he was an innovator in antiquarian method and that his name truly stands at the head of the roll of the antiquaries of a new age; but we have said, and we shall presently make the reason clearer, that in the matter of antiquarian thought and theory Leland did not exercise the critical sense that a scholar of his training might be supposed to possess in the sixteenth century. He remained medieval in mind, as many antiquaries of his day, and after his day, remained medieval; for he was the victim of that kind of patriotic fervour that permits no tampering with national faith in a dearly cherished national myth. We see him as a man two-faced, in one direction looking hopefully forward into a new era of empirical research and practical survey, and at the same time looking with affection backward to the writing-desk of the medieval scholastic chronicler-antiquary where a traditional fable might be repeated without unrestful inquiry or impertinent sixteenth century doubt. In both these directions we have now ourselves to travel, and we shall therefore meet Leland again,

---

[1] The subject in general is discussed by J. Seznec, *La Survivance des Dieux antiques*, London, 1940.

[2] This passage is from the *Genethliacon, Itinerary*, ed. Hearne, 1768–9, IX, p. xxiv.

first as a touchy patriot defending with fanatical devotion the doomed cause of medieval fancy, and afterwards as the alert and energetic guide of the great Tudor antiquaries who finally achieved that which had been Leland's own courageous ambition, the completion of the *Britannia* or the antiquarian "description of Britain".

V

The Medieval Tradition

THOUGH there was scepticism enough about the British
History and King Arthur even in the first half of the sixteenth
century, nevertheless much antiquarian thought tended to
remain medieval in kind—medieval in credulity and in recklessness
of conjecture—right through the sixteenth century. There was
no general Renaissance purging of antiquarian minds, no general
revolutionary conversion to a new way of thinking about the
past. The cult of King Arthur and the peculiar Tudor interest in
the British History has, perhaps, prepared us for this conclusion;
but, even so, it is not easy to understand the muddle-headed
deliberateness with which antiquaries of acknowledged learning
continued to adorn the already fantastic British History with
tatters and scraps of an even more nonsensical and irresponsible
guesswork.

For a first and very important example of the medievalist
tradition in antiquarian thought we must for the moment turn
from the fortunes of the Brut and consider briefly the antiquities
of Scotland as handled by that fine man, Hector Boece (d. 1536).
He had studied in Paris and had there met his countryman, John
Major, whose sensible and bravely sceptical views about the
medieval legends still passing as history, we shall presently honour;
Boece also knew Erasmus. We might expect him to show both
caution and some critical ability in presenting the early story of
his own land; but, on the contrary, the *Scotorum Historia*, published in 1527, opened with six long books, a quarter of the whole
volume, that, as an example of antiquarian method, might at
first reading be said to put the clock back about 400 years. Not
only did Boece give new currency to the story that Scotland was
named after Scota, daughter of the Pharaoh of the Oppression
and the wife of a Greek prince, but he also produced a mass of
Galfridian narrative, lively with speeches and detailed action,
about nearly forty ancient Scottish kings of whom no chronicler
before him had claimed to know much more than the names.[1]

---

[1] Thirty-five of Boece's thirty-nine kings come from previously existing medieval
lists. His genealogical table is an abridgment as he lessened the number of generations by

He filled, in short, the gap of over 700 years in Scottish history between Fergus I (fourth century B.C.) and Fergus II (fourth century A.D.) with a long, lively and agreeable story, just as Geoffrey of Monmouth in the twelfth century filled the 800-year gap in British history between the arrival of Brutus and the coming of the Romans. Like Geoffrey's narrative, Boece's presents what is to us an obviously anachronistic account of the social life of the ancient people he is describing.[1] Moreover, he told the old tale about possessing sources of information, denied to previous writers, that should silence all criticism, and, just as Geoffrey of Monmouth's boasted *vetustissimus liber* could not subsequently be found, so the most important of Boece's declared sources (in particular an ancient history by Veremund) were missing when they were wanted for examination by critics of a later day. Needless to say, as happened to Geoffrey, Boece was in the end accused of inventing his story of early Scotland.

Probably he did not invent it, but merely embellished and edited a forgery,[2] being cheated as some think Annius of Viterbo was cheated by spurious texts (p. 71) forty years earlier; but what we have to note, even though the first Principal of Aberdeen University be acquitted of the heavier charge, is that Boece took his preposterous material seriously, and worked hard to make it presentable and to defend it.[3] Thus, he recognized that there were what honest John Fordun, the medieval historian of Scotland, had described as *dissonantia historiarum*, and he was

making some names those of collaterals. See *Historians of Scotland* VIII, Innes's Essay, p. 130 ff. and cf. ib. Fordun II, p. 394; John Major *Hist. Maj. Brit.*, 1521, II, f. xxii b, sensibly shortened the medieval forty-five kings to fifteen kings.

[1] The anti-monarchical colouring seen in Boece's frequent introduction of regents and in his depositions of evil kings by popular right, was noted by Edward Stillingfleet, *Origines Britannicae*, 1689, pp. XII, XVII, and mercilessly exposed by Thomas Innes in the early eighteenth century.

[2] There was a "Veremund" MS. for it was seen by David Chambers in 1572. *Historians of Scotland*, VIII Innes's Essay, p. 172 ff. Generally, on this subject see Professor J.B. Black. *Boece's Scotorum Historiae* in *Quartercentury of the Death of Hector Boece*, University of Aberdeen, 1937.

[3] To give an instance of Boece's editing—or at least of his selection of sources—his Scota story is not taken directly from John of Fordun's chronicle, for Fordun, agreeing with the Biblical account of the Oppression and Exodus, knew only one Pharaoh, and he is an unnamed king. Boece has two Pharaohs, and names them, Amenophis and Bocchoris, so that he adds to the tale details that came originally from Manetho and Josephus. Either he had another source hardly likely to be a forgery, that included the addition to the story, or he looked the matter up for himself. The reference to two great finds of Roman coins in Scotland, one made in 1519, is obviously a contribution of archæological fact made by Boece. (Book V. c. XIII).

quite willing to point them out, and he felt he was right in maintaining that if Geoffrey of Monmouth or Roman historians were found to tell a different tale, in the matter of Scotland, Scottish authors were more dependable and should be preferred. He was just and kindly in his treatment of the Trojan Brutus, in whom he firmly believed, and he took the British History perfectly seriously. Occasionally he contributed a few details about kings only mentioned briefly by Geoffrey, telling us for instance that King Coel invaded Scotland and perished at Kyle, which was named after him. He was even prepared to give way to the Brut, when, for example, he accepted Fordun's date for the conversion of Scotland to Christianity, and was forced to admit that according to the British History the Britons became Christians sixteen years before the Scots were baptised. Here Boece was comforted by the reflection that, having accepted the Faith, the Britons thereafter had "bene sindry tymes aberrant from the samyn",[1] whereas the Scots, once converted, remained steadfast in their Christianity, untarnished by heresy.

There was no harm done here, but when his narrative reached the Roman period the *dissonantia historiarum* became somewhat startling, for Boece began to describe events about which his southern contemporaries held quite different opinions. He said that the Picts and the Scots had come south to help the British drive Julius Caesar out of the island after his first invasion, and he followed Fordun, and indeed Geoffrey of Monmouth, in believing that Caesar, on his second visit, had decided on the invasion of Scotland. All this he claimed was "nocht far discordand from the wourdis of Cesar in his Commentaris", and he went on, in the manner of a careful and accurate historian, to reject the statements of "vulgar authors" about Caesar actually fighting battles in Scotland; he would only allow here, following Fordun and Major, that Caesar had advanced threateningly as far as Carron Water in Stirlingshire, where he built the now destroyed "Arthur's Oon". Boece then proceeded to give what was to his British readers a very unpleasant Scottish twist to the whole story of the subsequent resistance to the Roman. He made Caractacus a King of the Scots; he placed the Silures in Ayrshire and the Brigantes in Galloway; he said Boadicea was the granddaughter of the Scot, Caractacus, and he described her army as

[1] Trans. Bellenden.

recruited from Man and Galloway. It made hard reading for British historians; but Boece was not making any claims that were from his point of view preposterous. Geoffrey of Monmouth had included a King of Albany among the allies of Cassivellaunus who routed Caesar; Caxton's *Chronicles of England* named this Scottish ally as King Gudian; Fordun had related that Caesar had advanced into Scotland and had treated with the Picts and the Scots. Polydore Vergil, who had no racial prejudice in the matter, satisfied himself that Caractacus was a Border chieftain and that the Silures were inhabitants of Argyll. If Boece could assume, as he did, that the Latin name of the Roman fort Camelon, near Falkirk, was Camulodunum, there was reason for transferring to the north the Roman history of Colchester. All this made up the kind of background to his narrative that justified him, he must have thought, in making his, to us extraordinary, claim that the writings of Caesar and Tacitus corroborated his account.

More and more divergences appeared when Boece reached the third and fourth centuries, and there were further difficulties when he came to King Arthur. His Scottish sources assured him that Arthur died on the shores of the Humber and that Guinevere was captured by the Scots; her grave, attested by an inscription, could still be seen at Meigle in Perthshire. The stories of the British hero's amazing conquests were, of course, ludicrous —such history could only "have faith with them that write the same"; indeed, Arthur had been very glad to make an alliance with Picts, and had promised Britain to the Pictish royal house after his death.[1]

There was quite enough already in Hector Boece's book to offend British pride without this last remark, and in due course British antiquaries showed their resentment. John Twyne of Canterbury (p. 105), who was one of the first to comment seriously, disputed Boece's account of the peopling of Scotland, and said his history showed a mistaken tendency to attribute to the author's native land things that were *Britannorum facta fortissima*;[2] more excitable antiquaries, like Leland, began to talk

---

[1] Boece did not know of a tradition that Arthur fought his battles in the north. Arthur's Oon was so-called before his day, but Boece followed Fordun in attributing it to Julius Caesar. He considered Arthur a southerner who won victories over the Saxons at York and at London, the Saxons being based on Northumbria.

[2] *De Rebus Albionicis*. London, 1590, p. 89.

about the book as a pack of lies,[1] and in 1568 the learned young physician and philologist of Denbigh, Humphrey Lhuyd, then a sick man, roused himself in his *Description* of Britain (p. 136) to describe Boece as a foolish and impudent writer, "a vaine reporter of fables", "a malicious falsifier", "the most beastlie man", "this monstre", an historian "with words a foote and a half long". "I do quite reject the fable of Scota," said Lhuyd,[2] and he mocked poor Boece's pages with a critical common sense that he was quite incapable of applying to the legendary history of his own people. This naturally led to a counter-charge, admirably handled on behalf of Scotland by the great George Buchanan, who saw that this kind of attack was a fine case of the pot calling the kettle black,[3] and, though what follows was not the point Buchanan made, it is indeed the fact that within a very few years of the publication of Boece's book, the British themselves became advocates of an antiquarian fantasy no less preposterous than that which had lately been delivered from Scotland.

The promulgator of this new essay in reconstructing the remote past was the Englishman, John Bale, Bishop of Ossory (d. 1563), a man of great learning who was nevertheless so blinded by religious prejudice that he could find no sympathy for the Renaissance doubts cast on Geoffrey of Monmouth's story. Ever since he was a young man and had renounced his monastic vows and had married, Bale had hated everything that a Roman said—and in his accustomed coarse-mouthed manner he declared that Polydore Vergil and his kind were "ad nauseam usque dedignabundi". He did not actually enter into direct controversy with the Italian scholar, thereby no doubt depriving West European antiquarian literature of its most violently expressed book; he did, however, in his catalogue of British authors[4] express his views about the origin of Britain, and his opinions are more than ordinarily important because he left the subject revolutionized by the

---

[1] *Encomia.* London, 1589, p. 60.

[2] I am using the English translation (*Breviary of Britaine,* 1573) made by Thomas Twyne, son of the John Twyne mentioned above, but the Latin original (*Comm. Brit. Descriptionis Fragmentum.* Cologne, 1572) is no less violent in expression. For Lhuyd's references to Polydore Vergil see p. 87.

[3] *Rerum Scoticarum Historia,* Edinburgh, 1582, f. 27 b.

[4] *Illustrium majoris Britanniae Scriptorum . . . summarium . . . per omnes aetates a Japheto sanctissimi Noah filio.* 4to, 1548. A second edition was published in 1557. *Scriptorum illustrium majoris Britanniae . . . catalogus: a Japheto per 3618 annos usque ad ann.* 1557, fol.; this larger volume contains copious extracts from Leland's then still unpublished work on the same lines.

detailed statement of a pre-Trojan population of Britain, founded by Samothes, son of Japhet.

Bale was a personal friend of Leland and a sincere admirer of the great antiquary; both believed in the British History, but Bale thought it would read better with a new opening chapter, giving the British a Biblical background. His contention was perfectly simple and perfectly sensible. Instead of denouncing like his poor friend, all Polydore Vergil's views about ancient Britain, Bale said he accepted the position that this island was first inhabited in the course of the natural expansion of mankind after the Flood; it was perfectly true, he said, and the record survived. He therefore announced in his 1548 volume, and in an expanded form in 1557, the following astonishing scheme for the remote history of Britain.

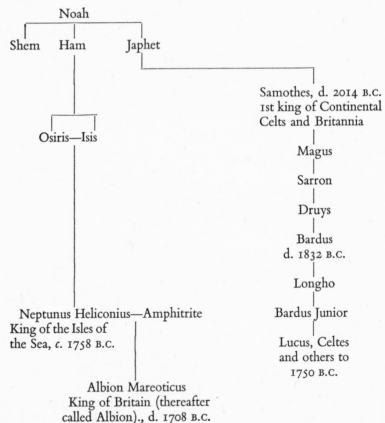

Noah

Shem   Ham   Japhet

Samothes, d. 2014 B.C.
1st king of Continental
Celts and Britannia

Osiris—Isis

Magus

Sarron

Druys

Bardus
d. 1832 B.C.

Longho

Bardus Junior

Neptunus Heliconius—Amphitrite
King of the Isles of
the Sea, *c.* 1758 B.C.

Lucus, Celtes
and others to
1750 B.C.

Albion Mareoticus
King of Britain (thereafter
called Albion)., d. 1708 B.C.

Samothes gave his people, the Britons and Gauls, laws and knowledge of astronomy and of political science. Magus taught them to build towns and dwellings; in Britain he founded Sito-magus, Neomagus (Chester),[1] Niomagus (Buckingham) and Noviomagus. He also instructed his subjects in the magic arts. Sarron established schools of philosophy. Druys founded the order of the Druids, in the first instance in Britain. Bardus taught music and poetry, and gave his name to the Bards. Osiris visited Britain, and he and Isis taught the people of the world agriculture, and from them the Britons learned to make beer. Albion, a wicked giant in the descent through Osiris and Neptune from the evil Ham, taught the Britons navigation and gave his name to the island.[2] All this time the world was getting a worse place; as long ago as the time of Sarron the Golden Age had become the Silver Age, but with the arrival of Albion, Britain had passed into a dreadful Iron Age (*tempus omnino ferreum, spurium, ac spurcum*) which endured for the interval of five centuries between the reign of Albion and the arrival of the Trojan Brutus about 1140 B.C.

There was no secret about the immediate origin of this elaborate essay in prehistory. Samothes, son of Japhet, had been mentioned in connection with Britain, so Bale thought, in a book published in 1498 by Annius of Viterbo (d. 1502) that contained among other allegedly ancient documents a spurious history of the peopling of the ancient world, based on Josephus, of which the first part, from the Flood to the founding of Troy, purported to be by Berosus, the Chaldæan historian and astrologer of the age of Alexander the Great, and the second part purported to be by the Egyptian historian, Manetho. This ingenious and convincing work, as even a superficial study of Continental antiquarian thought will show, was undoubtedly the most mischievous study of the remote past published during the

---

[1] Bale is quoting Sir Thomas Elyot, *Bibliotheca*, s.v. Neomagus.

[2] The story of Albion, son of Neptune, who was slain by Hercules in Liguria is antique, and the suggestion that this Albion gave his name to our island had been made by N. Perottus, *Cornucopiae*, Venice, 1489 (edn. 1521, col. 424, bl. 58), and by H. Ringmann (Philesius Vogesigena) in *Descriptio Europae, instructio ... in cartam ... M. Hilacomili*, 1511, p. ix. Cf. also Giraldus Lily, *Herculis Vita*, Basle, 1539 (*works*, ed. 1696, col. 583). In England it was approved by Sir Thomas Elyot, *Bibliotheca Eliotae*, 1542 and 1545, s.v. Albion, and adopted with the corollary of an "Albionic" civilization by Bale and Twyne (p. 106); Lhuyd and Camden later supported the derivation, but thought Albion was a kind of nickname conferred on this island by visiting Greeks. The pseudo-Manetho text (op cit. below, note 3, Z iiib) merely names an Olbius, king of the Celts.

Renaissance.[1]   It did harm almost everywhere in western
Europe, and it is not in the least surprising that Bale was deceived
by the passages designed to mislead French and English antiquaries.   According to this pseudo-Berosus, and to Annius's
commentary thereon, when Armenia could no longer hold
the ever-increasing descendants of Noah, the family of Japhet
took possession of Europe, and Samothes was made ruler of
those of Noah's children who were the Celts, and thereafter first the *Britones* and then the Gauls were called Samothei.
Samothes, the account went on, was also called Dis and he
succeeded by a long line of Kings of the Celts, who conferred
various benefits on their people and freely bestowed their
names on nations, cities, and institutions, as Bale related.   He
had convinced himself that the story concerned Britain in
particular, and he saw that it made excellent sense; moreover,
though Samothes was not actually mentioned in the Bible, his
father and brothers were, and thus the Scriptures must henceforth take their place in front of the Aeneid as the paramount
source-book in which we should seek the origin of the Britons.
Bale most carefully insisted on this in his title; the story of the
British began with Japhet.   There was even a further advantage
in his scheme, for by adopting Albion, son of Neptune, and
making him and his race bad men, there was an explanation not
only of Britain's other name, but of the savage pre-Trojan giants
whom Brutus had found here.

It was some time before antiquarian opinion in Britain took
notice of the Samotheans; but Bale's interpretation of the pseudo-
Berosus seemed sense to John Caius (d. 1573), of Cambridge, a
learned medical man and naturalist who in other fields of knowledge knew how to distrust traditional opinion, but nevertheless
found no difficulty in accepting the more preposterous sorts of
ancient history, provided they were not part of the ancient history of the University of Oxford (see p. 77).   In the first book
of his *De Antiquitate Cantebrigiensis Academiae* (1568) he agreed
that the first inhabitants of this island were post-Diluvian
migrants, the Samotheans of Celtica; he named the early kings
and praised their glorious attainments in learning and the arts.[2]
Eight years after he had thus shown his approval of the new

---

[1] *Commentaria super opera diversor. auctor. de antiquitatibus loquentium.* Rome, 1498.
[2] *Works*, ed. Venn, 1912. pp. 14–16.

chapter added to the British History, the matter of Samothes was presented to the learned world by William Lambarde in 1576,[1] and, subsequently, in a more popular form in 1577 by Ralph Holinshed and William Harrison in the famous *Chronicle*. Holinshed knew that there were doubts about the Berosus text, but he felt that what was good enough for Bale was good enough for him, and it was obvious that scholars had not finally rejected the Samotheans. Thus, in 1597 they were again offered to the learned world as a subject of serious study by the painstaking antiquary, Richard White of Basingstoke (1539–1611), the author of a long history of early Britain written throughout in the medieval tradition.

White came of a wealthy Hampshire family and was a Fellow of New College when Elizabeth came to the throne; but thereafter he lived abroad as a Catholic exile. He was a scholar of considerable repute on the Continent, and became a Professor of Law in Douai University and a Count Palatine, and after he had been twice widowed, a Canon of St. Peter's at Douai. His first antiquarian essay (1568) was an attempt to interpret the enigmatic *Aelia Laelia Crispis* inscription near Bologna, a forgery that was the subject of considerable discussion;[2] he also wrote a defence of the legend of St. Ursula and the 11,000 virgins (1610); but his principal work was the early history of Britain from the Flood to the Norman Conquest in eleven books, of which the first five were published in 1597 and the last in 1607.[3] He tells us that he had been urged to write a complete history of England by some of his fellow exiles,[4] but his main encouragement to embark on the early books came from his friend, Cardinal Baronius, the great librarian of the Vatican, who had declared in print that the British History was in part a respectable source and could be trusted in matters such as the story of St. Ursula.[5] White had no difficulty in believing that Geoffrey of Monmouth's tale was in the main true; but he followed Baronius in admitting that it could not be so in every detail. Who, he asked, could take serious notice of the prophecies of Merlin after they had been condemned by

[1] *Perambulation of Kent*, p. 13.
[2] *C.I.L.* XI, 1, 88.
[3] *Historiarum (Britanniae)* . . . *libri*, Douai, 1597–1607.
[4] Goldwell, Bp. of St. Asaph, Sir Francis Englefield, and Robert Peckham—see Pref. to Book II; cf. also the preface to Book I by his son Thomas White with its reference to Polydore Vergil and to the risks of dealing with recent and contemporary history.
[5] *Martyrologium Romanum*. Antwerp, 1589. October 21, p. 466.

the Council of Trent? And what Continental scholar could be expected to believe Geoffrey's extraordinary story of King Arthur's European conquests?

He was writing on the Continent among Continental scholars, and he was acquainted with the many books on the origins of the Gauls and the Germans that had been published in the second half of the sixteenth century. He could believe that our first population consisted of antediluvian giants, refugees from Enochia (Genesis IV, 17), who, on being warned of the Flood, had escaped to *Anglia*, then an extremity of the Continent and the most remote *angulus* of the world;[1] but when he came to the Samotheans, he saw that certain absurdities in Bale's outline would not do, and he cut out Albion Mareoticus. White's Olbion was not the son of Neptune, but an ordinary Samothean king who was not remarkable for much more than the fact that he had bestowed his name on Albi in France and upon this island. White had even some doubts about Samothes himself, for he thought that Berosus might really be referring to Magog.[2] Nevertheless, whenever he could support a fable against sixteenth century doubt White did so—for instance by insisting, in opposition to Camden, that Hercules Libyus, the son of Osiris, had visited Britain,[3] and in general he gave the full story of the Samotheans in Britain with an unruffled credulity; moreover his account is in narrative form and has a copious apparatus of notes and chronological summaries, and it is to-day, so to speak, the standard work on the subject of the children of Japhet in Britain.

Another antiquary who believed in Samothes was the trusting John Lewis,[4] and another was William Slatyer (1587–1647), a rather troublesome rector of Romney and Otterden in Kent. Slatyer was convinced his countrymen did not take a sufficient interest in their past history—"yet then I feare we should not be the true, plaine, downe-right, shall I say, or fantastique Englishmen, if Apes, Toyes, Monkeyes, Parrots and Baboones, or yond-Sea owles, other country far-fetcht and new-fangle fashions, were not more fancyable to our brain-sicke humours, and

---

[1] The theory that this island was called Anglia *ab angulo orbis* is medieval, cf. *Polychronicon* I, 39 (Rolls ed. 41, II, p. 4). See White, *op. cit.*, pp. 13, 59.

[2] *Historiarum*, I, p. 67.

[3] Ib., pp. 20, 93–4; cf. Camden, *Britannia* s.v. Damnonii, Herculis Prom.

[4] *History of Great Britain*. London, 1729. Lewis wrote 1603–12.

plausible to our palats, then wiser and better objects . . . nearer concerning both ourselves and native home".[1] He was a friend of Michael Drayton, and a great admirer of the antiquarian lore in *Poly-Olbion* (p. 103); but Drayton had said nothing about Samothes, and Slatyer felt there was room for another poem:

> Thy Poly-Olbion did invite
> My Palæ-Albion thus to write

he said, and in 1621 he published his chronicle, a most elaborate book set out in parallel columns of Latin and English verse tricked with copious notes and explanations.[2] Slatyer believed in the entire fabric of medieval legend; he even believed in the arrival in Britain of Albina and the other daughters of Danaus—who

> —meete such mates in our wild Groves
> You'ld think unfit for Ladies loves——

these being the wicked giants brought here by Bale's Albion Mareoticus. Slatyer then makes his own little contribution to the British History, by saying that from the union of these and the ladies sprang a further race of giants "of whom nothing is memorable beside their rudeness, disorder, and overthrow by Brute, save that Leon-Gavere built Caerleon . . . now called Chester."[3] The protestant Slatyer followed Bale in his main outlines, and had no difficulty in accommodating the pre-Trojan kings:

> This joy we more, that not our land
> From teeth of Hydra sowne in sand,
> Receive her Peoples, they their birth,
> Like wat'ry Mushromes from the earth!
> Since Gaules and Britons, both of these
> Are said to come of Samothes.[4]

It sounded very grand and very certain, but by this time, late

---

[1] *Palæ-Albion* (see note below), preface.

[2] *Palæ-Albion or The History of Great Britanie*. London, 1621. Slatyer also published in 1630 a complicated genealogical table beginning with God and Adam and setting forth the full ancestry of King James I; it is called *Genethliacon sive Stemma Jacobi*.

[3] *Palæ-Albion*, heading to Canto III, p. 65, and note p. 67.

[4] Ib., p. 15. White had said that the term aborigines did not mean that *in principio homines more fungorum e terra germinarent*, *loc. cit.*, p. 11.

in the reign of James I, English antiquaries had had over seventy years to consider the matter of Samothes, and the truth is that he had arrived on the scene too late to be a permanent success. A few felt there was something in the general underlying idea, and Sir Robert Filmer,[1] writing in the time of Charles I, found that "most of the civilized nations of earth labour to fetch their Originall from some one of the sons or nephews of Noah"; Lambarde had wondered if Samothes might not be Mesbech, a son of Japhet, actually named in the Bible,[2] but the medieval world that loved these legendary founders was at last beginning to pass away, and in this case Samothes was at a disadvantage special to himself, for he was not actually mentioned in the Bible, and the "Berosus" text—on which he depended—had been completely exposed as a forgery.[3] Slatyer was the last who took Samothes seriously, and he was not a good enough poet, as he very charmingly confesses, to make this shadowy newcomer an immortal in English literature. As late as 1676 the pre-Trojan Celtic kings made one more appearance, this time in the hospitable and omnivorous pages of the *Antiquities* by Aylett Sammes (p. 133) who did not believe in them at all; and that is the end of them. "If all published authority were a legitimate brother to truth's certainty," wrote John Selden in 1610, "then could I affirm that their common father, old Time, once saw a Samothean race in this isle of Britany."[4] John Stow (1580) and John Speed (1611) shared this view, though they put the matter more simply; William Camden did not think the Samotheans worth mention.

The mention of the founder of Caius College as a believer in Samothes will remind us that John Caius was a participant in a controversy about the antiquity of Oxford and Cambridge, in which the preposterous accounts collected and studied by John Rous (p. 25) were once again restated and were the subject of prolonged argument. The occasion of the sixteenth century dispute was a speech made by the Cambridge orator, inspired by

[1] *Patriarcha.*, London, 1680, p. 14.

[2] *Perambulation of Kent*, London, 1576, p. 13.

[3] Vives (*Comm.* St. Augustine, De Civitate Dei; Book VII, IV) had suspected this in 1522; the fraud was fully exposed by Gaspar Barreiros, *Censure in quandam auctorem qui sub falsa inscriptione Berosi Chaldaei circumfertur*, Rome, 1565.

[4] *England's Epinomis*, cap. 1; . . . cf. *Analecton Anglo-Britannicon*, 1607 (published 1615), Bk. 1, cap. 1.

John Caius, before Queen Elizabeth in 1564. This brought Cantaber, son-in-law of Gurguntius Brabtruc, into the open again, and in 1566 an answering "assertion" of the greater antiquity of Oxford was presented to the Queen, which in turn used Cricklade and the Greek philosophers to prepare the way for the crowning work of Alfred the Great. The Oxford champion was Thomas Caius, a Fellow of All Souls and one time Registrar of the University, and according to his own account the assertion was not intended for public use; but in 1568 John Caius, claiming to write not as the master of a Cambridge college, but as a neutral Londoner who had left Cambridge thirty years ago,[1] published the book referred to above, together with the Oxford document; subsequently Thomas Caius wrote some animadversions on John Caius's book, and the learned world was therefore treated to an unashamed display of medieval antiquarian argument that was allowed to thrive until at least as late as 1620, the date of the second edition of Bryan Twyne's seventeenth century defence of the Oxford position.[2]

The story of the renewed dispute about the age of the two Universities is in itself sufficient to establish our immediate thesis that the struggle to apply to the British History the critical machinery of a new scholarship did not speedily result in an easy and inevitable triumph of the Renaissance mind, but was one that had to be sustained for over a century against a formidable deadweight of contrary opinion jealously preserved and defended by reactionary scholars of great learning and repute. We may indeed feel that for the moment we have had enough of sixteenth and seventeenth century medievalism in antiquarian matters to satisfy even the most eager collector of mistaken theories about the past, and the time has now come to refresh ourselves with the wholesome tonic of some wiser and cleansing thought on the subject of the time-honoured legends about Trojans in Britain and the great King Arthur.

---

[1] *De Ant. Cant. Acad.* London, 1568, p. 7. There was no secret about his identity, and to sixteenth century readers his pseudonym *Londiniensis* was probably justifiable, as Caius did live a London as well as a Cambridge life. On this book see H. R. Plomer, *The Library* S.4 VII (1926–7), p. 253 ff.

[2] *Antiq. Acad. Oxon. Apologia*, 1st ed. 1608. For the whole story of the controversy, see Parker, op. cit., p. 25 here; note that neither side was in a position to confound the opposing case by pointing out that the British History was a discredited source, and it is not until John Caius examines the Alfredian origin of Oxford that some sensible Renaissance criticism can be found in the literature of the dispute.

VI

The Battle over the British History

THE persistent devotion to the confused, fabulous nonsense that could be found in, or added to, the British History was a complex matter involving real learning, ingenious argument, and an intense and emotional patriotism; in contrast, the story of the cooler and quieter currents of thought that purged our early history of these obviously preposterous legends is relatively simple. It is the tale of a few scholars who could look at the British History objectively, and there is less and less to say about their comments on the Brut as they became more and more silent about it; for it was eventually seen that one of the best ways of getting rid of this embarrassing material was to ignore it.

The story of the attack on the Brut is centred on the great figure of the Italian, Polydore Vergil, who is the principal character in the first part of this chapter, which covers the period 1521–82; but, as a beginning, there is the opinion of a Scotsman to note, and we must later make a short reference to the views of another Scot. The British do not speak here until the second half of the chapter, when we shall see them coming bravely to the defence of the British History. In a following chapter we shall study the slow passing of this almost immortal collection of legends from the pages of serious history books.

The medieval Scottish historians had not been completely taken in by the British History. John of Fordun in the late fourteenth century had had doubts about Brutus, and Andrew of Wyntoun in the early fifteenth century did not believe in the British account of Arthur; but here we begin with John Major (1469–1550), for he, wasting no words, sought to smash down the entire top-heavy structure of British and Scottish fabulous history with a few adroit and powerful blows. He was a divine and an historian who had spent many years in the University of Paris, and it was in 1521, three years after his return to Scotland, that he published his *Historia Majoris Britanniae*,[1] the greater part

---

[1] For a translation and biography of the author, see *Scottish History Society*, Vol. X. 1892. The title introducing for the first time the name Great Britain is probably a pun on the author's name.

of which must have been prepared, if not written, abroad. In it he dismissed with good humour, but nevertheless with unmistakable firmness, the legendary history of England and Scotland. The story of Albina giving her name to Albion was the nonsense of dreams; the legend of Brutus was self-condemned as rubbish by the absurd episode of the oracle of Diana. He denounced with equal severity the legends of his own country. The medieval tale that Scotland was named after Scota, the daughter of the Pharaoh of the Oppression, seemed to him to be wholly improbable; but he thought there might be a basis of truth in those alleged travels of Scota's people that suggested the Scots were originally connected through Ireland with Spain. His book, in short, has a brilliant, sensible, and honourable beginning, sweeping aside, as it does, with the sound sense of the cosmopolitan Renaissance scholar most of the medieval fables that were making the early history of England and Scotland ridiculous.

Major escaped the wrath of the upholders of the British History, and by the time Polydore Vergil in a really much milder manner had provoked the defence beyond endurance, Major's book had been overshadowed by that of his trusting fellow-countryman, Boece; moreover, Major offered the British considerable consolation for the loss of Brutus, because he took King Arthur and Merlin's prophecies seriously. It is probable, however, that he shocked the antiquaries of his own country. Boece's history is a proof of this, and we know that Gavin Douglas (1474–1522), Bishop of Dunkeld, who in the last years of his life was at the Court of Henry VIII, expressly warned Polydore Vergil against the *Historia Majoris Britanniae* in so far as the beginnings of Scotland were concerned. He offered to supply the full facts, and in due course he handed to Polydore, much to the embarrassment of the Italian, the old medieval legend of Scota, in which Douglas and Boece still believed.

Polydore Vergil, the central figure in the battle of the British History, was an Italian scholar who came to England in 1502 as a collector of Peter's Pence, being at that time a young man of about thirty who had already written two widely read books. He was a relative of Adrian de Castello, who had been kindly received by Henry VII, and Polydore likewise won the King's favour, and also the friendship of the principal English scholars.

It was the king who asked him to write a history of England, the justly renowned *Anglica Historia*, and it was first published in Basle in 1534,[1] just after Leland had taken up his court appointment. By this time Polydore had been made Archdeacon of Wells, and become a naturalized Englishman, and had been for a short time imprisoned, as a result of a diplomatic indiscretion that had offended Wolsey. He had not, however, lost favour at court, and he continued to spend much of his time in London, receiving several Treasury grants in the reigns of Henry VIII and Edward VI; but early in Mary's reign he was an old man, over eighty, back again in his native Urbino, and there he died in 1555,[2] three years after Leland.

It is possible to say something about Polydore Vergil as an antiquary on the evidence of one of the two books he had written before he came to England, and while he was still in the twenties. Both books were in a sense collections of classified notes made by a young man in the course of a prodigiously thorough reading of the classics and of Christian literature, and the first, his *Adagia*[3] or *Proverbs*, does not concern us here; but the second, *De Inventoribus Rerum*, is of great antiquarian importance, because it inquired into the origin of man, and of man's thought and sciences and arts and crafts. It was published in 1499, and was first a small volume of three books that are mainly anthropological in scope; but to this, twenty years later and long after he had gone to live in England, he added five books (the volume of eight books was first published in 1521) dealing with the origin and growth of the Christian faith and of the Church's ceremonies, institutions, and rites. The book seemed to Vergil's readers original in plan[4] and so interesting that edition after edition was needed, of which over seventy were in Latin, and there were, moreover, translations into six languages.[5] There

[1] *Polydori Vergilii Urbinatis Anglicae Historiae Libri XXVI.* Basle, 1534. Later editions contain twenty-seven books.

[2] For recent biographical notices see E. A. Whitney and P. P. Oram, *The Will of Polydore Vergil*, *Trans. R. Hist. Soc.* 4th S. XI (1928), p. 117; J. F. Fulton, *Bull. Hist. Medicine.* Supp. 3, 1944, p. 65.

[3] Polydore established, after some acrimonious argument with Erasmus, that he had in fact anticipated his friend's better-known work with the same title.

[4] Gulielmus Pastregicus (d.c. 1370) had written his *De Originibus Rerum Libellus* over a hundred years before Polydore was born; but it remained in manuscript until 1547, and is an index rather than a full-dress study such as Polydore attempted.

[5] See John Ferguson's hand list of the editions, *Yale University School of Medicine*, 1944, and, for an account of the work, the same author's posthumous paper, *Isis* (pub-

were, however, some passages relating to the Church that gave offence, and after being placed on the Index, an official expurgated edition appeared in 1576.

Polydore's book is very far from being a mere list of references; he wrote in chapters of continuous prose, and he often states his own opinion when there were rival claimants for the honour of being an inventor; moreover, in matters of Church history he permitted himself a good deal of comment, and, in the manner of a Renaissance "Golden Bough", wrote much about possible pagan origins of Christian ceremonial practice. In short, the *De Inventoribus*, at any rate in the form it had reached by 1546, was a literary wonder, and is now comparable in significance with the seventh century *Etymologia* of Isidore of Seville, and, with the *Etymologia*, has a place in the category of famous books like Pliny's *Natural History*.

The passages that gave offence were mostly references to the doctrine and custom of the church.[1] What we have just called his "Golden Bough" studies were not considered harmful, though in the expurgated edition there are one or two excisions of some really gross comparisons, for example the inept reference to Apuleius in connection with the custom of the priest turning towards the people at the salutations.[2]

Polydore was not a great antiquary with a warm and—in his day—revolutionary interest in the real past. In fact, except when dealing with such a matter as the history of printing, he regarded his subject very much as Pliny and Isidore had done. All three considered the antiquary's task as finished when one could name an inventor or a founder, that is to say if he could discover in ancient literature the legendary originator of an art or of a

lished Bruges), XVII, 1932, p. 71. To illustrate the vogue of the book, observe that when in 1577 Alessandro Sardi published his *De Rerum Inventoribus*, he added on his title-page *Iis maxime quarum nulla mentio est apud Polydorum.*

[1] The expurgated edition of 1576 is a revision of that of 1546, and not of the expanded posthumous edition of 1570. The censored passages referred to topics such as the marriage of priests; contemporary bad preaching; the sacrificial character of the Eucharist; the original absence of ceremony in the celebration of the Eucharist; a charge that ceremonies tended to supplant devout private prayer; an attack on the gift of gold and jewels to images in the place of alms to the poor; the disconcerting differences between the religious practices of various orders of monks; the outrageous conduct of the mendicants; and a reference to the orders to hold decannial councils and twice-yearly episcopal senates. Evidently Polydore could be interpreted as suggesting that the Reformers among whom he lived had some right on their side.

[2] Ed. 1546, p. 360; ed. 1570, p. 452; cf. ed. 1576, pp. 336–7. Polydore's reference is presumably to the *Metamorphoseon* VIII, 27.

science, or the names of the men who had built towns and founded states. Medieval tradition, that had succeeded in keeping the pagan gods and goddesses alive as deified humans honoured for this very reason, that is to say as originators of the arts and habits of mature mankind, naturally influenced Polydore Vergil's attitude very strongly, and did much to blunt his antiquarian feeling. Pliny had rejected the romantic vision of primitive humanity glimpsed by the poets, and only a few unappreciated traces of the Lucretian understanding survived in the works of the medieval and the Renaissance author. Isidore, for example, noted that bronze was used before iron, and both writers speak of primitive man living in caves; Polydore, indeed, quotes Lucretius, and refers to war's origin in a primitive bout of fisti-cuffs; but neither he nor Isidore showed any real interest in this vaguer sort of antiquarian speculation; they wanted pseudo-history and facts out of books. Thus the Eusebius-Jerome *Chronicon* was an invaluable quarry: "Throcilus or Proclytas is said to have been the first to harness a team of four horses", was the kind of statement Polydore was seeking, and presupposes the kind of question he was trying to answer, just like Isidore. The first war was waged by Ninus the Assyrian, Isidore had said; by Tubalcain, said Polydore. The Lydians made the first ship, said Isidore; Noah did, said Polydore Vergil. Minerva, Ceres, and Bacchus are the inventors they like to cite, though Polydore using the Bible and Josephus, ventures more frequently outside the legends of Greece and Rome; thus he said that Cain was the probable inventor of agriculture.[1] Occasionally he seems to show a genuine antiquarian interest in some small matters, such as the history of the signet ring[2] and of sealing in wax; but the general character of his researches is revealed in such statement as (Book II, XIX): *Ignem e silice Pyrodes Cilicis filius invenit, at eundem servare in ferula Prometheus docuit*, which he took word for word from Pliny.[3]

The *De Inventoribus*, therefore, in its archæological aspect does not reveal the youthful Polydore Vergil as an antiquary possessed of new and dangerous powers; but that in middle age he did be-come a man of uncommon ability in the testing of sources and in

---

[1] Pastregicus (see p. 80, n. 4) had said so too.

[2] His references (Book VIII, II) to the O.T. use of the signet (e.g., Genesis 38, 18) appear in the posthumous edition of 1570 (p. 617).

[3] *N.H.* VII, 198.

extracting reason out of muddled and one-sided evidence was made clear by the publication of his history of England. It has been described as the first of the modern histories, and it is in general true that nobody in England before him had approached distant historical problems with such objective sense and critical ability. He did, in fact, establish a new and admirable standard in appraising sources and the veracity of chroniclers. He had illustrated his method of approach in 1525 when he published an edition of Gildas's *De Excidio*, a work he knew to be crucially important, and also excessively difficult to obtain. It is only a tiny volume of forty-five pages, but it is the first serious study of an early historical source attempted in England, for it was a collation of two texts. His co-editor was Robert Ridley, chaplain of Tunstall, then Bishop of London, to whom one of the two manuscripts belonged; they tried to correct obvious errors, to restore words to their right order, and to verify Gildas's scriptural quotations. As a result of this study, Polydore was able to denounce a pseudo-Gildas, based on the British History.

It is obvious that the British History and King Arthur were not likely to survive Polydore's scrutiny without some candid comment. "He pincheth somewhat smartly upon the antiquity of Britain," it was said of him,[1] and his book gave rise to clamorous and angry indignation. It might seem curious that what an already internationally famous scholar said on these subjects earned no respect from a young student with Continental training like Leland; but Polydore was setting foot on ground where Tudor patriotism prevented any cool judgment. Brutus, King Arthur, the Welsh, the prophecy that Arthur would return, Henry Tudor, Prince Arthur, Henry VIII, every link in this chain was a focal point for the unswerving admiration of Leland and those like him. How could a foreigner know anything about these intimately national matters?

Yet what Polydore Vergil said on these subjects was neither unpleasantly sarcastic nor conclusively destructive. To him, a foreigner, the question of the origin of the British presented no difficulties at all. Man had arrived here as the result of normal post-Diluvian expansion, finally crossing from the Continent as the adjacent lands became more and more fully occupied. What need, he asked, was there for theories of an empty land

[1] John Nichols. *Leicestershire* III, I, p. 538—quoting William Burton.

"intertaining the exiled or hurtfull roge runninge away owt of
Spaine, Germaine, Fraunce, or Italie, as late Historians make
report?"[1] Gildas, he pointed out, was on his side here. He was
forced to admit, however, that the *nova historia*, as he called the
Brut, had swept all reason away; and he said that Geoffrey of
Monmouth had immoderately extolled his people, "feininge of
them things to be laughed at" and enhancing his stories "with
most impudent lyeing"; indeed, by working up the material to
be found "in the olde lesings of the Brittons" he had concocted
the great fable of King Arthur, "taking unto him bothe the
coloure of Latin speeche and the honest pretext of an Historie".
Polydore then made what seemed to him to be the obvious
historical and chronological objections to the whole narrative.
"But yet nether Livie, nether Dionisius Halicarnaseus . . . nor
divers other writers, did ever once make rehersall of this Brutus."
In particular, there was the glaring case of the Brennus who
sacked Rome, for if this character in the British History is supposed to be the historical Brennus who attacked Rome, then he
lived over three hundred years too soon. Polydore made one or
two other points, but in the end he did not feel himself entitled
to suppress all these legends that he knew many of his readers
dearly loved. "Albeit not altogether without indignation," he
summarized the British History, and its accretions such as the
Glastonbury Legend of St. Joseph of Arimathea, for he said that,
above everything, he would not be guilty of suppressing a
people's own account of themselves, nor would he "intermeddle"
in such matters. This was why he included the tale of Scota
giving her name to the Scots, though we know he was of the
mind of John Major and considered the story ridiculous.

The extreme sensitiveness of the British to the Italian's rather
mild twitting of their traditional history is one of the curiosities
of the Tudor period; but before we come to the shocked and
often extremely angry protests, first voiced by Leland, we must
note a further trial inflicted some twenty years later on the
defenders of the Brut, this time, and it made matters even worse,
coming from another brusque and out-spoken Scot. The *Rerum
Scoticarum Historia* of the great scholar and Latin poet, George
Buchanan, was published in the last year of his life, 1582. The

---

[1] Polydore Vergil's English History, ed. Sir Henry Ellis. Camden Soc. 1846, p. 32.
The translation is from a MS. (*Royal* 18 C. *VIII, IX*) of Leland's age.

author was a man who, in his youth, had heard John Major lecture; he had lived abroad, and he had lived at the Scottish court in an atmosphere that was most certainly not one of dreamy antiquarian isolation; he was aware of the ribald scorn with which the British had treated the fanciful early history of his own country written by Hector Boece. When he set out to write about the origins of the people in Britain, Buchanan, though he said the Scota story was a mere fable, was not by any means prepared to abandon all the extremely suspicious material in Boece's book; but he took care to show with the clear-headed candour of a cosmopolitan scholar that historians south of the Border were believers in stories of obvious absurdity. He denounced the story of Diocletian and Albina, and he denounced the Trojan part of the British History, and he showed by a string of taunting questions how obviously ridiculous these stories were. He called attention to the difficulties of the voyages involved; he made fun of the oracle of Diana, and raised awkward points about language and the antiquity of the name Brutus. He asked how it was possible that twenty years after the arrival of a tiny band of Trojans in an empty island, each of Brutus's three sons could find· himself possessed of a large and obviously populous kingdom with thriving towns? Buchanan himself had sensible views about the derivation of the ancient peoples of Great Britain from Gaul and Spain and Germany; he said, indeed, that it could be shown from Greek and Latin sources that the early British were an insular branch of the Celtic peoples represented on the Continent by the Gauls, and that there was no need to invent eponymous founders from distant lands like Brutus. In fact, Buchanan was as severe a critic as the British History had yet had.

The antiquarian controversy that took place after Polydore's history had appeared was hard-fought and long-sustained, and often accompanied on the British side by the intemperate language to be expected of a fundamentalist Tudor patriot of the Reformation who was inclined to suspect that such damaging denigration of his country's past by an Italian might be one of the more dangerously subtle moves of the Holy See. The first champion of the British cause was Leland, who wrote in 1536 an angry pamphlet of nine or ten pages called *Codrus, sive Laus et*

Defensio Gallofridi Arturii Monumetensis contra Polydorum Vergilium,[1] in which Polydore is the Codrus, that is to say a conceited and ignorant person, of the title; subsequently he expanded this into a tract of forty pages, the *Assertio inclytissimi Arturii Regis Britanniae*,[2] which was published in 1544; both these papers, in spite of their confused form and indignant mood, contain certain valid antiquarian arguments that we shall presently notice; but before we examine the case for the British History, let us be clearly aware of the undercurrents of downright anger that disturb so many of the British outpourings on the subject of the Italian's offence. This feeling is illustrated, for example, in the rhyming *Chronycle* by Arthur Kelton, who proudly proclaimed himself a Welshman. He had a good knowledge of history and the classics, and was in a position to argue seriously; but his poem, which was published in 1547, is full of gross flattery of Edward VI, fervent praise of the Welsh, and a surprisingly furious attack on Polydore Vergil and all Romans, past and present. He describes Polydore as a man raging violently abroad with lies and vile slanders and grossly false accusations reflecting on the honour of the Welsh; and whatever he could find discreditable in the history of ancient Rome and of the Roman Church he paraded with a gloating satisfaction, for Kelton believed that their own shameful past made it necessary for Italians deliberately to suppress the British History. The Brut proved the Welsh to be an older and nobler people than the Romans. Kelton reminded Polydore's countrymen of:

> The honour ye lost, your knights manly slain
> by princes notable, kynges of Britain

and scornfully he cries:

> Remember Rome, thy olde abasion
> Thy infamed, and cursed governance
> Thy tyranny, and false extorsion
> Thy great adultrie, and foul dalliance
> Way these together, al in one balance

---

[1] Hearne, *Coll.* 2nd ed. 1770–4, V, p. 2.

[2] Also printed by Hearne, *Coll.* 2nd ed., 1770–4, V, p. 17, and by W. E. Mead, with Middleton's *Chinon* and Richard Robinson's translation of the *Assertio*, E.E.T.S. 165. London, 1925.

And thou shalt not fynd, any rightful sentence
Against the Brutes, to give evidence.[1]

This mood of anger lasted long among the Welsh. Thirty
years or more after Kelton had raged in verse, we find David
Powel (d. 1598), an historian and antiquary in the diocese of
St. Asaph, writing thus in a passage relating to the twelfth century
discovery of the remains of King Arthur:

"Therefore let William Parvus (i.e., William of Newburgh) and Polydore Vergil, with their complices, stoppe their lieing mouthes, and
desist to obscure and darken the glittering fame and noble renowne of
so invincible and victorious a prince, with the envious detraction and
malicious slander of their reproachful and venomous toongs, thinking
that they may cover with the cloud of oblivion, and burie in the pit of
darkenesse those noble acts and princelie deeds by their wilful ignorance and dogged envie, whereof the trumpet of fame hath sounded,
not onelie in Brytaine, but also throughout all Europe."

Powel said he would leave the exposure of these cankered
minds so determined to belittle the fame of the Britons to such as
could better paint them in true colours,[2] and there were indeed others after him ready to storm at the mere mention of the
attack on King Arthur and the British History. Powel, however,
was commenting upon a passage in Humphrey Lhuyd's translation of a medieval history of Wales, and Lhuyd had shown himself to be a man of the same mind in the topographical book
(p. 136) in which he also rages against Hector Boece (p. 69);
Polydore "uttereth his ignorance," said Lhuyd; "he doth in all
places nippe and girde at the Britaynes" and he was "an infamous
baggage-groome, ful fraught wt. envie and hatred."[3]

The Brut and *King Arthur* were, however, to find one Welsh
champion who could put the case for the defence not only with
learning and sound judgment, but also with a becoming restraint.

[1] Kelton's antiquarian arguments need no comment, but his verses include an example
of the kind of mistake possible in repeating a statement. Referring, as he must be, to the
lead cross found in the grave of King Arthur in the twelfth century, he says "in the thirtie
yere, or there about" of Henry VIII, i.e., *c.* 1540, "ye blinded Romans to put out of
doubte", a cross with an inscription in gold letters was found at Glastonbury; the inscription declared the place of Arthur's grave, and concluded with a prayer for his soul
and for the continued spreading of his name (cf. p. 97, and fig. 1).
[2] *Historie of Cambria*, trans. H. Lhuyd, corrected and augmented by David Powel.
London, 1584, p. 239.
[3] The quotations are from Thomas Twyne's English translation, see p. 69, n. 2

This was Sir John Price, and it is in the calm, well-ordered pages of his *Historiae Britannicae Defensio* that we find the principal scholarly affirmation of the medievalist's position.[1] His is the first of the great books on the subject of the antiquity of the British, and in it we see as in no other work what the Brut meant to a thoughtful antiquary of British nationality in the middle of the sixteenth century. Price (d. *c.* 1573) was one of the visitors of the monasteries, and a lawyer who by constant practice was thoroughly expert in writing up a case or profession, and his antiquarian knowledge was not inferior to that of Leland and Bale. He indulged in no violence of expression; he described Polydore Vergil as in general an honest man of great learning; but his considered judgment was that Polydore, able and ingenious though he might be, had not disturbed the faith of a reasonably instructed antiquary in Geoffrey of Monmouth's story.

The history of antiquarian thought in Britain cannot ignore the defence of the medievalist position as it was stated by Leland, Price, and Lhuyd, and we must briefly summarize their case, using each author as contributors to the general thesis. Price opened his book by disposing of some initial objections to the British History. In the first place, the fact that Roman historians ignored the Trojan kings of Britain seemed to him to be of little significance. Why should Livy and Dionysius Halicarnassus mention Brutus among the descendants of Aeneas? They were pre-occupied with Latium and the direct genealogies of the Latin kings, and Brutus did not come into their story. That was the point—Roman writers were chroniclers of their own people, and there was no reason why they should record the early history of Britain at a time when their people had nothing to do with this island. One looks for the genuine Mosaic history of the Jews in the Bible and not in the writings of Tacitus; and if Tacitus could so bungle his account of the Jewish past—and the Jews were an important people—why should we expect Latin authors to have taken the trouble to ascertain and record the past of a distant and almost unknown island? In any case, said Price, the Romans had a very imperfect knowledge of their own early history, and they did not understand the traditional past.

[1] A rough draft of the *Historiae Britannicae Defensio* in the British Museum (Cotton MSS. Titus F. III, p. 170 ff) has a preface addressed to Brian Tuke (d. 1545). The printed work has an author's preface dedicated to Edward VI (d. 1553), but it was not published till 1573; it is a 4to. book of 160 pages.

It was, on the contrary, in this very matter that the Britons, above all people, excelled. It was said—and this was the second objection to the Brut—that there were no very ancient annals in Britain; but, said Price, it could be shown that the Britons deliberately cultivated oral tradition and possessed in the Druids a college of very carefully trained historians. There was nothing, therefore, against the veracity of the Brut in the fact that this history did not appear in written form until a comparatively late date. In fact, Price thought that the Trojan ancestry of the British had been demonstrated by Giraldus Cambrensis, who had pointed to the survival of Greek words in Welsh, and to the continued use in Britain, even to his own day, of personal names like Oeneus, Rhesus, Aeneas, Hector, Achilles, Heliodorus, Theodorus, Ajax, Evander, Ulysses, Helena, Elissa, and Wendoloena. It was conceivable, indeed, as Giraldus had said, that the Welsh language, Kymraeg, might be in name "Cam-graec", i.e. distorted Greek.

Then came the question of the credibility of Geoffrey of Monmouth. On this subject Leland had already conceded as much as was prudent. "I am not so stupid," he had said (in Latin), "as to think that Geoffrey was such a stickler for accuracy that he never made a mistake, for obviously he sometimes assumes uncertainties to be facts, and presents us with vanities masquerading as verities; but what historian does not so err?"[1] The point that Leland then made, and that Price underlined, was that Geoffrey most carefully explains he was not an author at all, but a translator. There might be embroidery or misinterpretation, but Geoffrey's *Historia Regum Britanniae* was a version of a *vetustissimus liber*. Price took the matter further. Geoffrey was a responsible and respectable ecclesiastic; he became a bishop, and it is obvious that distinguished contemporaries like the Duke of Gloucester were genuinely interested in his work. Fellow-historians like Giraldus Cambrensis and Henry of Huntingdon believed his history, in outline at least, to be true, and it is these knowledgeable contemporaries, said Price, who would have told us emphatically and at once if the Brut were a twelfth-century invention without any background in British tradition. Price added that, after all, Geoffrey's trustworthiness could be tested by comparing the account of the invasions of Julius Caesar

---

[1] *Commentarii*, p. 190; the passage is repeated in the *Codrus*.

as given first by Caesar himself and later by Geoffrey. It is at once obvious that Geoffrey was using a different source for personal names. His "Androgeus" is not a later and mistaken rendering of Caesar's name for the same person "Mandubracius"; on the contrary, Geoffrey was following Bede and preserving for us an understandably mutilated form of a real British name, Arvaroius Afarwy. Moreover, Geoffrey was following a different tradition in the relation of British affairs; for instance, he says Tenvantius was the brother of Androgeus, whereas Caesar makes his "Imanventius",[1] the father of his Mandubracius. It is as clear, therefore, that Geoffrey was using a separate source for at least this part of his book, as it was ridiculous to suppose that he would deliberately alter details like this if he were writing a faked history.

Both Price and Leland thought it could be demonstrated that Geoffrey's story did have an immediate background in written British records. Price himself owned ancient manuscripts containing portions of the matter of the British History that he believed to be older than Geoffrey's *Historia*, or to depend on sources that were earlier;[2] he also pointed out that he had seen various Bruts that made no mention of Geoffrey as their originator and might therefore represent an independent version. He referred also to the Bardic poems, particularly to those of Taliessin, as confirming the general knowledge among the British of their Trojan ancestry. Leland was more concerned with establishing the ancient background of the Arthurian legend; for in his studies in the monastery library at Glastonbury and elsewhere, he had found what he regarded as important new material. He cited John of Glastonbury's history of the abbey, in which was a passage referring to Gawain and Arthur, and the burial of the King in Avalon, taken from the lost work of an extremely early bard, Melchin, a man who had lived before Merlin;[3] in the same book there were also passages from an ancient *Gesta Arturii*, and he found that in another medieval chronicle of Glastonbury (that of Adam of Domerham) there were new facts about the

---

[1] The name is a late interpolation, *D.B.G.* V, 20.

[2] A Nennius and another Latin chronicle, and a Llandaff MS. with Welsh charters, including a donation of King Arthur; also Lives of St. David and St. Dubricius.

[3] Leland did not seem to understand that Melchin could only prophesy concerning Arthur; but he had misread John of Glastonbury, for Melchin in fact refers only to Avalon and Joseph of Arimathea.

burial and translation of Arthur and Guinevere. Leland also had in his possession that most remarkable document, St. Patrick's Charter,[1] which so clearly demonstrated the immense antiquity of the Christian fraternity at Glastonbury—so how dare the mischievous Polydore Vergil suggest that there was no monastery there in Arthur's day? Finally, in a Nennius manuscript he had found the valuable notes of Nennius's contemporary, the ninth century Samuel, who was Leland's authority for, among other things, the story of the Arthurian relics at Wedale, near Melrose.[2]

The defenders of the British History now came to some more detailed matters in which the facts seemed to be on their side. First of all there was the name *Britannia*. Price said that whereas it naturally could not be proved beyond all doubt that the word was derived from Brutus, at least it could be shown that the alternative suggestions were in the highest degree improbable. He disposed of the objection that the name of the country should be *Brutannia* and its people *Brutans*, if the island and its inhabitants were really called after Brutus; for even in Latin, he said, we write *consilium* and not *consulium*, though the derivation (as he imagined) from *consulo* should lead one to expect the U form; in Welsh, he pointed out, u, y, and i often do each other's work, and in his language *Brytannia* was an equivalent of *Brutannia*. Price then went on to contest the claim that the Britons were called after the Bretons of Armorica, for there was clear historical evidence that it was the Britons of this country, having fled to Gaul in the time of Constantine the Great, who conferred their name on the Armoricans. It was obvious that Caesar and Ptolemy knew nothing about a Brittany as part of the Gaul of their day. Equally, Price and those of his way of thinking were not able to accept the suggestion of Sir Thomas Elyot that *Britannia* was originally a Greek work, *Prytania* derived from πρυτανεια, a reference to the abundance of metals here;[3] but it should be noted that the medievalists were not entirely in agreement about the

---

[1] *Coll.* ed. Hearne, 2nd ed. 1770–4, V, pp. 31, 42.

[2] Ib., V, p. 30; for Samuel, see ib., III, p. 47. The Wedale passage is a late addition to the Nennius text, see *M.G.H. Auct. Ant.* XIII, p. 200.

[3] Price did not object to Elyot's theory that Albion was originally a Greek word, but he argued that Albion was a later name than Britannia, and preferred as the root ἀλφός, white (really "white leprosy"), to Elyot's ὄλβιος, happy or rich. Price accepted the theory that Greek voyagers had reached Britain, and quoted the reference by Solinus to the altar set up by Ulysses in Caledonia. Full-dress Greek colonies here were first established by Aylett Sammes (p. 133) in the seventeenth century.

derivation of *Britannia* from Brutus, for Lhuyd was of the opinion that the ancient name of the island was *Prydain* and held the view that this was a compound of *pryd*, comeliness, and *cain*, white. He acknowledged, however, that the inhabitants of the island, the Britons or *Brituuns*, owed their name to their first founder, Brutus.

The champions of the Brut now moved to the attack. Price had little difficulty in showing that there were many mistakes about British names and places and history in Polydore Vergil's work. He had confused Mona, Anglesey, with the Isle of Man; he had assigned the Trinovantes and Ordovices to the wrong parts of Britain; he was guilty of a serious anti-British bias in his reading of the Roman historians; and he made no attempt to understand the British record. What did Polydore mean by talking of the Brut as a *nova historia*? In its known form it went back four hundred years, and behind even this was the antiquity of the *vetustissimus liber*. What did people like Polydore Vergil think had happened in Britain before the Romans came? Were there no kings, nothing, just chaos? Price felt he was now in a position to demolish his adversary on two further counts, the matter of Brennus and the matter of King Arthur.

Price dealt very fully with the difficulty pointed out by Polydore Vergil, for it was not easy to identify the historical Brennus, the Gaulish chieftain who captured Rome in B.C. 390, with the British Brennus of the Brut who, with his brother Belinus, conquered Gaul and sacked Rome, and ruled in Italy. Chronology, nationalities, and events were all hopelessly in contradiction, but the defenders of the Brut were undismayed. We need not follow their arguments in detail. Price maintained that the separate contingent of the "Gauls" who operated against Macedonia *duce Belgio*[1] were in fact fighting *duce Belio*, that is to say, under the leadership of Belinus. Lhuyd said that Brennus was a brave British gentleman who was remembered in many British placenames, such as that of his royal residence Dinas Bran, and he showed that Brennus's men abroad spoke the British language, for the reference by Pausanias[2] to the tactical cavalry organization of the "Gauls" as *trimarcisia* proved that the warriors concerned were Britons, for this was a British word meaning *three horses*. It was impossible, said Lhuyd, that Frenchmen used the British

[1] Justinus XXIV, V and VI.
[2] X, 19, §11.

tongue, and Brennus's followers were therefore Britons. He produced further proof of their nationality from the names of their continental settlements, and he waved aside the chronological discrepancies to which Polydore had called attention by observing that early dates were reckoned by several embarrassingly different systems of counting years. Geoffrey had simply lost his way in this well-known maze of time-scales.

We come now to the more important subject of King Arthur. An outstanding difficulty, then and now, about this all-conquering hero of the British, is that Gildas does not mention him. Lhuyd put the answer admirably when referring to what seemed to him to be the unfair use made of the *De Excidio* by Polydore Vergil. He said, "that I may at length stop Polydorus mouth, together with his Gildas: thus much I say, that if he sticks in any poynte unto him: he (Gildas) was no historiographer, but a Preist, and a Preacher. Whose custom is very sharply to inveigh against the faultes of their hearers. Wherfore, if we seeke authorities out of Sermons, as Polydorus Urbanus has done, what Parish, what Towne, what nation, or kyngedom, may escape infamie?"

The same thought had been in Leland's mind, but his argument was confused and angry. He began by pointing out that Gildas himself admits that he was a new-born babe in the year of the Battle of Badon, so that he would know little about the principal personages and events of that time. In any case, however, only a fragment of Gildas's total works had survived, and he may in fact have written much about Arthur in some more complete history, now lost—for was not Arthur the renowned victor in the memorable battle that took place in the year of Gildas's birth. Furthermore, added Leland, there was nothing in the fact that Gildas did not mention Arthur in the *De Excidio*. He did not mention Arviragus, or Lucius, or Constantine the Great, and is that a reason for supposing that these persons never lived? *O novum dialectices acumen!* Then in an outburst of scorn he denounced Gildas. There was no need to defend him, as Welsh writers had done, by saying that Arthur had killed Gildas's brother;[1] the truth was that Polydore's trusted author was a rogue who had foully slandered his own people, the British, by his false taunt, *Britanni nec in bello fortes, nec in pace fideles*. Giraldus

---

[1] Cf. Caradoc of Llancarfan, *Vita Gildae*. M.G.H. Auct. Ant. XIII, 108.

Cambrensis had already shown up his worthless countryman.[1] The British not brave? What about the defeat of Caesar by Cassivellamus? The conquest of Rome by Brennus and Belinus? What about Constantine the Great, son of our British Helen? What about the prowess of Aurelius Ambrosius? And what about the great men in the days of our illustrious King Arthur? Obviously the shifty evasions of such a wretch as Gildas could not be allowed to count at all.

Price discussed this difficult matter with scholarly seriousness. In the first place he thought it might be questioned whether Gildas really was the author of the *De Excidio*, for the writer of this tract had only an imperfect knowledge of the British tongue and knew so little of British history that he spoke of five British kings reigning simultaneously. He could not be the Gildas who wrote about the Molmutine laws and of the deeds of Aurelius Ambrosius, for he was just a vain and abusive pamphleteer, interested only in the disgrace of the Britons and not their prowess. For instance, he distorted the words of Caesar in order to disparage the conduct of his own people. Price believed that it was true that this Gildas of the *De Excidio* hated Arthur as the murderer of his brother, and so suppressed the name and fame of the great king; he knew that there still existed in Venedotio an inscribed stone commemorating this brother Hoel, and pointed out that the tradition of his death as a result of a quarrel with Arthur not only went back to the writings of Giraldus Cambrensis, but was confirmed by an ancient Life of Gildas. Gildas, in fact, was one of Mordred's men, an enemy of Arthur, and it can be proved by his faulty chronology that he was deliberately distorting history in order to keep Arthur's name out of his shameless tirade.

To explain the failure of Roman authors to mention King Arthur, Price offered a simple explanation. Arthur belonged to the Migration Period. Rome was being assailed on all sides by enemies, and Roman historians of Arthur's day had really no chance to write anything at all. As they were not likely to want to catalogue their defeats, and had little creditable history to record, probably they were glad enough to leave unwritten the ill-omened chapter of the story of their lost province in which the name of Arthur of Britain would appear.

[1] *Descriptio Cambriae* II, 11.

The defenders of the Brut now came to what they felt to be strong positive evidence in favour of the veracity of Geoffrey's account of King Arthur—by calling attention to folk-tradition, exemplified by placenames, and to easily verifiable archæological facts. Here Leland, much-travelled and observant, had most to say. At Pontperlus he was in some doubt; it was the bridge "wher men fable that Arture cast in his sword";[1] but he had been to many other places that still bore Arthur's name, and these seemed to him to afford convincing proof that the great king had indeed lived and been a famous man. There was, for instance, "Arthur's Gate", at Montgomery, and "Arthur's Hill" near Brecon. Price, who was born in Brecon, mentioned this "Arthur's Seat", as he called it, and also referred to "Arthur's Stone", a logan in Herefordshire, his adopted county; he said that elsewhere in Wales there were very many more places and rocks called after Arthur. Leland, naturally, spoke also of "Camelot", the South Cadbury hill-fort in Somerset whose great earthworks he had climbed, a place where Arthur was still remembered, and "bones and harneys" were often found by ploughmen, relics of Arthur's last battle;[2] he recorded, too, the existence of Arthurian memories and relics in Dover Castle.[3] In Wales Leland had seen inscriptions testifying that Arthur had resided at Caerleon,[4] and even in Scotland there was an Arthurian tradition, for fragments of an image of the Virgin brought back by King Arthur from Jerusalem were preserved at Wedale near Melrose.[5]

If all this did not shake the doubting Polydore, there was in addition an overwhelming archæological case. Leland had seen the Round Table itself hanging on the wall of Winchester Castle;[6] he had seen the wax impression of King Arthur's seal in Westminster Abbey; and, above all, he had seen Arthur's tomb in the presbytery of the Abbey Church at Glastonbury, and he had examined the lead cross from the original wooden coffin.

The impression of Arthur's Great Seal hung by the shrine of the Confessor in Westminster Abbey, side by side with costly jewelled offerings. Its existence is mentioned by Caxton in the

[1] *It.* I, p. 148.
[2] *Coll.* ed. Hearne, 2nd ed. 1770-4, V, p. 29; cf. *It.* I, p. 316.
[3] Cf. Caxton, pref. to *Morte D'Arthur*, for a different account of these.
[4] *Coll.* ed. Hearne, 2nd ed., 1770-4, pp. 5-6.
[5] See ante, p. 91, n. 2.
[6] Paolo Giovio gives an interesting reference to this. *Descriptio Brit. Scot. etc.* Venice, 1548, p. 6.

preface to Malory's *Morte d'Arthur* (1485), and it is there described
as being of red wax enclosed in crystal, the legend reading
"*Patricius Arthurus Britannie Gallie Germanie Dacie Imperator*".
It was also known to John Rastell, who had been told at Westminster that the seal came off some gift or grant made by King
Arthur to the monastery, the parchment itself having perished;[1]
but this story rather spoilt things for Rastell, as we have said
(p. 41), and he had his doubts about the whole affair. Was there
really a monastery at Westminster in the time of Arthur? Could
wax have lasted so long, almost a thousand years? And were
documents sealed with wax in Arthur's day? Rastell decided to
leave "every man—at his lyberte to beleve therin what he lyste".
Leland, in his turn, went to see this famous seal; he was allowed
to examine it very carefully and his guide did not tell him any
improbable stories about it; needless to say he left the Abbey
completely convinced about the seal's authenticity. It was, he
said, most skilfully carved and very imposing, though the wax
was hardened with age and cracking in places; for this reason, he
tells us, the reverse and the edges were protected by a silver
mount, and the obverse by a removable crystal covering. The
king, who had a big beard, was crowned and seated in majesty
on an arc-like rainbow; he held a sceptre with a fleur-de-lys tip
and an orb with a cross. Leland was deeply impressed. "Certes
Reader, I pray God I be deade but that thou wouldest desire to
see the same, such and so greate is both the antiquitie and also the
majestey of the thing. Neither surely is there anything apparent
(that I doe knowe of) which more evidently approveth that
Arthur was living, then the same seal doth."[2] Moreover the
inscription revealed Arthur's glory to be even greater than was
supposed, for he was *Patricius* and *Imperator*, and had territorial
cognomina derived from those very triumphs that were now so
basely doubted.

It was, however, at Glastonbury itself that there was the really
incontrovertible evidence of Arthur's existence; for the king was
buried there and his grave could be seen. Like William of Worcester, some sixty years earlier, Leland had been shown the two
carved and inscribed crosses in the graveyard between which the
bones of Arthur had been found in 1191. Inside the church, in

---

[1] *The Pastyme of People*, 1529.
[2] *Ass. Art.* trans. Richard Robinson, 1582, ed. Mead E.E.T.S., 165, pp. 40–1.

the presbytery in the place of honour between the graves of Edward the Elder and Edmund Ironside, was the grand tomb of black marble[1] in which the headless remains of Arthur and Guinevere had been lying since the exhumation in the presence of

FIG. I

Lead Cross found in King Arthur's grave.
Camden, 1607

Edward I in 1278. Even this was not all there was to see; for in the Treasury Leland was allowed to handle and measure the lead cross that had been found face downwards on the wooden coffin

[1] For Leland's description, see *Coll.* ed. Hearne, 2nd ed., 1770–4, V, p. 55.

at the time of the original discovery of the King's remains, and he tells us that he was deeply moved by this impressive and venerable relic. It was about a foot long, and the famous inscription on it was in Roman capitals rather roughly cut in ancient characters.[1] Small wonder that the total effect of all this evidence seemed overwhelming. After this let anyone try to deny that Arthur had existed and had been a great hero! The patriot could no longer restrain his indignation. "Undoubtedly it were a greate and greevouse crime, not only worthie of stripes, but also of all kinde of punishment, if any man should derogate from her the glory due to his Cuntrie, should envy the fame of his Princes which have most justly deserved well of the common weale, and should not finally stand up with valiancy and famouse actes by all meanes to adorn and illustrate the same."[2]

[1] Like those on west country crosses of the Dark Ages, as Mr. Martin Holmes, F.S.A., has remarked to me.
[2] *Ass. Art.* trans. Richard Robinson, ed. Mead, p. 78.

VII

The Eclipse of the British History

SUCH was the defence of the Brut. There were others, of course, who joined battle in the cause, for instance William Lambarde (pp. 73, 139), who had something to say on this subject in his *Perambulation of Kent* (1576). Moreover, George Buchanan's taunts in the *Rerum Scoticarum Historia* (1582) had given rise to another outburst of anger, and in 1593 the young Cambridge astrologist, Richard Harvey, a brother of the poet Gabriel Harvey, appeared as a new champion of the fundamentalists. He must have been about thirty-five when he wrote *Philadelphus* to reproach the memory of "the trumpet of Scotland" who "plaieth the Terrible schoolemaster". His arguments are not always easy to understand. To the difficulty raised by Buchanan about the Trojans not speaking British, Harvey asks whether an eagle, swooping to secure his prey, must know the language of lambs and kids and geese and swans? But he took care to see that there was no doubt about his own position. "I saye, Puissant *Brute* is no fabulous *Prince*, but a true example, no counterfeit man, but a corporall possessor of this land; let them saye what they can." To show his faith Harvey then gave a most remarkable summary of the Trojan Brut, arranged, apparently, to demonstrate the historical probability of its narrative; for, in addition to a chronological essay dealing with each dynasty of kings, he classified the acts and events related of its various rulers in a section that he called "anthropology", that is to say, he grouped them as items of accustomed later history—good deeds and bad deeds, exhibitions of temperance or intemperance, lawgiving, fighting, seizing territory, slaying heirs, building cities, acting as allies, bravery and cowardice, and so on, and so on; thus Harvey was able to show very easily and successfully that the kings of the British History moved on a perfectly normal historical stage.

It is not necessary to follow in detail the continued upholding of the fundamentalist position at the end of the sixteenth century and thereafter; but at least the headings of the story must be recorded, lest it be supposed that the redoubtable Brut was blown away with one strong breath in the days of the early Stuarts. Harvey stood by no means alone. In 1592 Henry Lyte of Lytescary, whose family used the motto "Fuimus Troies", still convinced that the noble Britons were the posterity of Mars and Hercules, said that Camden, "beinge stroken blinde withe the Chaffe and duste of Wheathamstedes barne or grange" had done so much harm with his doubting *Britannia* that the book ought to be called in. "I wolde to God . . . master Camden or some others wolde write a new Britannia with better advisement," added this determined champion of the Welsh cause.[1] In 1607 John Ross of Waddesdon, Bucks, who had been admitted to the Inner Temple in 1583, published a version of the British History, from Brutus to Cadwallader, in Latin verse, and, after having summoned to earth the troubled shade of Cadwallader in order to inform him of the scandal of the Gunpowder Plot, he gave a short and perfectly serious defence in prose of the traditional story.[2] The Welsh lawyer and historian, John Lewis, writing in the period 1603–12, improved on this by giving a full-scale restatement of the whole case for the Samotheans and the British History.[3] Edmund Howes inserted into his edition of John Stow's *Annals* (1615 and 1631) a chapter that he called *A Briefe Proofe of Brute*, and in this Polydore Vergil was reproached with the often-quoted lament on the enormity of his offence against the British History, "this man with one dash of a pen cashireth threescore princes together with all their histories and historians, yea and some ancient laws also". Lewis also made this same reproach. "I rather commend them who have added twenty-four more from Samothes to Francius" was his verdict.

Even in the Society of Antiquaries (p. 144), where no doubt the sceptical modernist view prevailed, there were Fellows who took the British History seriously. One of them, Arthur Agard (d. 1615), alluded to the story in such terms that we can only

[1] Bodleian, *Twyne MS.* 2, ff. 165, 161; the passages quoted are from Lytes's *Mysticall Oxons of Oxonforde*, and *Recordes of the true originall of the noble Britaynes*; cf. his *Light of Britayne*, 1588 (reprinted 1814). For the motto see B. M. *Harley* 1559, f. 35.

[2] *Britannica, sive de regibus veteris Britanniae.* Frankfort, 1607.

[3] *History of Great Britain*, London, 1729. Lewis wavered on one point, Brutus's descent from the Trojans; but "tho I never liked it, yet will I excuse him (Geoffrey of Monmouth)", for Nennius had already connected Brutus with Aeneas. Lewis also spurned Albion, son of Neptune, for he thought Albion was derived from *Gal-Bian*, little Gaul.

assume he regarded it as fact;[1] another, Joseph Holland, was able to declare Totnes the oldest town in the country because Brutus landed there, and he said it could still show the stone on which Brutus himself had rested;[2] another, James Ley, the first Earl of Marlborough (d. 1629), accepted Geoffrey of Monmouth's account of the Arthurian heraldry.[3] Then, too, and still in the first half of the seventeenth century, there was a firm protest against the growing scepticism of his age made by the Welsh lexicographer Dr. John Davies (d. 1644), though he admitted its then considerable force.[4] Again, we find that immediately after the accession of Charles II, Percy Enderby, a man from Lincoln who lived in Monmouthshire and was a fanatical admirer of the Welsh, gave the British History in full and with evident approval in his *Cambria Triumphans* (1661), an uncritical work written in the excitement of the Restoration with the purpose of showing that "the manner of Great Brittains Government was ever princely" and of informing the Stuarts of their Welsh ancestry. Then, in 1670, the Trojan story was defended with vigour by a Fellow of Caius, Robert Sheringham, a great linguist who was able to bring forward new material in support of the old claim that the British tongue and the Greek language were very much alike.[5] Another serious protagonist, whose word was as weighty as that of Davies and Sheringham, was Daniel Langhorne, a Fellow of Corpus, Cambridge, and for a time University Preacher. In his *Introduction to the History of England*, published in 1676, he took an honest central position, rejecting, of course, Albina and the Samotheans, but maintaining that Geoffrey of Monmouth should be "neither absolutely followed nor rejected" and that it was wrong to "explode the whole Narration of Brutus". The Brut appeared, unaccompanied by any disparaging comment, in the respectable pages of a history written about this time by Sir Bulstrode Whitelock,[6] and the Trojan

---

[1] Hearne, *Curious Discourses*, Oxford, 1720, pp. 71, 157.

[2] Ib., pp. 62, 154. West country topographers like Carew, who maintained that Arthur was Cornish-born, and the Devon antiquaries Hooker and Whitbourne, who refused to yield in the matter of the antiquity of Totnes, were of the same mind. On the subject of Brutus and Totnes see R. N. Worth, *Trans. Devon Assoc.* XII (1880), pp. 560–3, 566 ff.

[3] Ib., p. 186. In contrast to these opinions note that of Arnold Oldisworth, ib., p. 163.

[4] Preface to *Antiquae Linguae Britannicae Dictionarium Duplex*, 1632.

[5] *De Anglorum Gentis Origine Disceptatio*, Cambridge, 1670.

[6] Whitelock died 1675; the history, published in 1709, is called *Memorials of English*

kings of Britons were taken seriously by Sir Winston Churchill in his *Divi Britannici*, published in 1675. There was, it must be admitted, little sign in these works of the original Tudor enthusiasm for the Trojan legend; but right up to the end of the seventeenth century and beyond, the Brut could still find champions prepared to do battle in this almost hopeless cause.

The most important writers who took the trouble at this late hour to speak well of Geoffrey of Monmouth and the story he had told were William Wynne, Fellow of Jesus College, Oxford, and Aaron Thompson, graduate of Queen's College, Oxford, and later Vicar of Broad Chalke, Wiltshire, from 1724 until his death in 1751. Both were prepared to argue at great length on the familiar lines of the sixteenth century defence of the Brut, but the upshot of their mighty outpouring words was in truth now only a modest claim. Wynne, publishing in 1697 an augmented English version of Caradoc of Lancarvan's *History of Wales*, concluded that "there is some real Foundation lodged in the Ruins of the Story of Brutus". Aaron Thompson, who published an English translation of the *Historia Regum Britanniae* in 1718, when he was thirty-six, declared in his preface with a surprising harmony of thought and language that there was "at least some Foundation of Truth discoverable in the ruins of this ancient Story of Brutus and his Successors", and it is clear that neither he nor Wynne saw anything archæologically improbable about the arrival of the Trojans in Britain. Thompson, in fact, added nothing of importance to the discussion, and he got no praise at first; "indeed, he is but a dabbler", said Hearne.[1] But Thompson's translation had subsequently the success of a standard work, and was eventually revised and reprinted by Dr. J. A. Giles,[2] so that the part the young man played in keeping alive an interest in the British History is in effect important.

It is less surprising that there should have been poets ready to declare themselves in favour of the British History with the full passion of a determined fundamentalist, for the fine old tale had a romantic and approved literary interest that no modernist antiquarian speculation could disturb. We must note, for instance, the poem on King Arthur, a summary of the Leland-Robinson

affairs from the Suppos'd Expedition of Brute to this island to the End of the Reign of King James the First.

[1] *Remarks and Collections.* Oxford Hist. Soc. VI (1902), p. 169; cf., pp. 164, 358.
[2] London, 1842, and in *Six Old English Chronicles*, 1848.

defence of its historicity (p. 86 n.), by Robert Chester,[1] whose *Phœnix and Turtle* sequences contain many allusions to the kings of the Brut; there was also Heywood's *Troia Britannica* (1609); and, most important of all, there was *Poly-Olbion* (1612-22), the great poem that contains what is perhaps the most spirited and the most direct exposition in the seventeenth century of the factual content of the Trojan legend. Michael Drayton was a midlander, but the story of the ancient Britons had bewitched him, and he refers to "my loved Wales" as though he were the most impassioned bard of the Welsh, and he delights in recording the stories of the Brut "by Cambro-Britons still maintained". There is no note of hesitancy about Drayton's attitude to the British History, nor reason to suppose that he used the material therein as something that was just poetically appropriate for his purpose. On the contrary; he regarded the Brut as containing much of the genuine lore of the land, a lore in danger of being forgotten. The Dart boasts she is the chief of British rivers because she was—

> . . . predestinate to meet
> My Britaine-founding Brute, when with his puissant fleet
>   At Totnesse first he touchte: which shall renowne my streame
> (Which now the envious world doth slander for a dreame).

and he glorifies the Cambro-Britons at the expense of the Saxons

> My Wales, then hold thine own, and let thy Britons stand
> Upon their rights to be the noblest of the land.
> Think how much better 'tis, for thee, and those of thine
> From Gods and heroes old to draw your famous line,
> Than from the Scythian poor; whence they themselves derive,
> Whose multitude did first you to the mountains drive.

Drayton was equally plain spoken on the subject of King Arthur. He said:

> Ignorance had broght the world to such a pass
> As now, which scarce believes that Arthur ever was.

---

[1] *Love's Martyr*, 1601; reissued as *Annals of Great Brittaine*, 1611.

> Heere then I cannot chuse but bitterlie exclame
> Against those fooles that all Antiquities defame,
> Because they have found out, some credulous ages layd
> Slight fictions with the truth, whilst truth on rumor stayd.

And the poem, of course, includes the great theme of the Tudor revival, suitably enlarged to admit of compliments to the Stuarts:

> By whom three sever'd Realmes in one shall firmly stand
> As Britain-founding *Brute* first monarchised the Land.

And here in this pleasant and eminently suitable atmosphere of half-truth, fancy and flattery we may leave the British History and King Arthur to survive as long as poets and romantics have a use for them.

The purpose of this chapter, however, is to study not these final evidences of faith in the British History, but the abandoning of belief in it, and we must return to the sixteenth century in order to find the roots of the antiquarian thought that eventually thrust the treasured fable aside. This is a first task, the examination of such varieties of experimentalist opinion as offered alternative and more plausible views about the origin of the British; but there is a second and no less important subject, the transfer of interest to the practical past, that is to say to new studies that resulted in our antiquaries becoming too busy to bother with Brutus and his problems.

The development of antiquarian thought in the sixteenth century had been complex, almost to the point of becoming entirely contradictory and confusing, and in an atmosphere of popular emotion, passionate British nationalism, and the most obstinate medievalism, it is extremely difficult to determine at any given time what the wiser antiquaries really thought. As we have said, however, (p. 41) it is certain that Polydore Vergil had more sympathizers among British scholars than might be imagined after reading Leland, Lhuyd, Price, and their followers, and the time has come to consider the evidence of two writers informing us, one in the first half and the other in the second half of the sixteenth century, of an antiquarian opinion in a quieter, different mood, and one that was by no means friendly to the British History.

The first illustration of this line of thought is given to us by one of the most original antiquaries of the sixteenth century, John Twyne (d. 1581). He was Headmaster of King's School, Canterbury, for twenty years, and a prominent man in the city, being Mayor in 1554 and for a time a member of Parliament. In the two printed accounts of him[1] a reference to Twyne is quoted that includes the words "ryot and drunkenness", but these are not used, it seems, in any particularly opprobrious sense, and we need only remember him as a most unusual antiquary in the humanist tradition, a great reader and an archæologist who had a large collection of Romano-British coins, pottery, and glass. He was interested in earthworks and megaliths; he knew of great camps near Chilham, Tilbury, Danebury, Kingsclere, Highclere, and Burghclere; he knew Kit's Coty House,[2] the Rollright Stones, and Stonehenge; and he had studied the results of the excavation of an important barrow on Barham Downs in which had been found a large cinerary urn containing fragments of bones of exceptional size, accompanied by helmets and shields of vast proportions.[3]

Our estimate of him as an antiquary has to be based on one shortish book, *De Rebus Albionicis Britannicis atque Anglicis*, that was published after his death by his son, Thomas Twyne, the translator who gave us Lhuyd's *Breviary of Britain* (p. 69 n.), and there is no evidence that John Twyne's contemporaries attached much importance to his views, though he earned the singular honour of having been praised as an antiquary both by Leland and by Camden. The book appeared in 1590; but it was in the main composed before 1550 and purports to be the record of a supper-party held about 1530 in the summer lodgings of the last Abbot of St. Augustine's at Sturry, near Canterbury. Obviously, a literary conversation piece of this kind must not be taken too seriously as the actual record of a real talk; but Twyne makes it quite clear that the occasion is supposed to be shortly

[1] D.N.B., and C. E. Woodruff and H. J. Cape, *Schola Regia Cantuariensis*. London, 1908, p. 60 ff.

[2] *De Rebus Albionicis*, p. 74. I so interpret his reference to Aylesford.

[3] Ib., p. 75. The excavation was carried out by order of Henry VIII at the expense of Sir Christopher Hales, Master of the Rolls (d. 1541), under the direction of William Digges. The investigation was the result of a shepherd's dreams.

before the suppression of the monasteries and in the early youth of one of the speakers, Nicholas Wotton, afterwards the diplomatist and the first Dean of Canterbury, and before a second speaker, Dygon, then a monk of St. Augustine's, had become, as we know he did, Prior; moreover, the principal speaker, John Foche, the last Abbot of St. Augustine's, expresses his confidence that the spirit of King Arthur had been reborn in the persons of Henry VII and Prince Arthur, with a mere postscript reference, as it were, to Henry VIII, which is certainly antiquarian thought of the Abbot's day; furthermore, the book mentions Margaret Tudor (d. 1541) as though she were still alive; so that it does seem probable that Twyne drafted his book within ten years or so of a party at which he and other young men had discussed British antiquities with the revered Abbot, whose views Twyne no doubt subsequently developed according to his own lights.[1]

Wotton and Dygon had just returned from conducting the great scholar Vives from Louvain to Oxford, and the Abbot began the conversation by asking what the crossing had been like. He told them there was a time when this island was joined to France, so that once they would have been able to have walked to Louvain, and he added that in those days our promontory was called *Albion* after the first settler therein, Albion, son of Neptune, a descendant of the original prediluvian stock. This would not have sounded at all strange or ridiculous to his hearers, for it was then customary to speak of the ancient gods as though they had been just rather important men, that is to say heroes of old who had really lived. Albion and his companions, because of their immediate prediluvian connections, were giants, and the huge earthworks and megaliths still to be seen in Britain were relics of the Albionic inhabitants. Unlike the highly civilized and sumptuously clothed Trojans (Pl. 120), the Albionic folk were primitives; they lived in caves and pit-dwellings; their dress was usually the hide of beasts and they were food-gatherers, and they had as yet little skill in the chase and in fishing. And there we come at once to antiquarian thought of a classical inspiration that was for sixteenth century England both rare and revolutionary.

After the isthmus connecting Britain with the Continent had been severed, *Albion* became an island called *Britannia*, this name

---

[1]Allowance must be made for some re-editing as the book is addressed to Thomas Twyne (b. 1543) after he had gone to Oxford.

being derived from a British word *brit*, a separated piece. "Don't you think then, that it was called after Brutus?" asked the astonished young Wotton. "No more after Brutus," is the answer, "than after *brutish* beings, or the *Bruti* of the Lucanians, or from the vi¬gin, *Britona* or *Britomart*, or from the drink Bryton." There was no Trojan Brutus at all, and our claim to Trojan ancestry is absurd. Geoffrey of Monmouth, *ille Homerus, ac mendiciorum pater* had actually pretended that Julius Caesar recognized the Britons as relations. Twyne then quoted what Caesar had in fact written. Where was any mention of cousinship there? *Ubi de Bruto verbum illo.* Twyne thought it a great pity that Geoffrey had not looked after his precious *vetustissimus liber* more carefully; for if he had kept it, he might have cleared himself of the charge of having invented all these tales.

Twyne went on to make the extraordinary suggestion, well over a hundred years ahead of his time, that our second important colonizers were the Phœnicians. He was a great admirer of the Carthaginian empire, and thought that the Phœnicians were the heirs of Babylonian greatness; he had been struck by a passage in the commentary by Vives on St. Augustine's *City of God* in which the Spanish scholar talks of the disaster to learning in Spain caused by the Phœnicians when they went there in order to exploit the Spanish minerals. Twyne said that as it was but an irresistible step on to the tin of Cornwall, this celebrated seafaring folk could be counted on to have got as far, and, once here, they would naturally spread themselves over the whole island. The effect of their arrival was considerable. The language of the inhabitants henceforth contained many Phœnician elements; our familiar *caer*, for instance, was a Phœnician word for an occupied or fortified site. Coracles are relics of the Phœnicians; so are moustaches; the primitive hut-dwellings of Wales are of Phœnician origin, and in Wales women actually preserve a Phœnician form of dress. The Phœnicians, of course, introduced the famous magic of the East. They were folk of cunning and corrupt manners, and of a physique weakened by luxurious life, and they were originally a swarthy folk; but those who settled in Britain became pale as a result of our climate, and they therefore took to painting themselves with woad.

Twyne said much more than this; he thought there might be Moorish blood in the dark and curly-haired Silures, and that there must have been a northern or *Scythian* invasion to account for the red-headed Scots; and there were also invasions of this island from Gaul and Germany; but enough has been said to show that side by side with the touchy Leland, the indifferent Polydore Vergil, and the contemptuous Lily, there must have been a group of antiquaries at Canterbury in the first half of the sixteenth century with vigorously independent views of the whole matter of ancient Britain, views that swept Brutus and his Trojans right off the picture.

The second and no less important indication of a serious revulsion from the story of Brutus and the Trojans is supplied by the first edition (1586) of Camden's *Britannia*, for very gently, but with unmistakable meaning, this modest little octavo volume announced to intelligent readers that the astonishingly learned young author, soon to be regarded as the foremost antiquary of the age, was prepared to admit that Polydore Vergil had, after all, been right.

By 1600 the *Britannia* had reached its fifth edition, and had grown into a thick quarto volume with many illustrations; a folio edition appeared in 1607, and Philemon Holland's translation of the work into English was published in 1610. In the early seventeenth century, therefore, the book had been established as a quite exceptional success, and it is obvious that its ever-increasing popularity could not fail to do the Brut great harm. Camden had been polite to the Trojan story. He said that so far from labouring to discredit that history, he had often strained his invention to the utmost in order to support it; but he had pointed out that it was rejected for what were obviously weighty reasons by many important scholars, both Continental and British; he went on to say that though he could not himself contradict the Brut, he found that the most that could be said in favour of the Trojan descent of the British was that Ammianus reported the settlement of some fugitive Trojans in Gaul, so that if it were admitted the Britons had originally come from Gaul, there was a possibility, through the Gauls, of their having ultimately a Trojan ancestry. This was indeed poor comfort, and to make things even more difficult for the believers in the Brut, Camden suggested a sensible alternative theory of the peopling of Britain, and an alternative derivation for the name of the island. He said that *Britannia* had nothing to do with *Brutus*, but was a Celtic and Greek compound meaning "land of the painted people"; and that we were originally an off-shoot of the Gauls, who were themselves the posterity of Gomer, son of Japhet, that is to say Gomerians, later known as the Cimbri or Cymry. Camden then made a convincing comparison between the language, religion, and customs of the Gauls and the Britons.

There is no doubt that Camden's modernist views made a great impression, and in particular a number of lawyer-antiquaries of the early seventeenth century declared themselves on the same side; for, like John Rastell of the earlier generation, their training made many of them suspicious of the sort of evidence on which the British History depended. Thus the young John Clapham (d. 1618) began his sensible matter-of-fact history of Roman Britain and Saxon England[1] by calling for a new and critical edition of the chronicles that had been too trustingly copied by Stow and Holinshed and Grafton; he rejected the story of Brutus and his Trojans, and he discovered the difference between the Arthur of the Twelve Battles in Nennius and the fabulous King Arthur of the Continental conquests described by Geoffrey of Monmouth; for, said Clapham, history "ought to be a Register of things, either truly done, or at least warrantable by probabilitie". Similarly, John Selden (1584–1654), the jurist antiquary, also a young man at the time, clearly perceived that the Brut was not serious history. He liked the tale, but he would only take notice of it in his capacity "as an Advocat for the Muse", for in historical matters "we must excuse artists and poets," he said.[2] Thus when, still under thirty, he annotated his friend Michael Drayton's *Poly-Olbion*, a work weighty with the lore of the Brut, "I importune you," he wrote, "not to credit the material derived from the British story." Selden's opinion was shared by Sir Walter Raleigh, as may be inferred from the omission of the British from the list of races descended from the Trojans in his *History of the World*.[3]

The learned world, had, in truth, begun to delight in incredulity and doubt, and medieval antiquarian dogmas, now devoid of patriotic content, could no longer flourish in an atmosphere that welcomed the shock and disturbance of criticism directed against

---

[1] *Historie of England*, 1602; *Historie of Great Britannie*, 1606.
[2] Preface to *Analecton Anglo-Britannicon*, written in 1607, *Works*, ed. 1726, p. 866; cf. Selden's reference to Trojan laws in Britain, *Janus Anglorum*, ib., col. 974-5.
[3] Ed. 1614, p. 458, ed. 1760, p. 260..

almost sacred belief. "The chaste Queen Dido did never see Aeneas in her life,"[1] was a cry not of dismay, but of triumph in new and astonishing knowledge. The story of the British from Brutus to Cadwallader was similarly seen to be in the greater part just a fairy-tale, as hitherto only a few had had the courage to hint, and now it might be openly mocked. In 1593 John More in his *Table from the Beginning of the World to this day* illustrated the now general opinion by questioning the value of the traditional entry referring to Brutus,[2] and in 1612 the sensible courtier-poet and historian, Samuel Daniel, also refused to take the British History seriously. The early Britons were unlettered, he said, so how could their history have survived? He did not believe in these wonderful kings who ruled over all Britain, for in those ancient days the country was more probably "a multitude of pettie regiments", just as in the "west world, lately discovered". As for Arthur, he may indeed have been the noblest of Britons, but it was a pity his deeds should not have been soberly recorded by other than irresponsible "legendary writers".[3] Similarly, Digory Whear in his guide to historical literature advised his readers to consult Camden, Selden, George Lily, and Clain,[4] in the matter of early Britain rather than Geoffrey of Monmouth, whose book was "involved with mere fabulous Stories".[5] The mood of the seventeenth century is perhaps best revealed in the work of a young scholar of Exeter College, Matthias Prideaux (d. 1646), whose popular *Easy and Compendious Introduction for Reading all sorts of Histories*, published posthumously under the supervision of his father, the Bishop of Worcester, conveniently summarizes the incredulity that the British History had now to face. One should inquire, he said, whether the story of Brutus and his line be as uncertain as that of Samothes and Albion? whether it can be positively set down who brought Christianity first into this island? Whether the passages between Lucius and Pope Eleutherius, especially the answer terming him God's Vicar in his owne kingdom be forged? Whether the story

---

[1] R. Verstegan. *Restitution of Decayed Intelligence*. Antwerp, 1605, p. 102.

[2] Op. cit., p. 19, *s.a.* A.M. 2911–2951.

[3] *The First Part of the Historie of England*. London, 1612. On this book see May McKisack, *Review of English Studies* XXIII (1947), p. 226 ff.

[4] J. T. Clain, *Historia Britannica*. Hamburg, 1603. This work does include a perfunctory narrative of the Brut, but is wisely reticent on the subject of King Arthur.

[5] *Relectiones Hyemales de ratione et Methodo legendi utrasque Historias*. Oxford, 1637, pp. 133, 139. English trans., *Method and Order of Reading . . . Histories*. London, 1694.

of Ursula and the 11,000 Virgins . . . be of any credit? Whether
the story of Arthur be for the most part fabulous? We cannot
be surprised, therefore, that about 1675 the name of King Brutus
was dropped from the Oxford University Almanac,[1] or that
Sir William Temple in his *Introduction to the History of England*
(1695) said in his preface that the tales of Brute and his Trojans
were "forged at pleasure, by the Wit or Folly of their first
Authors, and not to be regarded", or that James Tyrrell in his
General History of England (1696) gave the traditional outline of
the Brut accompanied by the chilling remark that he "would
have been much better satisfied in wholly omitting it". In the
same year Bishop Nicolson said "for the main, I am of Camden's
judgment."[2]

Geoffrey of Monmouth's narrative of the early Trojan kings
was not the only subject thus discussed throughout the seventeenth
century; there were also the legends about early Christianity in
this country for which Geoffrey of Monmouth was not primarily
responsible. Though only briefly, we must say something about
their fate, and first of them is the story of St. Joseph of Arimathea,
who was said to have come to this country from Palestine by
way of France and to have founded a church at Glastonbury.
As we have said (p. 16), in the Middle Ages this tale was held
to make the English church in origin agreeably independent of
Rome, and Archbishop Parker very emphatically restated this
claim in 1572,[3] and ecclesiastical controversialists like Sir John
Hastings and Father Parsons, the Jesuit, were engaged in argument on this same subject in the opening years of the seventeenth century, at which time the Roman Catholic case appeared to be very strong; for, as Parsons pointed out,[4] even the
earliest "sparkles" of Christian faith in this country must have
been sparkles of the Roman faith as professed by the Apostles;
and another Catholic historian, Richard Broughton, was prepared to smash the Anglican claim by supporting the view that

---

[1] George Gordon. *The Discipline of Letters.* Oxford, 1946, p. 36 n.
[2] *Eng. Hist. Lib.* ed. 1776, p. 30.
[3] *De Antiquitate Brit. Ecclesiae,* 1572, pp. 1–15. A more moderate position is that of
James Pilkington, Bishop of Durham. "*Confutacion of an Addicion . . .*," 1561, in *Works,*
Parker Society, Cambridge, 1842, p. 511.
[4] *Treatise of Three Conversions of England,* by N. D. 1603, pp. 6, 25.

St. Peter had visited Britain and preached here, and was in fact the founder of the Christian religion in this Kingdom. St. Joseph of Arimathea, he said, had not preached to the Britons; he came merely "to profess the penetentiall contemplative Eremiticall Religious life".[1]

In the seventeenth century Protestant antiquaries, however, reviewed the position with a creditable objectivity, studiously avoiding the Reformation twist that had been given to the subject of St. Joseph in Britain. Archbishop Ussher considered the matter with his customary care and thoroughness in 1634, and concluded that the Glastonbury legend might be believed; but in the honest atmosphere of the best seventeenth century antiquarian scholarship it was not long before doubts about the whole story were expressed. In 1639 the aged and respected antiquary Sir Henry Spelman published in the opening pages of his *Concilia* a rubbing of the brass plate vouching for the arrival of St. Joseph in A.D. 31, that had formerly been fixed to one of the pillars of the church at Glastonbury; he also published a picture of St. Joseph's primitive church; but he pointed out that the lettering of the brass was fourteenth century, that it was in the highest degree improbable that a church at this early date would be dedicated to the Virgin, and that there were other very suspicious features in the Glastonbury story; in fact, he used the word "dreams". Thomas Fuller in his *Church History* of 1655 was impressed by the appropriately primitive nature of this oldest of all churches, and he wrote "we dare not wholly deny the substance of the story, though the leaven of Monkery hath much swol'n, and puff'd up the Circumstance thereof"; but he went so far as to describe the Glastonbury legend of St. Joseph as "his drossy history". It was left to Edward Stillingfleet, Bishop of Worcester, to end the business in 1685 by speaking plainly the doubts of his age. He reviewed the evidence in his *Origines Britannicae*, and "I decline the Tradition of *Joseph* of *Arimathea's* coming hither to Preach the Gospel," he said.

The story of the conversion of Britain to Christianity during the reign of King Lucius in the second century was one that it was much more difficult to doubt and to discredit. The Centuriators of Magdeburg disliked it; but the English were loth to let it go.

---

[1] *Ecclesiasticall Historie of Great Britaine.* Douai, 1633; cf., *True Memorial of . . . Great Britain*, 1650; 2nd ed. 1654 (with title *Monastichon Britanicum*).

It was a tale of great antiquity, for the Venerable Bede could be quoted as one who vouched for its general truth, and all that was apparently wrong with it was that the existence of a King of Britain in the middle of the Roman occupation needed some explanation; for most of the antiquaries of the seventeenth century saw that a most tendencious and recently publicized letter from Eleutherius, the Bishop of Rome, to Lucius, telling him that he was head of the church in his own country and Christ's Vicar in Britain, must be admitted a forgery.[1] John Clapham tried to make a more reasonable figure of Lucius by supposing him to be a person "who by permission of the Roman Lieutenant, did governe, as King, a great part of the Province".[2] Ussher agreed that some such explanation was probable, and observed that two coins of King Lucius had been found, whereon the letters LVC could still be distinguished, and the sign of the cross.[3] Fuller confessed to doubts, but concluded with an assertion of faith in Lucius. Stillingfleet likewise seemed to feel the need for caution, but he felt it was impossible to ignore the evidence of Archbishop Ussher's two coins. He decided that Lucius succeeded Cogidunus as a quisling king of the Regni, and he pointed out in support of this view that the Romans themselves had left singularly few remains in the Surrey and Sussex territories of this tribe. Lucius therefore escaped safely into the eighteenth century, and from the eighteenth century into the nineteenth;[4] indeed he continued to hold his own until he was brusquely expelled from the pages of history by Haddan and Stubbs.

---

[1] The letter was quoted in controversy by John Jewell, Bp. of Salisbury, in 1565 *Replie unto M. Hardinges Answeare*, p. 191 (*Works*, ed. Jelf. Oxford, 1848, VI, 341, and 11, 76); it was published by Lambarde in 1568, 'APXAIONOMIA, f. 131. Stow, Holinshed, John Clapham, Selden, Speed, and William Prynne accepted it; but Father Parsons, *Three Conversions*, 1603, p. 98 and ante, suspected it, and Sir Henry Spelman (*Concilia*, 1639) showed that the document was indeed in the highest degree suspicious. The original is in a fourteenth century hand, B.M. MS., *Claudius* D.11, f. 33; cf *Munimenta Gild. Lond. . . . Liber Custumarum.* ed. *Rolls*, 12, 11, pf. 2., p. 632.

[2] Cf. Baronius, *Martyr. Rom.*, May 26, note.

[3] *Works*, ed. 1864, V. p. 58. Dr. John Allan, C.B., formerly Keeper of Coins and Medals, tells me the actual coins (ex Cotton Colln.) cannot be identified and are not necessarily in the British Museum, as has been stated. The coins would be seventh century thrymsas or sceattas of a type struck in Frisia and Eastern England, B.M. *Cat. Anglo-Saxon Coins*, Pl. 11, 19; 111, 10. Ussher probably read LVC for ΛV G.

[4] In 1839 the Rev. M. A. Tierney, F.S.A., editing *Dodd's Church History* wrote (p. 4), "Of the precise motives which influenced the conduct of Lucius on this occasion, we can know nothing. The facts, however, remain undisputed. . . ."

The most important cause of the weakening of interest in the British History was that the British antiquary was changing into a new kind of person with much more important things to do than bother about unverifiable legends. Thus, when, probably somewhere about 1580,[1] a Society of Antiquaries was formed in London, the fellowship was not a company of tender-skinned patriots puffing themselves up with pride in Brutus and King Arthur, but a group of sober-minded gentlemen interested in what has been called the "practical" past, the past that was immediately important in their own lives and thoughts, and discoverable through the study of subjects of portentous anti-quarian solemnity, such as ancient law, the origin of institutions, offices, customs, privileges, and the like, and in the history of land-tenure and of the measurement of land.[2]

It was, in fact, the modern antiquary who thus made his appearance in England late in the reign of Queen Elizabeth, and to get a quick picture of him, we might say he was one-third herald, one-third lawyer, and one-third theological disputant— or, to put it in another way, we may regard him as the offspring of the College of Arms, the Inns of Court, and the propaganda departments of the Anglican and Roman Churches. To discuss fully the influences that led to his emergence, we should have to study some external forces that would make too big a subject for this book; but, at least, these foreign influences must be briefly mentioned. They are, firstly, the pressure of the continental humanist tradition; secondly, the influence of religious contro-versy; thirdly, the first appearance in print of the Antonine Itineraries; fourthly, the numismatic achievement of Budé;

[1] Frequent reference is made in modern works to a Society of Antiquaries founded by Archbishop Matthew Parker in 1572, the existence of this depending on Spelman's state-ment in 1614 that such a society had been formed forty-two years earlier, coming to an end twenty years later (i.e. 1592). Spelman would have been only about eight years old in 1572, and he can have had no personal knowledge of a foundation by Matthew Parker, whom he does not mention in this connection. On the other hand, there is evidence that the real founder of the Society was not Matthew Parker, but Dr. John Parker (d. 1592), Archbishop Whitgift being the second president, (*Proc. Soc. Ant.* XXIX, (1917), p. 169), and its surviving papers—cf. B.M. MS. *Faustina* E.V. and Hearne, *Curious Discourses*—include none dating before 1590. This society was revived by Sir Robert Cotton in 1614. Note that Camden's appeal *ad Antiquitatis Senatum* is taken to be a refer-ence to Matthew Parker's Society of Antiquaries (cf. *Britannia*, trans. Philemon Holland, 1610, p. 6, and ed. Gough, 1789, I. p. IV); but this does not appear in the editions of 1586, 1587 and 1590, and occurs first in the 1594 *Britannia* (p. 5, bottom). On the subject generally see *Proc. Soc. Ant.* XXIX (1917), p. 168.
[2] Hearne, *Curious Discourses*. Oxford, 1720 and (2 vols.) London, 1775. Note in particular Mr. Tate's studies, pref., p. cxiv (ed. 1775, I, p. lviii).

fifthly, the personal influence and persuasiveness of Abraham Ortelius; and lastly, the antiquarian results of the discovery of the New World.

` In their continental aspect these matters are outside our scope, but two of them directly affected the fate of the British History, and therefore their consequences in England are part of our story. These results are the rise of English studies that had its origin in the religious controversies, and, secondly, the revival of primitivism that is to be connected with the finding of the American Indians.

Francis Bacon said in the *Advancement of Learning* that Martin Luther had been "enforced to awake all antiquity and to call former times to his succours . . . so that the ancient authors, both in divinity and humanity, which had a long time slept in libraries, began generally to be read and resolved". In our country, Leland tells us in his *Antiphilarchia* that Henry VIII was aware of this need for research and was encouraging it, and that before about 1540 the antiquities of the Saxon Church were being studied as a source of Reformation propaganda. The most important activity of this kind, however, one almost comparable with the prodigious efforts of the Centuriators of Magdeburg,[1] was the work, both controversial and also of a disinterested and purely scholarly nature, of the team of historians and language-experts that was directed by Archbishop Parker in the third quarter of the sixteenth century,[2] and the fact that Parker had an Anglo-Saxon type cut by John Day, who printed a Saxon sermon (1566) and the Saxon Gospels (1571), and the great number of Anglo-Saxon manuscripts in his library, prove that he and his secretary Joscelin attached special importance to pre-Conquest history, religious institutions, and laws. For us, the principal interest of this research aimed at establishing the antiquity of the thought and customs of the Reformed Church, is that out of it there emerged not only a knowledge of the Saxon tongue and of the Saxon elements in English placenames, and of Saxon law, but also a dawning interest in the Saxons themselves. Ab-

---

[1] Matthias, *Ecclesiastica Historia*. The Centuries began to appear at Basle in 1559.
[2] On this subject see Sir Edwyn Hoskins. *Cambridge Sermons*. S.P.C.K., 1938. *The Importance of the Parker MSS.*

sorbed as we have been in the matter of the ancient Britons, it is almost with a shock that we notice how little interested Shakespeare's England had been in the early history of the English themselves. One might extol to the skies the glorious significance of the Welsh blood in Queen Elizabeth, but the more remote Saxon ancestry of the Sovereign was, it seems, by general consent left alone as a kind of dark side to the picture. The Saxons were heathen boors, "a multitude of whelps", and Gildas had indeed been right. This is how Richard Harvey expressed it:

"If I omit some histories of Saxons I do but my dutie: what have I to do with them, unless it were to make them tributary to *Brutans*. . . . Let them lie in dead forgetfulness like stones . . . let their names be clean put out, and not come among the righteous. When men play the part of beasts, let them goe among the numbers of cattel as Zoography and keepe their fit place. . . . Arise, ye sons of Ebranke, and ye kinsmen of the true auncient *Brutans* and make those stone-hearted creatures know that they are made to be your servants and drudges: let not any double-forked toong perswade you that *Brutanie* is under any part of the earth."[1]

Though it is obvious from this that even at the end of the century it needed some courage to study Saxon antiquities for their own sake, it was probably antiquarian and topographical interests that in the first instance inspired the Saxon researches of Laurence Nowell, Dean of Lichfield, whose knowledge and collections bore fruit in the topographical dictionary of his friend William Lambarde,[2] and at least as early as 1574 some respect for even the pagan Saxons had already become noticeable, for Christopher Watson (d. 1581), the translator of Polybius and the author of a *History of Duresme*, still in manuscript, spoke up for them as a people of the most honourable antiquity because they were descended from gods, and not, like the Britons, from mere mortals such as Priam.[3] A much more important championship, however, was that of a young man who had been learning Anglo-Saxon at Oxford in the '60s; this was Richard Rowland, or Verstegan (d. 1620), and he published a book in 1605 that marks the beginning of English studies directed expressly towards the

[1] *Philadelphus*, 1593, p. 97.
[2] On this subject generally see D. C. Douglas, *English Scholars*, London, 1939.
[3] British Museum, *Vitellius* C.IX, p. 104.

a DONIERT STONE

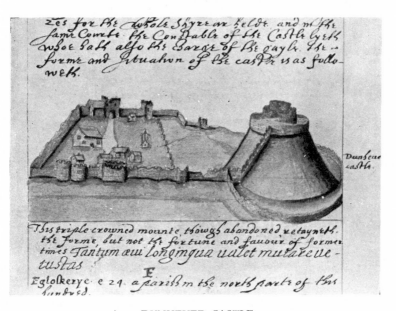

b DUNHEVED CASTLE

Illustrations from Norden's *Cornwall*, Manuscript of c. 1610

British Museum, MS. Harley 6252, pp. 85, 93

X

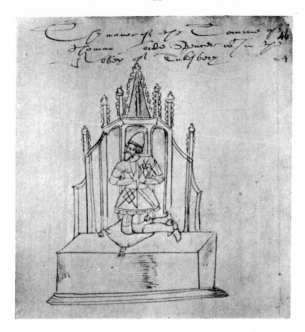

a   EDWARD, LORD DESPENSER, TEWKESBURY

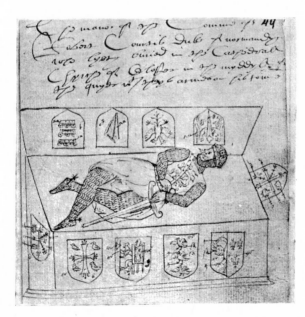

b   ROBERT, DUKE OF NORMANDY, GLOUCESTER

Drawings of Tombs by Robert Cooke, Clarenceux, 1569

College of Arms MS. CN. 1569

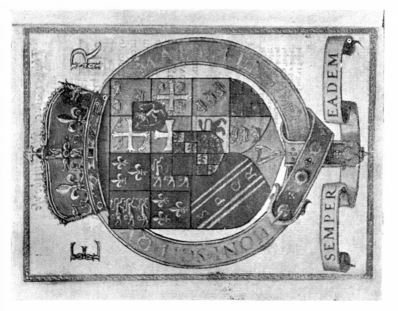

a BRUTUS

From Godet's *Chronicle*, c. 1562

b ROYAL ARMS OF QUEEN ELIZABETH

From Norden's *Hertfordshire*, 1598

b A NATIVE OF BRITAIN

British Museum

Drawings by John White, c. 1585.

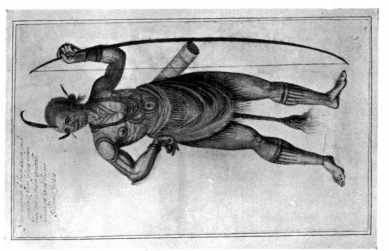

a A RED INDIAN

XIII

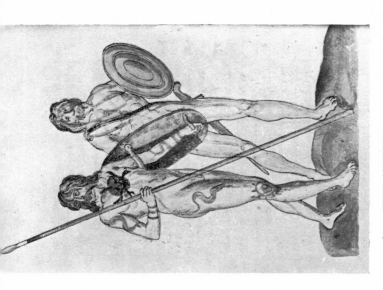

b   TWO ANCIENT BRITONS
Drawing from Lucas de Heere's *Description of Britain, c. 1575. British Museum, Add. MSS. 28, 330, f.8b*

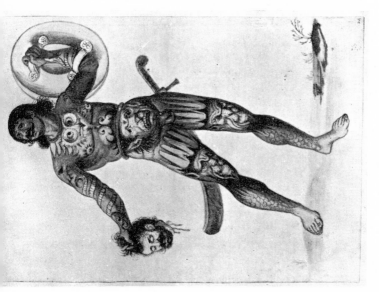

a   A PICT
Drawing by John White, c. 1585
British Museum

a MALE NEIGHBOUR UNTO THE PICTS

b WOMAN NEIGHBOUR UNTO THE PICTS

Engravings by Theodore de Bry, 1590

ILLUSTRATIONS OF THE ANCIENT BRITONS
From Speed's *Historie*, 1611

TITLE-PAGE OF SPEED'S *THEATRE*, 1611

matter of the origin of the English people. Verstegan came of a Dutch family settled in England, and was a student of Christ Church, but he was afterwards a Catholic exile and a noted printer of Antwerp, having resumed his Dutch name. He called his book the *Restitution of Decayed Intelligence in Antiquities concerning the most Noble and Renowned* English *Nation*,[1] and dedicated it to James I who was "descended of the chiefest Blood-Royal of our ancient English-Saxon Kings"; it contained, he said, material "so extraordinary and unwonted, that perhaps not any (especially of our Nation) hath thereof written before". England had been his "sweet birth-place" and he counted himself an Englishman, and the English "my most noble nation, most dear unto me of any National in the world"; he said he could not understand the persistence with which English writers "are found to stand so much upon the descent of the Britains" and "permit us to remain ignorant of our own ancestry". The Britons, he went on, would never make the mistake of confusing their past with that of the English, so why should we forget our own English ancestors by this constant talk about Aeneas and Trojans and Brutus and his Britons? Verstegan therefore set out to show the honourable ancestry of the English themselves, and his book must have made very strange reading for a conservative antiquary in this country. He said that the Anglo-Saxons were a branch of the Germans, a people of the most honourable antiquity, being of direct and unpolluted descent from Japhet; these Germans had long occupied their European territory without, unlike the Britons, ever submitting to conquest, and they were distinguished for prowess in war and for the irresistible migrations of their adventurous children such as the Franks, and Lombards, and Goths; they were honest, continent, and sober; they were the stock of which Charlemagne was descended; indeed, the present Roman Emperor was a German and lived on German soil; they were distinguished for their learning; they had invented printing; they had constructed a marvellous clockwork planisphere of silver, and a wooden flying-machine in the form of an eagle.

This glorification did not have to be taken very seriously, but Verstegan became an important writer when he went on to show the general increase in knowledge that resulted from learning Anglo-Saxon. He explained that reference to the Saxon

[1] Antwerp, 1605. Republished in London, 1673

vocabulary made nonsense of many often-repeated explanations of familiar placenames, gave a meaning to English personal names, and threw light on the development of English social structure and law. He gave a short glossary of "our owne ancient words", and his book ends with sections headed "Etyomolgies of the ancient Saxon proper Names of Men andWomen"; "How by the Surnames of the Families of England, it may be discerned from whence they take their Originals . . ."; "Of our ancient English Titles of Honour, Dignities and Offices: and what they signifie. Also the signification of our English names of disgrace or contempt". No English antiquary had written such a stimulating book before, and we must note that to increase the delights of this unexpected vision of the English past, Verstegan himself engraved for his book a number of charming illustrations of the ancient gods of the Germans and of two great events in Anglo-Saxon history, the landing of Hengist and Horsa and the conversion of King Ethelbert.

Nowell and Lambarde had already found out for themselves all and more than Verstegan knew about the importance of English studies, and in Verstegan's time their interest had also been recognized on the Continent; Joseph Scaliger learnt Anglo-Saxon at the end of his life because he thought it one of the *primitive* languages,[1] and Verstegan's friend, Abraham Ortelius saw nothing absurd in the view that the old German tongue, or Cimbric, of which Anglo-Saxon was a valuable representative, had been the language of Adam and Eve in the Garden of Eden.[2] What Verstegan contributed was a new enthusiasm and true antiquarian vision. He gloried in the ancient tongue of his people. It was he who proudly pointed out that the Normans "could not conquer the English language as they did the land".[3] He begged that English be kept pure; his glossary was intended to provide poets with words that could be taken into use again in order to avoid the incorporation of foreign words. He disliked minglers. Edmund Spenser had been able to honour Chaucer as "the well of English undefiled"; but not so Richard

[1] William Lisle. *Saxon Treatise*, 1623. Preface.

[2] A theory advanced by Goropius Becanus, *Origines Antwerpianae*, 1569, p. 534, and cf. Verstegan, *Restitution*, p. 207. Verstegan himself agreed with the orthodox view that Hebrew was the language of Eden, and that Anglo-Saxon was not older than the Tower of Babel.

[3] Ib., p. 222. Cf. William Lisle, op. cit. Preface. "Thanks be to God that he who conquered the land could not so conquer the language."

Verstegan; he thought Chaucer was a great poet, but reproached him for the very reason that he "had not kept his English un-defiled"; Chaucer was indeed "a great mingler of *English* with *French*". Camden, be it noted, took a different view. "Our tongue is mixed," he said, "but that is no disgrace."

Needless to say Verstegan made mistakes in his etymologies, and his little pictures are now a source of amusement to modern archæologists;[1] but his book is nevertheless a landmark in the history of antiquarian thought. He knew he was working on the right lines, that his knowledge of our ancient tongue was being used to create new and practical interests in the Saxon past, that it was, moreover, a real past that could be reached and examined. He had something to offer in place of the old profitless spec-ulations about British legends. However imperfect the materials and equipment—there was no Saxon dictionary in print till 1659—Verstegan's lively demonstration of the rich field for inquiry presented by Anglo-Saxon studies, supported by the more majestic essays on Saxon law, land-tenure, and social structure by Sir Henry Spelman, and discussions at the Society of Antiquaries like those on the origins of shires,[2] contributed to the seventeenth century determination not to allow our swaggering and all-too-familiar British forefathers to crowd the hitherto little-loved Saxon out of the picture. Verstegan's book remained as a standard work to direct the reading public to this newly dis-covered interest. There was a second edition in 1673, and in 1696 it was said that "the book has taken and sold very well".[3]

William Camden owed all his considerable knowledge of Saxon to the Elizabethan scholars of the earlier generation, Nowell, Lambarde, and Joscelin, and to his contemporary Francis Tate. Much that he learnt from these friends has been incor-porated in the *Britannia*, but a more explicit statement of his genuine interest in English studies is to be found in his *Remains Concerning Britain*, the first edition of which appeared in 1607, the year that also saw the publication of Verstegan's *Restitution*. There is, of course, much else in the *Remains* that has no special

---

[1] Cf. *London and the Saxons*. London Museum, 1935, p. 114.
[2] *Curious Discourses*, Nos. 43, 47, 70. See in general *English Scholars* by David C. Douglas. London, 1939.
[3] *English Historical Library*, ed. 1776, p. 40.
Bp. Nicolson admits this somewhat grudgingly; he preferred Sheringham's *De Anglo-rum Gentis Origine Disceptatio* of 1670.

connection with the Saxons or the Saxon tongue, and the book did not convey the challenge that Verstegan so deliberately made; but it proved extremely popular—it achieved its seventh edition the year after the *Restitution* reached its second—and it had such a marked English bias, that its influence in creating the new antiquarian concept of the English must have been important. Our ancestors, the Germans, Camden said, were a great people, and in his day they were represented on the Continent by a nation "the most glorious of all now extant in Europe"; the Saxons who invaded Britain had been "a warlike, victorious, stiffe, stout, and rigorous Nation", and of Saxon England it could be boasted that "foure Englishmen have converted to Christianitie eight Nations of Europe".[1] Camden shared Verstegan's admiration for the Saxon tongue, for it "could express most aptly all the conceits of the mind", and he gave a short list of words showing the glory of our ancient English language. His treatment of personal names is much better than that of Verstegan, being based on the sound principle "that the Saxons, Danish, Norman, and British tongues", and in lesser measure Hebrew, Greek, and Latin, "were the fittest Keyes to open the entrance"; but Camden said plainly that in general "old English names" were "the scope" of his care.[2]

The return of the Saxons was a calamity for the ancient Britons of medieval imagining, and one as bad was the discovery of an ancient Briton's probable appearance. Obviously Brutus himself and Belinus and the other Trojan kings were pictured as very gorgeous personages in grand armour, as we can see in the handsome illustrations of Godet's *Chronicle* (Pl. XI), published about 1562; and we can be sure that their glory would be woefully diminished when men began to think of their followers as halfnaked savages. To do this, however, demanded realistic antiquarian vision, and in sixteenth century England this was rare as, indeed, it had been rare in the Middle Ages, even though John Rous of Warwick had tried to show us the rulers of Warwick looking progressively more old-fashioned as they receded into the past (Pls. III, IV). One kind of antiquarian

[1] Camden, *Remains*, ed. 1629, p. 11.
[2] Camden, *Remains*, ed. 1629, p. 47.

vision that we have now in mind is a product of the later Renaissance and is attributable to the influence of the classical texts; for it was in classical thought, in the writings of ancient Greeks and Romans, that the first adequate picture of primitive man and of the life of savages is to be found. For example, the opening of the second book of Vitruvius's *De Architectura*, which contains a dramatic reference to early men, born like wild creatures in caves and woods, and to the slow progress towards man-made shelters and simple hut-dwellings, was faithfully and convincingly presented to sixteenth century readers by two illustrations in a French translation published in 1547,[1] and it is not unimportant that the Renaissance student should be thus pointedly directed to the contemplation of a credible, and indeed probable, reconstruction of the past. Another instance of the return of antiquarian vision is provided by the *Aurei Saeculi Imago* of Abraham Ortelius, published in 1596, for this contains an account of the ancient Germans derived from Tacitus and other classical authors, and it is illustrated by pictures of primitive life among the Teutons. We may, indeed, be sure that John Twyne got his notion of the manner of life of our Albionic inhabitants from his classical studies, and we may expect that sooner or later English imagination would comprehend the ancient Britons as semi-wild men, running about nearly naked, savage, shaggy, and woad-stained.

But patriotic feeling about the Britons being what it was, and our Brutus being so obviously a well-clothed man (Pl. XI, a) there was bound to be resistance to this concept of the ancient British as an extremely simple and rustic folk. It needed a shock and a strong-minded antiquary to make us admit that we had once been noble savages; and it seems probable that the shock was provided by the Red Indians and that the courageous antiquary was John Speed.

It is difficult for us to realize the impression that the discovery of the New World made on antiquarian thought of the sixteenth century; but a spectacle such as the Brazilian tableau staged in Rouen in 1550, a luxuriant Garden of Eden in which real and dummy Indians were discovered leading a primitive and happy natural life, was the kind of thing, added to travellers' accounts and exciting pictures in books, that was bound eventually to give

[1] Jan Martin. *Architecture ou art de bien bastir*. Paris, 1547, p. 15, 15b.

rise to reflections other than those of the greedy colonist intent
on taking advantage of a simple folk. It was, indeed, not many
years later that Montaigne in his two famous essays on Coaches
and on Cannibals pleaded for the kindly treatment of the Indians
and spoke of them in a way that both delighted and perplexed
his readers,

"Our world hath of late discovered another . . . no lesse large, fully
peopled, all-things yeelding, and mighty in strength than ours: never-
thelesse so new and infantine, that he is got to learne his A.B.C. It is
not yet full fifty yeeres that he knew neither letters, nor weight, nor
measures, nor apparell, nor corne, nor vines. But all was naked, simply-
pure, in Natures lappe, and lived but with such measure and food as
his mother-nurse affoorded him".[1]

No primitive people in the Old World could possibly be the
cause of such astonishment.   Across a prodigiously vast ocean
had been found a new land, and in it a people for whom time
had stood still, original men, so it seemed, in their natural innocence, an anthropological discovery that amazed the thinker into
doubting the value of western civilization and of the Christian
faith. Might it not be the Indians, asked Montaigne, and not the
Europeans, who were the sane and proper representatives of
mankind? Once, alas, we had been as they were now.

In England, though Eden's *Gatherings from Writers on the New
World* was published in 1555, and Hakluyt's *Voyages* in 1582, it is
probable that the Elizabethans were not thus easily moved to
sentimental reflections about the Indians. They had been in-
formed of somewhat drearier contacts with the inhabitants of the
New World than those that had captured the imagination of
Montaigne. Frobisher had spoken fairly enough of the Eskimos
of Baffin Island, but he had not been enthusiastic about them; Sir
Humphrey Gilbert had advised colonists to approach the
Beothuks of Newfoundland with kindness and peaceful intentions, but he had also shown, on the authority of Scripture, that
it might be necessary to treat such graceless people very harshly.
It was not until near the end of Elizabeth's reign that the English
heard a different tale from their own people, for instance, an
illustrated account of the life and manners of the Indians of Vir-

[1] Essays, Bk. III, VI. Trans. Florio. See in general on this subject G. Chinard.
L'Exotisme Américaine . . . au XVIe siècle. Paris, 1911.

ginia (1588), and Raleigh's description of the goodly, well-favoured, and manly inhabitants of certain parts of Guiana (1596). And by this time travellers' tales from abroad had been in circulation; the bitter lament of Las Casas over the shocking cruelty shown to the Indians by the Spaniards had become known in England as a reproach to that race; Montaigne's Essays were familiar and had been translated into English by Florio (1603). Pictures of the Indians and of their life were now often to be found in books from abroad, and references to Indians began to appear in English literature. Spenser, for instance, gave this description of Maleger:

> And in his hand a bended bow was seene,
> And many arrows under his right side,
> All deadly dangerous, all cruell keene,
> Headed with flint, and fethers bloody dide;
> Such as the Indians in their quivers hide.[1]

Inevitably, comparisons were made between Red Indians and Ancient Britons. Samuel Daniel, as we have seen, suggested that the tribal divisions of the Indians gave a clue to the real social organization of the ancient Britons, and Raleigh in his *History of the World*, referring to the ridiculous colonization stories of fabulous European history, for instance the migrations headed by Tubal and Gomer after the Flood, remarked that in certain parts of the West Indies, it had taken the Spaniards ten years to penetrate ten miles into an unknown and tractless country.

Exactly in what way Red Indians became a pattern for ancient Britons is not known, but the important links were the pictures of the tattoo'd Indians, and the idea that an ancient Pict, a painted man, must have looked very like such an Indian. In the Print Room of the British Museum there is a famous series of Tudor records of America made by John White, the Virginia pioneer, about 1585, and these show various types of Indian, chiefly of Roanoke, and also illustrate their villages and customs; and with them are a number of drawings, intended for a kind of "Races of the World" book, that include some oriental persons and a remarkable team of individuals now labelled "Ancient Britons". It is not difficult to see how close is the connection between

[1] *FQ*, II, XI, 21.

"Indian" and "Early Man in Europe" (Pls. XII, XIII, a); but we must remember that, as far as we know, John White did not call his early Europeans "ancient Britons", and when his or a similar set of drawings of these primitive people was engraved by De Bry and published in 1590,[1] we find they are supposed to represent not Britons, but "Picts" and the "Neighbours to the Picts", that is, presumably, the Scots (Pl. XIV); just as Indian-type costumes with feathered head-dresses were deemed more suitable for the Scots than the British by the illustrator of the 1577 edition of Holinshed's *Chronicle*.[2] Before this, however, the cruel thought that the woad-painted ancient Britons must also have looked very like this had occurred to someone; for the Dutchman, Lucas de Heere, included a picture of two naked natives (Pl. XIII, b) in his *Description of Britain*, written about 1575, and there is no doubt whatever that he intended it to be an illustration of the early Britons, for one copy of the picture is so labelled by him.[3]

The great antiquary who settled the matter for us was John Speed, for in his *Historie of Great Britanie*, first published in 1611, he used four of the De Bry engravings in the chapter called "The Portraiture of the Ancient Britaines",[4] and he had a great deal to say about them and knew exactly who they are (Pl. XV). Indeed, when he came to deal with the "more civil ancient Britons", that is to say White's rather better-dressed natives and De Bry's "Neighbours to the Picts", Speed was prepared to take matters into his own hands, and choosing the figure formerly described as a "Woman Neighbour to the Picts", he caused his own engraver to put more and grander clothes on her, and he then told his readers she was Boadicea (Pl. XIV, b; XV, b).

Speed, like his contemporary Camden, was a great organizer of antiquarian knowledge; he believed in system, and he even forced the chaotic fabulous heraldry of our ancient rulers into something that must have been welcomed as a plausible and intelligent arrangement. In our matter he seems to have realized that it was no use quoting classical authors to the effect that the

[1] In Thomas Hariot's *Briefe and True Report of the new found land of Virginia*. Frankfort, 1590.

[2] See especially History of Scotland, p. 40.

[3] Th. M. Chotzen and A. M. T. Draate, *Beschrijving den Britsche Eilande door Lucas de Heere*. Antwerp, 1937. The drawing of the ancient Britons in the London manuscript of de Heere's work (Pl. XIII, b) is B.M., *Add.* 28, 330, f. 8 b.

[4] *Hist.*, ed. 1611, pp. 180–1; ed. 1632, pp. 39–40.

ancient Britons wore few, if any, clothes, and painted themselves, if at the same time one refused to recognize that the picture of a naked and painted person would give some idea of the probable appearance of an ancient Briton. There was no question of any disgrace here, but rather an occasion for pride; for nakedness implies hardiness, and painting one's self is, after all, art. Where an ancient Briton was concerned, there could be no doubt that savagery must include the idea of nobility.

Speed, therefore, not only took De Bry's engravings of the Picts and the Scots as serious visual aids in the reconstruction of the British past, but he was prepared to take a step further and to honour one particular Pict as a type-Briton, the standard representative of his race; for we may be sure that Speed was directly responsible for the inclusion of the famous ancient Briton in the place of honour on the title-page of his *Theatre* (Pl. XVI), which was engraved by Hondius, a figure subsequently made more familiar still by the versions of it in the atlases of Janssen and Blaeu. We may smile at the Roman and the Saxon and the Dane and the Norman, with their baroque plumes and swagger clothes; but that Speed's half-naked woad-stained Briton was an important newcomer into the world of the Tudor and Stuart antiquaries, no student of antiquarian thought could possibly deny.

Though in the preceding pages we have become aware of an ever-growing contempt for the British History and a corresponding lack of interest in it, we have not thereby finished with this inescapable subject. The neutral opinion expressed by Daniel Langhorne in 1676 and William Wynne's defence of the Brut in 1697 with its modestly expressed, but definite, conclusion that the story was based upon truth, will have warned us of the existence of a school of thought that did not countenance total belief or total disbelief in the British History, but preferred a position that may be described as that of the institutionalist. This was the man who saluted it, so to speak, as a time-honoured tale, and was prepared to admit that, though it was mostly nonsense, it might contain at least "the footsteps and reliques of something true"; and added, that whether this be so or not, the British History did possess the merit of calling attention to an admitted lacuna. It could be regarded, in fact, as a challenge to study the past, and find out what had really happened, and, therefore, the institutionalist maintained that, if the proper reservations were made, the British History could be legitimately used as an understandable allusion to the true past that it so guilelessly represented.

The quotation about the footsteps and reliques is taken from Milton's *History of England* that was published in 1670, four years before the poet's death. Milton would not have anything to do with Albina and Samothes; but the Trojan Brut seemed to him to be a story of another kind, a collection of tales that might very well be founded upon fact, tales suitable for "English poets and rhetoricians who, by their art, will know how to use them judiciously". This is a typical institutionalist point of view, and it was also that of his contemporary Edward Stillingfleet, Bishop of Worcester, who said of the British History that there might be "somewhat of truth in it under a mighty heape of monkish forgeries".

An example of another kind is the polite use that Sir William Dugdale made in his *Warwickshire* (1656) of John Rous's views about the early history of Warwick (p. 23). Dugdale thought it was reasonably certain that the Britons did make an early settlement there, and that Rous's highly improbable rigmarole did at least have the merit of calling attention to the gap in our knowledge; and, after all, said Dugdale, there might be something in what he said, for the old man had been a most diligent antiquary and had access to many manuscripts, since lost.

It will be appreciated that a very considerable subject is here opening before us, and it would be interesting to follow this line of thought into the eighteenth century and even to modern times; but in this book our period must be restricted, and, in truth, the account given here of the general collapse of the British History in the seventeenth century does not to any serious extent have to be altered in order to accommodate this generous hat-raising to out-moded antiquarian dogma. It is more important for us to go back in time to the sixteenth century and take note of the attitude of the first of the great institutionalists, Edmund Spenser, who died in 1599 at the age of forty-seven.

As antiquaries we should study the *Faerie Queene* seriously, because Spenser was a serious antiquary. He had made collections for a book on the antiquities of Ireland, where he resided off and on for some twenty years, and in his *View of the Present State of Ireland* (1596) he wrote of the prehistory of that country with a noteworthy sagacity. He had done some work on Irish place-names; he could offer ethnographical explanations of the customs, dress, and arms of the Irish; he was aware that there were two kinds of *rath*,[1] and that Irish megaliths were ancient burial-places, and were neither the work of giants nor natural formations. He had studied the legends concerning the origin of the Irish, and he thought it was possible to make some sense of them, because he was sure that in these stories were "reliques of the true antiquities, though disguised, which a well-eyde man may happily discover and fynde out". He recognized allusions in these tales, though they were in themselves fabulous, to actual invasions of Ireland at an early date from Spain and from Scotland, and he maintained that there was still surviving evidence in Irish customs to prove that these invasions were real. Those familiar to-day with the theories identifying the *Fir Bolg* with the *Belgi*, or the *Fir Dumain* with the *Dumnonii*, will agree that Irish legend does indeed present opportunities for a "well-eyde" man.

It is not necessary for us to discuss here the question of the re-casting of the *Faerie Queene* and the consequent intimate matters of chronology, for there is little doubt that the verses[2] containing the main narrative of the British History were originally written as part of an earlier and different poem. We can accept the *Faerie Queene* as we find it, a prodigious compliment to Queen Elizabeth that deliberately linked the Tudor Queen with the Prince Arthur of the poem, and, through him, with Brutus and the Trojans. Spenser, therefore, could hardly avoid making use of the British History, for the action of the poem takes place in the time of Uther Pendragon's Saxon wars, that is to say in Book VIII of Geoffrey's narrative, and if his characters were to have a glorious past, it could only be the glorious past that Geoffrey had invented for them. We must sympathize with Spenser. Neither Virgil nor Ariosto could give him guidance here, for he had to introduce with apparent seriousness something that all his intelligent friends considered to be completely bogus history, and we

---

[1] Cf. Giraldus Cambriensis, *De Top. Hib.*: caps. XXXVII, XXXVIII.

[2] *FQ*, II, IX, 59, 60; II, X, 5 ff.; III, III, 22 ff.; III, IX, 38 ff.; and there are other references in the Thames and Medway canto (IV, XI). For a full study see Miss C.A. Harper, *Sources of the British Chronicle History in Spenser's Faerie Queene*, 1910. Bryn Mawr Monographs, 7.

may be sure that Spenser knew that he was running the risk of
making his lovely poem ridiculous if he solemnly regaled his
readers with the substance of the early part of the Brut. Yet that
is what he did.

For Spenser did not believe in the British History. In one
manuscript of the *View* he went out of his way to remark that the
story of Brutus was an invention;[1] but even without that evidence it can be taken as certain that a man who was the friend
of Sir Philip Sidney and Sir Walter Raleigh would smile at the
story of the Trojans in Britain. The idea that he was a fundamentalist is intolerable, and Spenser took care, it seems, to make
it obvious to his friends that he was not.

In Book II, Canto X, verse 10, there is an entirely orthodox
and up-to-date reference to the turf-figures on Plymouth Hoe
(p. 161) commemorating the famous struggle between Goemagot
and Brutus's lieutenant Corineus,

> The westerne Hogh, besprinkled with the gore
> Of mighty Goemot, whome in stout fray
> Corineus conquered, and cruelly did slay.

Everybody knew the story of this famous wrestling-match, and
Spenser gave us here the latest antiquarian news, following Camden, about the location of the fight; but the next verse must have
come as a very great surprise to any well-read antiquary:

> And eke that ample Pit, yet farre renownd,
> For the large leape, which Debon did compell
> Coulin to make, being eight lugs of grownd;
> Into the which retourning backe, he fell.
> But—But those three monstrous stones doe most excell
> Which that huge sonne of hideous Albion,
> Whose father Hercules in Fruance did quell,
> Great Godmer threw, in fierce contention,
> At bold Canutus; but of him was slaine anon.

Nobody had heard of Debon and Canutus before; but Spenser,
not content with this mention of their prowess, went on to tell
us that just as Corineus became Duke of Cornwall, as in the

---

[1] *View of the Present State of Ireland*, ed. W. L. Renwick, London, 1934, p. 261.

British History he did, so in turn Debon became Duke of Devonshire, and Canutus Duke of Kent.

There are other surprises of this kind for the well-eyde antiquary, but the most astonishing of all is the statement that Brutus founded Lincoln as well as London, a really gross outrage against the poor British History, which had been entirely consistent throughout 450 years in telling us no more than that Brutus had founded a single city, his new Troy, that is London. But here is Spenser saying:

> His worke great Troynovant, his worke is eke
> Faire Lincolne, both renowmed far away,
> That who from East to West will endlong seeke,
> Cannot two fairer Cities find this day,
> Except Cleopolis:[1]

Devonshire, Kent, and Lincoln. The puzzling references must surely be little complimentary allusions to Sir Walter Raleigh, to whom the *Faerie Queene* is dedicated, and to Sir Philip Sidney,[2] and to the great antiquary, Thomas Cooper, who was Bishop of Lincoln from 1571 to 1584, the part-author of *Cooper's Chronicle*. They were just signals assuring Spenser's friends that the British History was in detail such nonsense that almost any liberties could be taken with it. Spenser even tampered with it to the extent of introducing a mention of the Holy Grail, an offence that none of its genuine protagonists would have committed; but what perhaps most clearly reveals the poet's attitude to the Brut as a record of fact, is his refusal to damage his beautiful Prince Arthur by the prophecy that he was to become the bogus Galfredian king who overcame Frollo, the Roman tribune ruling the Franks, and the united armies of the eastern and western worlds under the procurator of the Republic, Lucius Hiberius; for when Merlin does prophesy to Britomart, the Arthurian period is pointedly omitted, and we pass from Uther Pendragon to Geoffrey's Constantine, who succeeded Arthur.

Yet Spenser had two institutionalist uses for this famous and

---

[1] *FQ.* III, IX, 51. Cleopolis is Tudor London contrasted with Troynovant, British London.

[2] The "three monstrous stones" are probably the High Rocks, or some similar notable outcrop, near the Sidney home at Penshurst in Kent.

familiar account of early Britain. "The general end," he said of his poem, is "to fashion a gentleman or noble person"; and though there was prolonged argument on this very point in the various celebrated text-books on the subject of fashioning a gentleman, Spenser believed that to be of good birth and to be aware of your past and of the obligations imposed upon you by your past was an urgent first rule.[1] In general, "what minde is so fainte . . . that in reading the actes and greatnesse of Caesar, Alexander, Scipio, Hannibalt and so many other, is not incensed with a most fervent longing to be like them?"[2] and, in particular, "The first member and part of nobleness is that which ariseth to any person from the bright shine and worthiness of his ancestors.[3] Clearly, if the perfection of all virtues were to be embodied in Prince Arthur, he must be shown to appreciate this essential duty of understanding his own and his people's past; and so Spenser revealed him to us as amazed with delight after he had read about the glittering and romantic Trojan origin of the British and about the names and deeds of their illustrious kings,

> And wonder of antiquity long stopt his speech.
>
> At last quite ravisht with delight to heare
> The royall Ofspring of his native land,
> Cryde out, Deare countrey, O how dearely deare
> Ought thy remembraunce, and perpetuall band
> Be to thy foster Childe, that from thy hand
> Did commun breath and nouriture receave?
> How brutish is it not to understand,
> How much to her we owe, that all us gave,
> That gave unto us all, what ever good we have.[4]

Here then, as a first use for the British History, is the invitation to study the past; but Spenser had something more to say, for he was deeply interested in problems involving relationship in time, being influenced possibly by such Irish myths as that of the

---

[1] Spenser was, however, well aware of the contrary view, see his verse in the preliminaries to *Nennio or A Treatise of Nobilities*, trans. by William Jones, London, 1595, and cf. Jones's preface, and the summing-up, p. 96 b.
[2] Thomas Hoby. *The Book of the Courtier*, 1561, f. H.IIIb.
[3] John Ferne. *Blazon of Gentrie*, 1586, p. 15.
[4] *FQ*. II, X, 68–9.

Tuatha de Danaan and of the timeless *Tir-na-nog* into which living men could enter in just the same way as Tudor knights could enter *Faerie Land*. There was nothing specially remarkable, be it admitted, in his division of the British History into two parts that were from the point of view of the characters in the poem their past and their future; indeed, the prophecy made to Britomart, a recital of the subsequent history of the British kings from the sixth century to the accession of the Tudors, opens almost with the same words as the prophecy to Bradamant made by the same seer, Merlin, in *Orlando Furioso*,[1] but the poet's special study of his characters' attitude to the future introduces an unexpected line of thought. We find that Prince Arthur, the Redcrosse Knight, and Arthegal are persons struggling in a misty present from origins they know not towards a destiny that is hidden from them, needing the guidance of the prophet who has knowledge both of the past and the future: thus from the special view-point of his poem, Spenser presented us with a vision of the whole British History, whether performed or to be performed, as itself a destiny; and so he conveyed to us the idea that the past is evolutionary, a preparation for the future that in this case is a striving forward to reach Elizabethan England. Even though this famous Elizabethan theme in the *Faerie Queene* be the result of a final rearrangement and expansion of a poem never intended to contain this obsession with Tudor glory and the Tudor queen,[2] there cannot be any doubt that in the form in which the poem was finally cast, Arthur, who sets forth magnificence, the virtue that is the perfection of all the rest, is a man seeking fulfilment in the future of the Tudors, a man whose destiny demands that some day his magnificence will be shown again to the world in the magnificence of Queen Elizabeth.

In the *Faerie Queene* Spenser expressed this very beautiful antiquarian doctrine in its loveliest and most famous form, and the notion that all of her country's past is orientated upon Elizabeth is one of the minor graces of the poem. The investment of Britomart in Saxon armour and the praise of the

---

[1] *FQ.* III, III, 22; cf. *OF.* III, 16–17.
[2] On this subject see Miss Janet Spens, *Spenser's Faerie Queene*, London, 1934. The line that, in my view, shows that Spenser made use of older material is *FQ.* II, X, 49, 1.8, for it is Arthur himself who is reading the passage.

Anglians[1] are evidence of this governing idea; but, be it noted it was not Spenser's invention, for he was alluding to a generally acceptable antiquarian sentiment of the Tudor period, a feeling that all that had gone before, the total past of this country, could be interpreted as a preparation for England's glory in the last quarter of the sixteenth century; for the state of hopeful excitement that had connected King Arthur with Henry VII, the young Prince Arthur, and Henry VIII, had now changed into a state of complete assurance that the splendour of Elizabeth was in itself both an entire justification of the English past and also its full fruition.

In the extraordinary complexity and ingenuity of his attitude to the British History Spenser is without a peer. In contrast let it be noted that Shakespeare would have nothing to do with this notion that the British History was an ingredient in the greatness of Elizabethan England. He used plots that derive ultimately from Geoffrey of Monmouth, and he made Cymbeline refer to the Molmutian laws; but he saw no contribution to the glory of Tudor England in these remote British kings. "Base Trojan, thou shalt die" might fairly stand as an expression of his attitude to the British History, and we even find that his references to King Arthur are but a few casual mentions by the common people in Henry IV and Henry V.

There is one final remark to be made in this chapter. Though, as we have seen, our Trojan ancestors in Britain had only a precarious footing in the land after the reign of Elizabeth, and though Britain henceforward lay open to any invaders that an ingenious antiquary might see fit to conduct to our shores, the new antiquarian interests of the seventeenth century were sufficiently absorbing and satisfactorily practical to prevent any immediate and sensational re-peopling of the almost empty island by invaders as glamorous as the departing Trojans. A direct invitation to do so came in 1646 when the great French theologian and philologist, Samuel Bochart (1599–1667), a scholar of colossal attainments and dominating prestige, planted the Phœnicians in Britain in his famous *Geographia Sacra* of 1646; but we had to wait another thirty years until this still lively

[1] *FQ*, III, III, 56.

element in our population, first sponsored by John Twyne of Canterbury (p. 105), was officially welcomed in impressive state by an English antiquary of the seventeenth century, namely Aylett Sammes, whose enchanting but bafflingly muddle-headed *Britannia Antiqua Illustrata* was first published in 1676.

VIII

Britannia

THE historian of topographical studies in Britain will not neglect the Middle Ages, for there was our William of Worcester before Leland, and, going further back in time past the fourteenth century descriptions of Britain in Ralph Higden's *Polychronicon* and in the *Eulogium Historiarum*; indeed, the writings of medieval chroniclers contain numerous topographical records that owe their origin to a genuine antiquarian interest. Giraldus Cambrensis, for instance, wrote a *Topography of Ireland* and a *Description of Wales*, and promised his readers a book on British topography.[1] Doubtless this would have been, like the two he did write, for the most part an irritably medieval mass of legends, marvels, and fancies; but it would certainly have contained scattered notes of permanent value, such as those in the *Itinerary* referring to the walls of Carmarthen[2] and to a submerged forest.[3] It is also well known that in the same century there are many excellent descriptions of buildings, and, in particular, William of Malmesbury delighted to give records of the work of the Saxon bishops and abbots.[4] We remember, too, William of Newburgh's description of Scarborough Castle,[5] and the detailed accounts of Lanfranc's cathedral at Canterbury, and the rebuilding of it after the fire of 1174;[6] and there is similar topographical information about St. Alban's Abbey.

In this chapter, however, our subject is not such nascent and rather casual medieval topography, but the more systematic Tudor topography after Leland's time, in other words the achievement of the Elizabethan description of Britain, the perfected *Britannia*, with all its antecedent and consequent enterprises; but before we come to our main business with the works of the Elizabethan topographers, there is one earlier Tudor anti-

[1] *Descr. Camb.*: praef. prima. Rolls 21, VI, p. 158.
[2] *It.*, I, X. Rolls 21, VI.
[3] *It.*, I, XIII.
[4] *Gesta Pont.* Rolls 52, e.g., p. 255 (Hexham), p. 363 (Wareham).
[5] *Hist. Rerum Ang.* Rolls 82, I, p. 104.
[6] Eadmer, *Hist. Novorum.* Rolls 81, pp. 13, 15; Gervase of Canterbury, *Chronicle.* Rolls 73, I, pp. 9 ff., 19 ff.

quary yet to be mentioned, a man whose contribution to the future *Britannia* was a creditable attempt to discover the general lay-out of Roman Britain by means of the Antonine Itineraries. This was Robert Talbot (*c.* 1505–58), a man within a year or two of the same age as Leland. He was at Winchester and New College, and then entered the Church, holding livings in Kent and Essex and Northamptonshire, the county of his birth, and becoming a prebendary of Wells; later he was appointed to a stall in Norwich Cathedral and to the living of Burlingham St. Peter in Norfolk. He became known for his elegant, if trifling, Latin poetry, and Leland addressed some highly complimentary verses to this fellow-poet;[1] but his antiquarian accomplishment was the identification of the Itinerary routes, and this was, of course, known to Leland and used by him; it was also known to, and used by, both Lambarde and Camden; it is frequently quoted by William Burton in his *Commentary* of 1658; but, in fact, Talbot's notes, relating to only six of the itineraries, were not published until the eighteenth century.[2]

Talbot's sources seem to have been two printed texts of the Itineraries published one at Paris in 1512, and the other at Venice in 1518.[3] His difficulties in dealing with the British material must have been considerable, for the versions before him were confusingly inaccurate, and the task of identifying ancient names was complicated by the fantastic crop of Latin names for English towns that had been recently invented for literary and poetical purposes. Yet Talbot was successful in plotting the main routes, and the short itineraries (III, IV) he solved correctly; in the longer lists he made many intelligent identifications, some of which are certainly correct, as, to give just one example, his placing of Caesaromagus at Chelmsford, and, though there are, of course, serious mistakes, this most ingenious man did provide the skeletal material for a map of Roman Britain. It was, for the times, a rare piece of practical research, and one of indisputable useful-

---

[1] *Encomii.* London, 1589, p. 75.

[2] *Leland's Itinerary*, ed. Hearne. Third ed. 1769, III, p. 162. Various manuscript copies exist, e.g., Corpus, Cambridge, MSS. 101, 379; Gonville and Caius MS. 391; British Museum, Vitellius D. VII, f. 203 ff. (damaged). Talbot's notes end with Iter VI, but Burton, p. 239, quotes a note to Iter IX. William Fulke (1538–89) is often named as an elaborator of Talbot's studies, but Hearne, subsequently, could find no evidence that he had made any noteworthy contribution to the elucidation of the Itineraries (Hearne, *Collections* IV, 161 *et passion*).

[3] For a medieval manuscript version in England, now lost, see contents list of Corpus, Cambridge, MS. 416.

ness. When the Elizabethan diplomatist and antiquary Daniel Rogers (c. 1538–91), wrote to Ortelius and remarked that his work "on the Roman dominion in Britain has been very laborious—no one before me has touched the subject",[1] he was doubtless expressing what was for an historian a just opinion; but the modern antiquary will rightly insist that Talbot's name should stand at the head of the sixteenth century students of Roman Britain.

About twenty years after Leland died, two descriptions of Britain appeared. The first was by the Welshman, Humphrey Lhuyd, an antiquary of great reputation,[2] who died in 1568 at the age of forty-one, and it is only a slender little book[3] written on a sick-bed in the year of the author's death. Lhuyd was directly inspired by the work and exhortations of Abraham Ortelius, and, though he knew Leland's published books, he did not have the advantage of seeing the notes of the Itinerary, which means that he knew little or nothing of Leland's notions of a topographical survey; his interests, indeed, were predominantly historical and linguistic, and he began his book by explaining the Welsh system of spelling and mutations, so that his special philological contribution might be understood. He defended the British History with a fervour equal to that of Leland, whom he much admired, and he was, as we have observed (pp. 69, 87), angry about the mistakes he discovered in the books by Polydore Vergil and Hector Boece; he was angry, in fact, with anyone whose views or actions were anti-British; he said William of Newburgh was "a greasie monk . . . more conversant in the kitchen than in the historie of olde writers", and he hated "the bloodthirsty monk whom men call Augustine" whom he believed to be responsible for the massacre of the British monks at Bangor-on-Dee. His talent for acrimonious argument, however, does not obscure a fine antiquary's contribution to the topographical picture of Britain, for Lhuyd did successfully use his knowledge of Welsh to clarify the study of placenames, and he did his best to restore the tribes of Britain to their correct position; moreover, there is a genuine, though slight, notion of the importance of "monuments" in his survey, for instance the

---

[1] Hessels. *Ecclesiae Londino-Batavae Archivum* I, No. 42.

[2] See the tribute paid to him by William Salesbury in a letter to Matthew Parker, c. 1566, quoted by Robin Flower, *Journ. Nat. Library of Wales* II (1941), p. 9.

[3] See p. 69, n. 2.

account of Caer Caradoc, which he discovered by accident, and of Offa's Dyke, and of St. Winifred's Well. The most complete description he gives is that of his own town, Denbigh: he says that Henry Lacy, Earl of Lincoln,

"erected a very stout castle, not only by natural situation, but also by a wall of wonderful thicknesse, made of a very harde kinde of stone, in my opinion the strongest and best defended thing in England, addyng also therto a towne walled about, which by the auncient name be called Dynbech. . . . This fine towne, and my sweet country, beynge compassed welnigh aboute with very fayre Parkes, and standyng in the entrance of an exceedynge pleasant Valley, aboundeth plentifully with all thinges that are necessarie to the use of man. The Hilles yeelde Fleash and white meates. The most fertile Valley: very good Corne and grasse. The sweet Rivers with the Sea at Hande minister all sortes of Fishe and Foule. Strange Wynes come thither foorth of Spayne, France, and Greece, abundantly. And being the chief towne of the shyre, standyng in the very middle of the countrie, it is a greate market Towne, famous, and much frequented with wares, and people, from al partes of Northwales. The indwellers have the use of both tongues, And beyng endued by kinges of England with many Priveledges and Liberties are ruled by their owne lawes."

It is not to reproach Lhuyd, but to illustrate the extraordinarily advanced scope of Leland's survey done some twenty or thirty years earlier that in contrast to this charming eulogy of Lhuyd's native city we now set forth what the visiting stranger had to say about this same town.

"This Lacy firste began the toun of Denbigh, walling it and making a castelle there. Afore his tyme I cannot lerne that there was another toun or castelle. The toune and castel of Denbighe standith on a craggy hille, and is nere a mile in cumpace, and ys *pene orbiculari figura*. The castelle lyith south on the toune: and the toun lyith to the castelle by north and est. In the toun be but 2 gates, the Escheker Gate and the Burges Gate. In the first was the lordes court kept: and in the other the burgesis. The Eskeker Gate lyith playne west, and the Burgess Gate plain north. These ii Gates as the cumpace of the waulle goith be a great flite Shot one from the other: and betwixt them in the waulle is never a Tower. And from the Eskeker Gate to the Castel is never a towre: but ther is a galery out of the castel into it. These towers be in the toune waulle by est from the Burgeses Gate to the south est side of the castelle. First a great *quadrata* tower . . . secondly the countes toure a goodly square tower of 2 loftes highe. The third the Goblin Hole *semicirculari figura*, the leades of which *in hominum memoria* about a 80 yeares agoe were with tempest carried awaye, as farre almost as St. Marcelles the paroche church, and so it hath lyen uncovered. There be 2 rounde toures beside. There hath beene diverse rowes of streates withyn the wald towne, of which the most part be now doone in maner: and at this tyme there be scant 80 howsolders. . . . I have not yet lernid the certente how this wallid toune decayed withyn: wither it were by fier or for lak of water, wher of there is litle or none, or for lak of good caryage into the toun standing sumwhat high and on rokky ground, I cannot surely telle. But the towne of Denbigh now occupied and yoining neere to the old toun hath beene totally made of later tyme, and set much more to commodite of cariage and water by many welles in it. And the encrease of this was the decay of the other. At this present tyme the newe is 3 tymes as bige as the oulde . . . and it lyeth all in one streete . . . and in the market place well builded, which is fayre and large, and pavid of late yeares. . . . There is a chapelle of ease in the midle of the new towne, of S. Anne. One Fleming was the builder of this, and yet it is caullid *Capelle Fleming*, and is of a good largeness. Ther was an almose house hard by this chapelle *ex saxo quadrato* made by the same Fleming. But now it is desolate. . . . The castelle is a very large thing, and hath many toures yn it. But the body of the worke was never finished. The gate house is a mervelus strong and great peace of work, but the *fastigia* of it were never finished. If they had beene, it might have beene countid emong the most memorable peaces of workys yn England. It hath diverse wardes and dyverse portcolicis. On the front of the gate is set the image of Hen. Lacy Erle of Lincoln in his stately long Robes."[1]

This is not all Leland has to tell us about Denbigh, for there are some notes about the history of the town and castle, and a reference to the Chapel of Ease in the old town "wither yet moste of the new Toun cumme"; but the passage quoted is sufficient to show the purpose and the power of our first great topographer. We must not blame others who had no intention of describing places in so thorough a way if their regional studies in this respect disappoint us; but it is Leland's kind of thoroughness, at least in intention if not always in performance, that is the principal antiquarian interest of this chapter, for the achievement of a *Britannia* depended far less on linguistic and historical scholarship, necessary though this was, than on the determination of the

[1] *It.*, III (Wales), pp. 96-8.

tough itinerant antiquary to go out into the country and look at places with an open-minded and all-embracing interest, as Leland had looked at them.

The first county history published in this country appeared in 1576, and in this there is no sign whatsoever of the new topographical interest that had begun with Leland's travels. The *Perambulation of Kent* by William Lambarde (1536-1601) is a history of the principal towns and villages in the county and an inquiry into the meaning of their names: it is a learned, very sensible, and most entertaining book, with many anti-Papist stories in it that are still good to read; but, except in the matter of placenames, it does not advance the main business of getting to know Britain.

Lambarde was a lawyer, and his chief antiquarian attainment was a knowledge of the Saxon language and the Saxon laws; in 1568 he published a book on these laws; he also made a huge collection of placename material for England and Wales which he arranged in the form of a dictionary,[1] but he wrote only the "Kent" chapter (it was his native county) of his projected description of the whole country, for this task he regarded as beyond the power of any one man, and he hoped that each shire would produce its own historian, so that by "joining our pennes and conferring our labours" a complete survey might be achieved.[2] Lambarde's interest being thus restricted to documentary research, we find in his book only a few scraps of information about the Kent of his own day and its visible or recorded antiquities; we heard that there were vessels of old wine and salt in Dover Castle that were supposed to be, though Lambarde doubted this, part of Julius Caesar's stores; he had much to say about the old wooden bridge at Rochester; he was of the opinion that the barrows on Blackheath were the graves of fourteenth century insurgents; and he tells us that there was a figure of St. Hildeferthe in the window of Swanscombe church; but there are no descriptions of towns, and no sign of any awakening archæological interest, even when he writes of the ruins at Richborough.

It is one of the principal curiosities of this admirable book that Lambarde had so little to say about the Romans in Kent. In the introductory historical account the four centuries of the

---

[1] *Dictionarium Angliae Topographicum et Historicum*, first published in 1730.
[2] *Perambulation*, s.v. Halling.

Roman occupation of Britain are referred to only in a most misleading allusion of six words,[1] and in the main body of the *Perambulation* there is, apart from one or two mentions of Julius Caesar that he could hardly avoid, a marked lack of interest in the whole subject. Lambarde was not only a Saxon scholar, but he was also a vigorous champion of the Reformation; and his view was that the history of Kent began properly with Hengist and Horsa, and first became really interesting in the time of the Danes; for whatever these dreadful folk had done, even if they had cut off the head of an archbishop of Canterbury, at least they did not bear a name suggesting that they were sprung from the very bosom of the Whore of Babylon; thus the chapter "Sandwich" is a long chapter about the Danes, and in the short chapter "Richeborrowe", though there is a mention of Roman coins, all we are really told about the great fort is that it probably was the royal city in which King Ethelbert entertained St. Augustine.

Lambarde believed in the British History, though he rightly distrusted the "new fantasies and follies" that had been added to the original story; he was even prepared to believe in the Samotheans; but these ancient matters did not seriously concern him; what he liked, in addition to his historical and placename collections, were the customs of Kent that had an ascertainable legal background, and here, as in the fine essay on gavelkind, he was making a significantly important contribution to English antiquarian studies; and he also liked to contemplate his favourite county as a scene of contemporary anti-Papist reform. He tells with undisguised relish the excellent story of the "Disgraceful Rood of Grace",[2] and of the fraudulent "Maid of Kent",[3] and of the "Growing Rood";[4] and he did not mince words about any writer, ancient or modern, whose Roman faith was likely to prejudice him. Thus, speaking of Bede, he began, "I wot well this writer is called Venerabilis, but . . ." [5]

The year after the publication of the *Perambulation of Kent* there appeared a topographical work of a quite different kind.

---

[1] *Perambulation*, p. 15.
[2] Ib. s.v. Boxley. On this see Aymer Vallance, *Greater English Church Scenes*. London, 1947, p. 9 ff.
[3] Ib. s.v. Court at Street.
[4] Ib. s.v. Asherst.
[5] Ib. s.v. Canterbury.

This was the *Description of Britaine* and the *Description of England* by William Harrison (1534–93), Canon of Windsor, that formed the first three books of Raphael Holinshed's *Chronicle*, first published in 1577. Their antiquarian content owed a very great deal to Leland's itinerary-notes, as the author, who himself did next to no travelling, most suitably and gratefully acknowledges; they also include direct borrowings from Lambarde's *Kent*; but in writing these books, Harrison had no time for original antiquarian research, and it was never his intention to concentrate on the antiquarian aspect of his "description". On the contrary, he had set himself the task of producing a general picture of the country he loved on the model of the discursive and fascinating *Historia de Gentibus Septentrionalibus* of Olaus Magnus, that had been published at Rome in 1555, and his successful achievement of this "portrait" style in topography is in itself a most valuable contribution to antiquarian studies that had a direct and stimulating influence on the county historians of the late sixteenth and early seventeenth century. Harrison, like Leland, knew how to put antiquities in their proper place and had the same omnivorous affection for everything within the scope of his survey—language, history, the Church, the Law, rivers, towns, markets, the Navy, marvels, food and dress, British cattle and dogs, and so forth—and his genial and discursive work was in effect an entertaining and abundantly informative guide to almost every aspect of daily life in Elizabethan England. He had, however, genuine antiquarian interests, for he was a collector of Roman coins, some of which he intended to have engraved for his unpublished "Chronologie"; he knew, moreover, what he was talking about when he came to a subject like Roman camps, for there was one at Great Chesterford, near his rectory at Radwinter in Essex, and he had first-hand knowledge of the ruins of St. Albans, which he described in the second edition of his work. He most sincerely admired Leland, though he complained about the dirty and chaotic condition of the manuscript of the itinerary-notes which he used, and he believed Leland had made it almost incomprehensible on purpose; but Harrison copied him both uncritically, as in repeating Leland's error about Chertsey lying up the river from Staines,[1] and with misinterpretations, as on the occasion when, whereas Leland says

[1] Cf. Leland, *Cygnea Cantio. It.*, ed. Hearne, 1769, IX, p. 11, l. 106.

that by Uresbie or Rosebie (Rauceby) in Lincolnshire a plough-
man found a cist with coins in it, Harrison says that near Ancaster
a cist was found "by one Uresbie or Rosebie, a plowman"; indeed
he delights in embroideries of Leland's laconic notes, as in the
example of the find at Harlaxton near Grantham, of which
Harrison says:

"an husbandman had far better lucke at Harleston—where he found
not onelie great plentie of this coine, but also a huge brasse pot, and
therein a large helmet of pure gold, richlie fretted with pearle, and set
with all kind of costlie stones: he took up also chaines much like unto
beads of silver, all of which, as being (if a man might ghesse aine cer-
teintie by their beautie) not likelie to be long hidden, he presented to
queene Katharine then lieng at Peterborow, and there withall a few
ancient rolles of parchment written long agone, though so defaced with
mouldinesse, and rotten for age, that no man could well hold them in
his hand without falling into peeces, much lesse read them by reason of
their blindnesse."[1]

What Leland had said was:

"a stone under the wich was a potte of brasse, and an helmet of gold,
sette with stones in it, the which was presentid to Catarine Princes
Dowager. There were bedes of silver in the potte, and writings cor-
ruptid."[2]

Topographical research based on personal observation and
of the kind that we shall shortly be able to call the *Britannia*
method was already in progress when Harrison was writing.
The heralds had begun to make detailed records and drawings of
tombs, and there were antiquarian tours, such as that undertaken
by an unidentified antiquary in 1574 in company with the Chancellor of Hereford, Dr. Edward Threlkeld.[3] The two men
travelled throughout the west country from Hereford to Chester,
and from Chester to Carlisle, and, in addition to a quantity of
heraldic notes our antiquary took a general interest in all he saw
and heard, just as Leland had done before him; he visited the

[1] Book II, XXIV (ed. 1807).
[2] *It.*, I, p. 28.
[3] B.M. *MS. Harley* 1046. The authorship was formerly attributed to Sampson Erdeswicke (cf. *D.N.B.*); the passages relating to northern England have been printed by M. A.
Richardson, *Reprints of Rare Tracts*. Newcastle 1893–9 (in vol. for 1848).

great hill-forts near Ledbury and on the Malverns, and he learnt of many archæological finds made in Chester, particularly of a gold ring inscribed *Gormandus Romanorum*;[1] he also transcribed two Romano-British inscriptions found in Cumberland. The whole tour, however, is reported on a few pages in a slender little note-book, and we find no sign here of the strong governing purpose that was necessary if the great *Britannia* Leland had planned was to be completed.

There can be no doubt that the first man possessed of the requisite generalship and judgment was William Camden, the great antiquary whose name is as familiar as that of Leland. Camden rejected the discursive Harrisonian model, and in setting himself the task of succeeding where Leland had failed, he saw that what was needed was not a mass of miscellaneous information, but the systematic handling of the material, whether it were already familiar or the results of new fieldwork. By one book, while still a young man, he raised topographical studies in Britain to a new dignity and usefulness.

William Camden (1551–1623) was a young schoolmaster at Westminster, aged thirty-five, when he published the *Britannia*, his first book. His father came from the Midlands and his mother of a Cumberland family, and he had been educated at Oxford. He tells us that between leaving Oxford and taking up his mastership at Westminster at the age of twenty-four he had travelled over a considerable part of Britain in order to visit antiquities, for he had been interested in the past ever since he had been a schoolboy. He was able to continue his investigations in the Westminster holidays, and it seems that even in these early days he had acquired a knowledge of Anglo-Saxon and Welsh. His talents as an antiquary were recognized when he was still a very young man, but the visit of Abraham Ortelius to England in 1577 was the most important event of his first years at Westminster, for it was Ortelius who advised him "to restore Britain to Antiquity, and Antiquity to Britain" by editing his topographical collections in the form of an antiquarian survey of the whole country, just as Ortelius also urged Humphrey Lhuyd to use his equally valuable placename and historical material.

[1] A commander in the Saxon wars and the first great figure in the history of Chester.

Camden's *Britannia* is not an easy book to discuss because even
in the author's lifetime it changed from a small octavo volume
to a robust and copiously illustrated folio of 860 pages, and we
to-day who use the great three- or four-volume editions of 1789
and 1806 with their heavy apparatus of supplements and addenda
of all kinds, have naturally enough almost lost sight of the book's
beginnings. The scope of Camden's survey was, however, from
the start ambitious. Leland had confined himself to England and
Wales; Camden included Scotland and Ireland, and outlying
islands from the Shetlands (his Ultima Thule) to the Scilly Islands
and the Channel Islands, and to Ushant and Oleron, and the islands
of the Frisian coast. It was not possible for him to see all these
places for himself, and he depended on others for help; indeed,
as his fame grew, he found himself in touch with such a useful
band of local correspondents that, even though he sometimes
edited their work without actual reference to the monuments
they were describing, the *Britannia* has throughout to a most
creditable extent the appearance of being work done on the spot.
But Camden was himself a very experienced traveller, and he
had seen much of England, certainly the eastern counties and
Lancashire and Yorkshire, before the *Britannia* was published;
before his last edition he had been to Wessex, and Wales, and to
the north midlands, and to Cumberland, He was therefore not
merely an efficient organizer, but a practical man undertaking
the antiquarian description of a land that he had taken the
trouble to know very well.[1]

It is possible that a first reaction on its publication in 1586 was
that antiquarian interests were obscuring the learning expected of
a sixteenth century schoolmaster, for Camden expanded the
second edition not only with new topographical information
but with additional references to the classics and appropriate
samples of a schoolman's wisdom. Nevertheless, the topographical theme prevailed, and, the plan of his book being
clear to him from the start, Camden made no important alterations in its essential structure. It opened with a general geographical note on the British Isles that was followed by a
discussion of their first inhabitants and of the origin of the

---

[1] His advantages after he became a herald must be noted in connection with his 1600
and 1607 editions; but it is also to be remembered that Camden made his visitations by
deputy (see p. 155).

name *Britain*; then came historical notices of the Romans in Britain, the Britons in Armorica, the Picts and Scots, the Saxons, the Danes, and the Normans; Camden then discussed the Roman and Saxon "divisions" of Britain and the creation of the shires; he next described the social orders and the government of the English, and included an apologetic note on the astrological sign under which Britain lies; then he proceeded to his detailed antiquarian account of the shires, which, in England and Wales, he arranged in groups that he thought represented the areas occupied by the ancient British tribes.

Before beginning the section *Danmonii* (Cornwall and Devon), Camden stated his general aim: "in each county I mean to describe its antient inhabitants, estymology of its name, its limits, soil, remarkable places both ancient and modern,[1] and its dukes or earls from the Norman Conquest." And then he says: "Aggreably to my principal design, I proceed now to describe the promontories, cities, and rivers, mentioned by the antients,"[2] and thereby he declared the central theme of his book; it was to be in the main an account of British antiquities written for antiquaries, and though Camden did not deny himself the pleasure of recording that which seemed delightful and interesting to him in Tudor England, whatever its age or nature, he was much more sparing in this matter than Leland had been, and on the whole the information he gave about the (in his day) present state of the country is a kind of stage-setting for the parade of antiquities he had in mind. He was not, like Leland, looking at nearly everything and liking nearly everything; he was professedly studying the past, and if there were no antiquities he lost interest: "In this low part of the County (Bucks), though stor'd sufficiently with towns and villages, we meet with few worth our observation,"[3] is a remark that Leland would not have understood; indeed, it is a remark typical of one kind of antiquary (now, as then) that to another kind of antiquary (now, as then) seems both inexplicable and unworthy. It would be very unjust, however, to the great Camden to suggest that his *Britannia* is to any serious extent marred by the limitations of the author's interests. The description of the counties proceeds in a full and even measure

[1] *Melioris notae. Britannia*, 1586, p. 65; Gibson, ed. 1722, I, cclxviii, translates "of the greatest eminence at present". The translation above is Gough's, ed. 1806, I, ccv.

[2] Ed. Gough, 1806 I, 3. Ed. 1586, p. 70.

[3] Ed. Gibson, 1722, I, 330.

exactly according to his declared plan, and the "soil", by which
he means scenery, natural history, and the occupations of the
people, is not a neglected subject. The noise of the anvils at
Birmingham,[1] the "diamonds" of Bristol,[2] the vineyards and
wines of Gloucestershire,[3] the perry (cold and flatulent) of
Worcester,[4] the lead and the bluejohn of the Peak,[5] the pearls of
the River Irt in Cumberland,[6] and the coal of Durham,[7] are
examples of Camden's detail concerning industries and produce; his admiration of scenery and of the sheep "whose fine soft
fleeces are in demand even in Asia" is noted at Ashridge, Bucks;[8]
he compared Crowland with Venice, and described its three
streets divided by canals of water, planted with willows, and
built on piles . . . and joined by a triangular bridge;[9] he paid
a fine tribute to the prospect from Windsor Castle.[10] He mentioned the fossils at Keynsham, Somerset,[11] and Alderley,
Gloucestershire,[12] the scurvy grass of the Thames estuary,[13]
the scordium of the Fens,[14] the medicinal plants of the Picts Wall,
introduced by the Romans and now sought after by Scottish
physicians;[15] he mentioned a fish, the ruff, common in the
River Yare,[16] the puffins and barnacles of the Calf of Man,[17] the
virtues of British dogs,[18] and the sweating sickness at Shrewsbury.[19]

The range of the individual antiquities recorded by Camden
is not much larger than that of Leland, but about the time of his
tour of the north in 1599 with Robert Cotton and aided by the
local researches of the Appleby schoolmaster, Reginald Bain-

[1] Ed. 1586, p. 318. Cf. Leland, *It.* II, 97.
[2] Ed. 1586, p. 111.
[3] Ed. 1586, p. 189.
[4] Ed. 1586, p. 323.
[5] Ed. 1586, p. 313 (lead only); cf. ed. 1590, p. 442 and ed. 1594, p. 429.
[6] Ed. 1586, p. 451.
[7] Ed. 1586, p. 438. Cf. for "sea-coal", ed. 1594, p. 612 and Leland, *It.* v, 140.
[8] Ed. 1586, p. 211.
[9] Ed. 1607, p. 399.
[10] Ed. 1586, p. 143.
[11] Ed. 1586, p. 109; cf. Leland, *It.*, v, 103.
[12] Ed. 1590, p. 278; cf. Leland, *It.*, v, 95.
[13] Ed. 1590, p. 244.
[14] Ed. 1590, p. 389.
[15] Ed. 1586, p. 464.
[16] Ed. 1586, p. 266.
[17] Ed. 1590, p. 725.
[18] Ed. 1586, p. 127; cf. ed. 1607, p. 190. John Caius had published his *De Canibus Britannicis* in 1570.
[19] Ed. 1607, p. 451. John Caius's work on this subject was published in 1552.

brigg (*c.* 1545–1606),[1] he made a very important beginning to a detailed survey of Romano-British inscriptions, and in the *Britannia* of 1607 he published nearly eighty from the northern counties; this is Camden's principal contribution to the serious study of antiquities in the field, but it is also true that in his orderly pages a number of sites and monuments are named that were not mentioned in Leland's notes—Stonehenge, the Boscawen-un stone circle, Kit's Coty House, Silbury Hill, the Bartlow barrows, Julieberry's Camp, and Maiden Bower are examples among the megaliths and earthworks. As scattered illustrations of Camden's interests we may mention his reference to the deneholes near Faversham and Tilbury,[2] the identification of the Coway stakes as the place where Caesar crossed the Thames, his survey of a Staffordshire section of Watling Street,[3] and the mention of the traces of streets still visible at Richborough and forming St. Augustine's Cross,[4] and the account of the discovery in Wensleydale of a statue of Commodus as Hercules, and of the Roman camp at Ambleside;[5] later antiquities that he considered worth notice are the Bewcastle cross, which he thought was erected by the Vaux family;[6] the Magnus inscription at Lewes (Fig. 2); the stained glass in Peterborough Cathedral containing a history of the abbots;[7] the effigies at Aldworth, which he said were not those of giants but of members of the de la Beche family;[8] King John's Cup at King's Lynn,[9] and the bronze font of the Scottish kings at St. Albans.[10]

In the main matter of the *Britannia*, the description of towns, Camden was workmanlike and informative, but in performance and in the interest of his work far inferior to Leland, as the modern antiquary knows from the much greater use that is made to-day of the *Itinerary* notes. Even though we consult Camden's 1607 edition, and even though it be acknowledged that there is much in the *Britannia* that is not in the *Itinerary*,

---

[1] For Bainbrigg, see Haverfield, *Cumb. and Westmorland Arch. Soc. Trans.* NS. **x** (1911), p. 343.
[2] Ed. 1607, p. 318 (references here are to entries not in first, 1586, edition).
[3] Ed. 1607, p. 439.
[4] Ed. 1594, p. 253.
[5] Ed. 1607, p. 624.
[6] Ed. 1607, p. 644.
[7] Ed. 1607, p. 379.
[8] Ed. 1607, p. 204, cf. ed. 1594, s.v. Bradfield.
[9] Ed. 1594, p. 386, cf. Spelman, *Icenia* in *English Works*, ed. 1723, p. 143.
[10] Ed. 1590, p. 318.

direct comparison in the case of such towns as Exeter, Bristol, Reading, Worcester, and York, shows that Leland's account of them is unquestionably the more valuable. Camden, however, is clear and sensible, and his "York", though far less interesting and less detailed than that of Leland, is nevertheless a fine example of the high standard he set himself and its successful achievement.

Much of Camden's historical detail comes, as is to be expected, out of easily accessible chronicles, and nobody in his position and at the age of thirty-five could have travelled, talked, and read sufficiently to write a *Britannia* without including much perfunctorily borrowed information, and his book is none the worse for this inevitable dependence on the scissors-and-paste method, or because of his obvious inclusion of other people's work that resulted from his use of local correspondents. The question of his sources ought not therefore to detain us, but the matter cannot be left without allusion to the very serious charge, made by a contemporary, that the *Britannia* represented a fraudulent misuse by Camden of the still unpublished notes of Leland's *Itinerary*, which we know he had studied. It was alleged that he had obtained John Stow's copy of Leland's work and had published it "with some additions and alterations . . . as his owne sole worke . . . it being well knowne at the first publishing thereof that he was never any travayler, neyther of abillitie to undertake such a worke".[1] A calumny, Camden called this accusation, and a calumny it certainly was; his later editors, Gibson and Gough, have each in turn agreed that it is only necessary to read the *Itinerary* and the *Britannia* side by side in order to see that the charge in its full implication is nonsense. No attentive reader could decide otherwise. The attentive reader will, however, discover that Camden does use much more of Leland's material than Gibson and Gough are willing to admit. He uses a very great deal, and he certainly does not, as he says he does, invariably acknowledge his borrowings. His account of Denbigh, for instance, is simply a conveniently shortened version of the admirable note on the town by Leland; but not to waste time on this undeniable debt, we need quote only one example of Camden's unacknowledged borrowing, namely his reference to Guy's Cliff, near Warwick.

[1] *Discoverie of Certaine Errours* by Ralph Brooke, ed. with additions 1723, II, p. 97.

Nemusculum ibi est spacum, fontes limpidi, et gemmei, antra muscosa, prata sempor verna, rivi levis et susurrans per saxa discursus, nec
non solitudo, et quies quae Musis amicissima.[1]

and here is Leland, whose jottings are sometimes a mixture of
English and Latin:

It is a place of pleasure, an howse mete for the Muses; there is silence,
a praty wood, *antra in vivo saxo*, the river rollynge with a praty noyse
over the stones, *nemusculum ibidem opacum, fontes liquidi et gemnei, prata
florida, antra muscosa, rivi levis et per saxa discursus, necnon solitudo et
quies musis amicissima.*[2]

The truth is, however, that in spite of such borrowings the
Britannia is in structure and form sturdily independent of the
Itinerary, so plainly so that it is possible to say that Camden's
book would have been much improved if he had made a more
systematic use of the chaotic notes that represented his great
predecessor's work.[3]

The accounts of Worcester or of York, or, on a smaller scale,
of Wallingford, or of Norwich—which Leland did not describe—
are typical examples of Camden's topographical work that are
obviously not stolen from the *Itinerary*. Camden himself explained[4] that his purposes were different from that of Leland,
who was obsessed with the idea of collecting material for a map;
in Camden's day map-making was the work of a professed
cartographer, and he, the antiquary, had no use for Leland's
laboriously recorded inter-town distances, and details about
bridges and notes on wayside scenery. He took a patronizing
view of Leland; he said that he himself had worked on British
topography for thirty years as against Leland's five; that he had
travelled just as much, and had read probably a great deal more.
He thought that on the historical side the *Itinerary* notes were by
no means satisfactory. Camden had, in short, an entirely different

[1] *Britannia*, ed. 1590, p. 452 (not in 1586 ed.)
[2] *It.* II, p. 46.
[3] Harrison complained that Leland's notes were "moth-eaten, mouldie, and rotten".
Camden probably used John Stow's copy, made in 1576, which has an inadequate index,
Bodleian MSS., *Tanner* 464, i–v (indexes in vols. II and III).
[4] Camden replies to the charge made against him in the *Ad Lectorem* of the *Britannia*,
ed. 1600; this is reprinted in the 1723 edition of the *Brief Discoverie*.

view of the task of compiling a *Britannia*; he did not eye a town in Leland's way; it was not for him a congregation of interesting buildings, but, primarily, a place with a history that might or might not be illustrated by reference to its more important buildings; he was not prepared to allow his carefully scaled and systematized account to be clogged with the detail Leland loved; there is no sense of joyous exploration in Camden's work, little of Leland's delight in any pretty building that caught his eye. Camden was efficient, thorough, and hard-headed, and in his slow-moving, dignified description of Britain he found little room to record the erratic enthusiasms of his famous predecessor.

Camden's achievement in writing the *Britannia* depended in the first instance on his wisdom in so limiting his task that he was actually able to perform it. Leland had failed, lost in the labyrinth of his notes, and Lambarde had declared that the task was beyond the power of one man; but Camden, prompted by Ortelius, devised a plan that was within one man's compass, created the *Britannia* single-handed, and maintained his book, when written, as a serviceable foundation-study to which all serious topographical work of his age must thence-forward necessarily be related. This directive power of the *Britannia* was the dominant influence upon antiquarian research in the seventeenth century; Camden had shown in his clear persuasive preface how to blow away the fogs and confusions of medievalism, and how to make a fresh start by the exercise of a little original thinking; he had shown that English studies were a necessary part of British antiquarian research, and he had made it henceforth obvious that this research must be conducted with reference to field work. As the book grew in edition after edition, Camden's leadership becomes more and more plain; he saw the kind of research that was wanted, and directed his readers thereto; in particular, he showed how great was the almost unexplored wealth of valid antiquarian evidence to be found by going to look for it. This was why he devoted more and more of his space to Romano-British inscriptions and to the description of British and Roman coins; and why he undertook the systematic recording of the epitaphs in Westminster Abbey.[1] It was prob-

---

[1] *Reges, Reginae, Nobiles, et alii in ecclesia collegiata B. Petri Westmonasterii Sepulti*, 1600, with subsequent editions in 1603 and 1606.

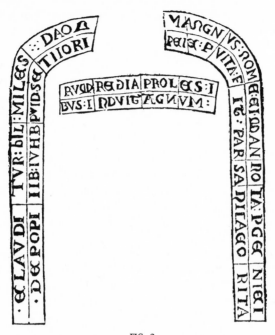

FIG. 2

Medieval inscription, St. John's-sub-Castro, Lewes.
Camden, 1586.

ably for this reason also that he demonstrated the advantages of illustrating an archæological book.[1]

Camden had not been very polite to heralds in the 1594 and the preceding editions of the *Britannia*, and he had made, as he

[1] The 1586 *Britannia* contains the first archæological illustration in an English book, the typographical arrangement (Fig. 2) representing the early medieval "Magnus" inscription at St. John's-sub-Castro, Lewes. In the 1590 edition Camden included four drawings of coins, and in 1600 the *Britannia* appeared with an important group of illustrations, including a title-page engraved by William Rogers on which is a map of early Britain and archæological insets, plates showing some of Sir Robert Cotton's coins (Pl. VIII, a), the well-known engraving of Stonehenge—itself based on an engraving by R. F. twenty-five years earlier (Pl. VII), and a plate illustrating a group of Romano-British altars (Pl. VIII, b); it also contained maps of Roman Britain, Saxon England, and ancient Ireland. The first folio edition of the *Britannia* (1607) has an even finer collection of pictures and maps, and includes for the first time the drawing of the Glastonbury cross (Fig. 1), which in 1590 and 1600 had been represented by a five-line inscription in archaic lettering. In the meantime Sir Henry Savile had published a plan showing the arrangement of a Roman camp (*View of certaine militar matters*, p. 59); but Camden, following Continental example, was certainly the pioneer in antiquarian book-illustration in this country.

could scarcely avoid doing, many mistakes in the genealogical sections of his books; yet, though it might be supposed he would not be popular in the College of Arms, in 1597, after he had been at Westminster for over twenty years and had become Head-master, he was suddenly made Clarenceux Herald. He entered the College to meet, so it fell out, a sour attack from within its walls on his antiquarian good faith and ability; and the ensuing quarrel is of some general interest.

The hard words charging him with the misuse of Leland's notes, which we quoted above, were those of York Herald, Ralph Brooke (1553–1625), who must have been busy preparing his *Discoverie of Certaine Errours . . . in the much-commended Brit-tannia 1594*, before Camden became Clarenceux; but though it is not certain whether the book was actually published before or after this, to Brooke, odious appointment of a mere "peddling armorist" to high office in the profession, it was out in time for the new Clarenceux to reply in the 1600 edition of the *Britannia*, and this set Brooke to work on an even more ill-tempered attack on his colleague, though, as it turned out, Brooke's *Second Dis-coverie* had to wait till 1723 before it was published. Brooke, who was in any case offended by Camden's modernist views and his readiness "to disperase newe opinions that impugne the anncient and Catholique veritie, as well concerning *Brute* as others",[1] wanted to show that instead of meddling with the difficult business of genealogy, a subject only an experienced herald could master, Camden ought to have stuck to his "inferior province of boy-beating". Camden had indeed made errors, and let it be added that he acknowledged them testily and tardily, preferring to show where Brooke himself had gone wrong; but our interest here is not in the rights or wrongs of the extremely complicated genealogical argument, but on the agreeable circum-stance that the contestants were quarrelling not about the misty material of legends, but about matters of fairly recent and usually ascertainable fact.

An example is the dispute that arose from Camden's state-ment that Henry Holland, Duke of Exeter (d.1473) had a daugh-ter who married a Neville; Brooke maintained that he died childless, and Camden, who was really referring to the Duke's half-sister, corrected his mistake in the 1600 edition of the *Brit-*

[1] *Discoverie*, 1723, II, p. 152.

annia without acknowledgment; Brooke then went on to say that the Duke was buried in Westminster Abbey in the tomb in St. Edmund's Chapel that Camden, following Westminster tradition, attributed to John of Eltham, Earl of Cornwall (1316-36). The effigy, he pointed out, wore a duke's crown not an earl's, and was that of a bearded man of sixty and not of a youth;[1] he added that the funeral shield hung above it was not old enough in appearance and not of the right fashion to belong to a burial of the first half of the fourteenth century; moreover, said Brooke, the arms thereon, and on the tomb itself, *England in a bordure of France*, were known to have been used by the Duke of Exeter on charters and deeds still in existence. Camden retorted that the arms were equally certainly those of John of Eltham, and he quoted the Roll of the tournament held at Dunstable in 1334 and also the Book of Thomas Jenyns. Brooke replied that he attached no importance to the Dunstable Roll; he did not even believe in the Dunstable Tournament, for Edward III was busy up in the north all that year; and as for Jenyns' book, he had possessed the original of that for thirty years and did not believe that Camden had ever seen it; he was happy to say that in fact it testified in precisely the opposite direction, establishing that the Plantagenet arms of an Earl of Cornwall must be *argent a lion rampant gules in a bordure sable bezanty*. Camden then appealed to the evidence of Queen Philippa's tomb in the Abbey—there, he said, in the first place of the row of shields on the left side would be found arms that, on the evidence of the other shields, could only be those of John of Eltham, and they were *England in a bordure of France*. "Let him goe to the tombe, lett him looke upon it," wrote Camden. "I have been to see," answered York Herald, and he insisted that Camden had "untruly reported these armes, there being no such armes in those places as he affirmed there are". In any case, he asked, why should John of Eltham's arms be on this tomb? He was only the Queen's brother-in-law—and he then proceeded to give Camden some expert instruction in the medieval use of arms; but the argument finally descended to the question of cross-legged effigies, like the one on what Camden called John of Eltham's tomb. Camden claimed that such effigies had gone

---

[1] "A verie great and large figure, with a beard more befitting a man of threescore yeares than one of nineteen." *Second Discoverie*, p. 126.

out of fashion long before 1473, so that this particular effigy could not possibly be that of Henry Holland. Brooke brushed this argument aside. Cross-legged effigies, he said, were supposed to be those of men who had been, or intended to go, to the Holy Land; if that were so, they might well be found up to about 1540 when Henry VIII suppressed the Order of Knights of St. John of Jerusalem; but even if it were not so, it could be shown that cross-legged effigies continued to be made at a very late date, and he cited an instance at Chew Magna[1] in Somerset and another at Bisham in Berkshire, that of Sir Thomas Hoby who died as late as 1566.

It is tempting to discuss this argument, in which on the main issue Camden was right; but our purpose is better served by another illustration of the new kind of antiquarian debate. Camden had given it as his opinion that the Bigots had built Norwich Castle because he had seen there "lions saliant in the same forme engraven in stone as the Bygots used in their seales before they obtained the honour and office of Marshall". Brooke criticized this statement first of all on the grounds that the arms of the Bigots at the time in question were "shieldes charged onelie with a plaine Crosse", in saying which he was correct; but he then took the matter up in terms of actual observation on the spot:

"I, for my better satisfaction therein, did ride to Norwich for to search the truth of your speach: and going into the said castle, I founde over the first gate, two great stones fixed, of some yarde square, and uppon each of them a Lyon passant cowardie, their tayles turning under their bellies, and comming over their backes, but in no Shielde or Escutcheon. And seeking more diligentlie all other places about the saide Castle, I did finde over the hall doore, other two like stones, with a Lyon also uppon each of them, but contrarie to the former, for these were passant, regardants with their tayles over their backes, and the endes in their mouthes: yet neither in Shielde, nor Escucheon. And therefore no such coats armour is there uppon the Castell of Norwich, as you sayde you had seene, that the Bygots did use in their Shieldes and Seales. In consideration of this my great paines, and journey, I desire but that you will from henceforth make a difference between

---

[1] A "Hawkewood", he says, whom some parishioners could remember. He is referring to the fourteenth century wooden effigy in this church, having probably been told that it had been moved thither from the church at Norton Hawkfield within living memory.

the Antique fictions of a carvers braine, and the right ensignes of our ancient Nobilitie."[1]

Brooke was right again; Camden had mistaken incidental Norman ornament for heraldic devices, and though in the eighteenth century Norfolk antiquaries were still prepared to consider these carvings to be armorial,[2] Brooke had settled the issue. He had done so by going to look at them, and we have come therefore to a development in antiquarian procedure that we must recognize as the end of our present inquiry; for whatever medieval obscurities were still embarrassing antiquarian thought, and however long they may have continued to do so, Camden with his: "Let him goe to the tombe, lett him looke upon it," and Brooke with his "I . . . did ride to Norwich to search the truth of your speech" are announcing plainly enough that a new age has begun.

Of Camden himself we need say little more. He published two works that had developed out of the preparations for the *Britannia*, one a collection of chronicles—which included the forged passage about King Alfred founding the University of Oxford that he inserted—it is thought innocently—in his *Asser*, and the other the *Remains* of which we have spoken (p. 119). Then he turned to the chronicling of recent history, and in 1615 published the first part of his "Annals" of the reign of Queen Elizabeth. His antiquarian work was now confined to assisting in the regional surveys that were being performed by his friends and correspondents, and such direction of it as he could give from his central position in the College of Arms. He did not himself invent the system of official visitation by deputy, but he exploited it—thus once again invoking the wrath and jealousy of his colleagues—to the great advantage of antiquarian studies by the employment he gave to the brilliant young heralds, Augustine Vincent and John Philipot. When he was nearly seventy and his health was beginning to fail, he made his last great contribution to the studies he loved by the foundation of

---

[1] *Discoverie of Certaine Errours*, London 1723 p. 51. The passage occurs in the first *Discoverie*.

[2] T. Gurdon, *Essay on . . . the Castle of Norwich*. Norwich 1728, p. 36, and Francis Blomefield, *Norfolk* II, 1745, p. 56; for an illustration of one of Brooke's second pair of lions see *Archæologia* xii (1796), Pl. xxvi, 3, and cf. Samuel Woodward, *Norwich Castle*, London and Norwich, 1847, Tab. IV.

the history chair at Oxford that bears his name; in 1623 he died in his home in Chislehurst, aged seventy-two. He was buried in Westminster Abbey where in the south transept is his monument, adorned with the bust of him, his hand resting on the *Britannia*.

> Camden! the nourice of antiquitie,
> And lanterne unto late succeeding age.

That was the way the antiquaries of his day thought of him, and it is well that an almost universal verdict should be spoken for us by that antiquary among his acquaintances who was also one of England's greatest poets.[1]

In this age the acknowledged masters of survey in the matter of genealogy and church-monuments were the Heralds. The broadening of the early Elizabethan visitation into the fine illustrated antiquarian catalogue of the first half of the seventeenth century is a subject that must be reserved for expert handling, but it is our duty to acknowledge the debt we owe to a body of men at whose head so far as our present interests are concerned stand Robert Glover (1544–88), Somerset, and Robert Cooke (*c.* 1537–93), Clarenceux, Francis Thynne (d. 1608), Lancaster, and Nicholas Charles (d. 1613), Lancaster. Their immense collections and visitations reveal a growing sense of the importance of the seals, monuments, and stained glass that provided the genealogical and heraldic information they sought, and a realization of the independent interest of these documents as—in themselves—antiquities. Cooke, Thynne, and Charles all made drawings of church monuments that were general antiquarian records rather than the professional notes of a herald; thus, in the tradition of the thirteenth century architectural drawings of Villard de Honnecourt,[2] Robert Cooke presents to us in church-notes as early as 1569 what he calls "the manner of the tomb" of Edward, Lord Despenser at Tewkesbury and of Robert, Duke of Normandy in Gloucester Cathedral (Pl. X) and of Lord Berkeley in the Temple Church, Bristol.[3] In this

---

[1] Spenser, *Ruines of Time*, 169.

[2] Of Cambrai. He travelled extensively on the Continent, and was an able draughtsman with general artistic, architectural, and antiquarian interests. See J. Quicherat, *Facsimile Sketchbook of V. d'H.* London, 1859. Pl. X.

[3] College of Arms MS., Cooke's CN, 1569, f. 49.

respect the drawings of Nicholas Charles, mostly some twenty or thirty years later, are particularly valuable, and he too has left many records of "the manner of the tomb", his best-known perhaps being his sketch of the tomb of the Black Prince in Canterbury Cathedral[1] and his drawings of the brasses at Cobham, Kent.[2]

Among the heralds of Camden's day, there was the fine antiquary William Smith (*c.* 1550–1618) of Cheshire who, after having been an innkeeper in Germany, entered the College in 1597, the same year as Camden; he was the author of a mass of papers on heraldic matters, but he is best-known for his short and charming *Particular Description of England* (1588), which is distinguished by its pretty coloured profiles of towns and a picture of Stonehenge;[3] and for his description of Cheshire,[4] which contains a fine bird's-eye view of the city. There was also William Wyrley (1565–1618), a herald and a famous collector of church-notes, and there were also Augustine Vincent (1584–1626), John Philipot (*c.* 1588–1645), Sir Richard St. George (d. 1635), and Sir Henry St. George (1581–1644).[5] It was indeed a praiseworthy company of men deserving to be remembered no less than the famous heralds of the next age, Dugdale, Ashmole, and Sandford.

Similarly, in Camden's time a distinguished company of antiquaries contributed by their regional researches to the antiquarian discovery of Britain. There was, for example, John Hooker or Vowell (*c.* 1526–1601) of Exeter, and the Devonshire antiquaries of the next generation, Sir William Pole (1561–1635), Thomas Westcote (b. 1567), and Tristram Risden (*c.* 1580–1640).

[1] College of Arms, Vincent MS. 225, p. 119.

[2] British Museum MS. *Lansdowne* 874, ff. 60b–61b.

[3] B.M. MS. *Sloane* 2596, f. 35b; the MS. was published by H. B. Wheatley and E. W. Ashbee, London, 1879.

[4] B.M. MS. *Harley* 1046; for the illustrations see ff. 172–4. The survey was published by Daniel Hall, *Vale-Royal of England.* London, 1656.

[5] Vincent, promoted to Windsor Herald in 1624, had been a clerk in the Tower Record Office before he entered the College in 1616; he published, in defence of his beloved Camden, a criticism of Brooke's *Catalogue of Nobility*, and he was a man of considerable influence in antiquarian matters, persuading William Burton to write the *Leicestershire* and having much to do with the preparation of John Weever's *Funerall Monuments.* Philipot was born at Folkestone and was Bailiff of Sandwich and M.P. for the Borough; he was also a citizen and draper of London, and entered the College in 1613, being appointed Somerset in 1624. Sir Richard St. George of Hatley St. George, Cambridge, entered the College in 1602, was knighted in 1616, and became Clarenceux in 1623 in succession to Camden. His son, Sir Henry, entered the College in 1610, and became Garter, and of Sir Richard's grandchildren two became Garter and one Ulster.

There was Thomas Churchyard (1520–1604), the Welsh patriot (p. 43), whose *Worthines of Wales* (1587) contains descriptions of effigies and of arms in Welsh churches. There was Thomas Habington (1560–1647), the first Worcestershire antiquary. There was James Strangman (*c.* 1555–*c.* 1595) in Essex, and for Norfolk there was the great Sir Henry Spelman (*c.* 1564–1641) who wrote an admirable description of his county, *Icenia*, notable to us for its practical archæological interest in the Roman fort at Brancaster.[1]

We must note too the good topographical sense of Sampson Erdeswicke (*d.* 1603), the historian of Staffordshire, who had learnt to look at buildings and places with some intention of noting their appearance and to take church-notes. He gave an account of Tickeshall House and Tutbury Castle, and a good description of Lichfield; he reported some antiquarian research of his own on the effigies in Dudley Church, and mentioned a monument bearing Saxon characters in the churchyard; at Burton he used his knowledge of style in effigies to correct the date of a tomb; he wrote an excellent note on Beeston Castle, and his collections for Cheshire have tricks of arms in the manner of the professed heralds.[2]

There are other names that cannot be omitted from even the shortest sketch of the rapidly widening interest in the *Britannia* kind of antiquarian research that distinguished the later part of the reign of Queen Elizabeth. For instance, there was John Stow (1525–1605), the London merchant-tailor, to whom Camden owed his knowledge of Leland's itinerary-notes. Stow was a man of fifty when the young Camden first went to Westminster, and though he was primarily an historian, he had amassed large topographical collections and even had materials for a general *Monasticon*; so, when eventually he became friends with Camden, who began his *Britannia* in 1577, he was in a position to be of great help to the junior man, and in return the young schoolmaster, who was more travelled and possessed of a wider learning and greater scholarship than the self-taught Stow, was

[1] *English Works . . . Posthumous Wbrks.* London, 1723. Part II, pp. 147, 149. Note also Spelman's *Villare Anglicanum*, a list of English towns and villages showing in what hundred and county they are situated; this useful compilation was organized and financed by Sir Henry.

[2] B.M. MS. *Harley* 506. Erdeswicke's *Survey of Staffordshire* was edited and published by T. Harwood (London, 1820 and 1844).

no doubt able to give some assistance to the author of the famous *Survey of London*. This was published in 1598, when Stow was over seventy, and it was the most detailed topographical study that had yet appeared, a laudable and lovable record based on the most extraordinarily patient observation and research. His purpose was to describe London as he saw it and to add an historical commentary and notes on social customs and interesting events; it is true that through the screen of reminiscences and topical information, the outline of his record is somewhat blurred; but a strong antiquarian interest is not difficult to recognize, and familiar examples of this to-day are his long account of the discoveries made in 1576 on the site of the Roman burial-ground at Spitalfields,[1] and the description of John Gower's tomb in Southwark Cathedral.[2] Stow had no difficulty in accepting the British History, and was able to pass on to us without any marked expression of incredulity the information that the first archbishop of London, Thean, aided by the chief butler of King Lucius, built St. Peter's, Cornhill, and that the second archbishop of London, Elvanus, built a library adjoining the church, which assisted in the conversion of the Druids to Christianity;[3] but where he could speak with knowledge of the circumstances, he was a dispeller of legend, for instance in correcting the story that Sir William Walworth's dagger had been added to the arms of the City, "which was the crosse and sword of St. Paule, and not the dagger of William Walworth";[4] in refusing to believe the exaggerated account of the famous feast given by Sir Bartholomew Reade in Goldsmiths' Hall;[5] and, again, in discrediting the fabled antiquity of Bakewell Hall.[6] Stow was at his best, however, in the plain recording of fairly recent fact, and a particularly good example of his work as a topographer is his description of the Eleanor Cross in West Cheap, a passage that illustrates not only the perils and tribulations endured by a late thirteenth century monument in the late sixteenth century, but also the strongly expressed concern of the Court for the preservation of the ancient monument in question.

[1] *Survey of London*, ed. C. L. Kingsford, Oxford, 1908 I, pp. 168–70.
[2] Ib. II, pp. 57–8.
[3] Ib. I, p. 194; cf. II, p. 125.
[4] Ib. I, p. 221.
[5] Ib. I, p. 305.
[6] Ib. I, p. 286.

Camden also knew, and was helped by, his contemporaries George Owen (1552–1613) of Henllys, Pembrokeshire, and Richard Carew (1555–1620) of Antony, Cornwall. Their works are very different from Stow's *London*, for both of them wrote general and discursive "portraits" of their respective counties, on the model of Harrison's *Description of Britain*, and they had much to say about physical features, natural history, and the pursuits and pastimes of the people. Owen completed his first volume in 1603, and did not live to finish the second volume in which the parishes were to be described; his antiquarian contribution is therefore not fully stated, but his book is a good one, and in it he has given us a serviceably accurate drawing of a megalith, the Pentre Evan chambered tomb, which he classes as one of the county's "wonders".[1] He was a good geographer, and among other interesting items of information includes a lively account of the game "knappan"; but Owen's work, which remained in manuscript until the end of the eighteenth century, is for all modern readers outshone by the greater brilliance and undeniable beauty of Carew's *Survey of Cornwall*, which was published in 1602.

Carew was a country gentleman with the county and parliamentary occupations befitting his station, and also scholarly tastes that were nourished by a considerable knowledge of languages, both ancient and modern; he had been at Oxford with Camden, was a member of the Society of Antiquaries, and was acquainted with all the new antiquarian interests of his day, as is shown by his warm-hearted and sympathetic praise of the English tongue.[2] He was indeed in a position to give the world an antiquarian survey of Cornwall that would be a long, dull, but, of course, invaluable enlargement of the Cornwall chapter of the *Britannia*, to which, Camden tells us, he had contributed so much; but in fact he did nothing of the kind, preferring to talk generally and discursively of Cornish affairs and Cornish worthies, of Cornish saints, of the Cornish language, of tin-mining, of games and fishing, and the elegant houses and the arms of his numerous

---

[1] B.M. *MS. Harley* 6250, f. 101; reproduced *Cymmrodorion Record Series*, No. 1 (1892), p. 251—later volumes of Owen's *Description of Pembrokeshire* in the same series were issued in 1906 and 1936.

[2] In his essay *The Excellencie of the English Tongue* contributed to the 1605, and later, edition of Camden's *Remains*. Carew defended "mingling" (cf. Verstegan's views, p. 119 above).

friends and relations, and on any other topic that arose as he spoke of the land and people he loved so much. It is, some may think, the best of all county surveys of the portrait kind, and it contains, as so learned an author would unfailingly contrive, a valuable admixture of antiquarian fact; for example, the figures of Gogmagog and Corineus cut in the turf on Plymouth Hoe,[1] the sea-covered land of Lyonesse, the image of the Magdalene at Launceston, the striking remains of Tintagel Castle, the unlucky excavation under an inscribed stone near Fowey, the "Doniert" stone (Fig. 3) and the story of the Hurlers, are antiquarian matters mentioned by this lovable wordy man; and he does not leave us in any doubt about his secret sympathy, in which all good west countrymen must have shared, with the British History. It was unfashionable Carew knew, but, after all, King Arthur was a Cornishman by birth, and there was much to be lost if men were allowed to "shake the irrefragable authoritie of the round tables Romants"; moreover, if there were a Brutus, he observed, then one could be quite happy about accepting Corineus as the first Duke of Cornwall.

The affection in which all readers must hold Carew's *Cornwall* being so warm, and its deserved praise even to-day being so high, it is remarkable that we should have to add that from the point of view of antiquarian observation in our present *Britannia* sense a visiting Englishman should have given us a much better account of Tudor Cornwall, imperfect and faulty though his survey may be. It is even more remarkable that this Englishman did not call himself or think of himself as an antiquary—indeed he wrote humbly "under the correction of learned antiquaries". This was the map-maker and surveyor, John Norden (1548–1625), of whom we have spoken (p. 35), a man only a few years older than Camden and Carew. He strikes us, in comparison with Carew, as a melancholy individual, much given to moralizing and the writing of religious books,[2] and he lived in a state of poverty that he often lamented, being paid not at all, or only a little, by Elizabeth and James I, for whom he laboured so long in his noble project for a detailed survey of England. He reverenced Camden and spoke highly of Carew and other antiquaries, and they in turn thought well of his maps, several of

[1] On these figures see R. N. Worth, *Trans. Devon Assoc.* XII (1880), p. 566.
[2] See A.W. Pollard, *The Unity of John Norden*, *The Library* NS. VII (1926), p. 233.

them being used in the 1607 edition of the *Britannia*; but no one seems to have realized what a fine topographical antiquary Norden was.

This is illustrated by his *Cornwall*, a fair copy of which with a dedication to James I was completed about 1610.[1] There is a greater wealth of detail—we hear for the first time of the curious prehistoric stone passages, the Cornish *fogous* (*ogos* or *googoos*, Norden called them); we have references to early cremation burials and to megalithic chambers; there is a note about stained glass at Fowey, and a splendid account of the ruins of Restormel, where "the ruyned Oven layeth open her entrayles that man

FIG. 3
Carew's illustration of the Doniert stone, 1602.

yet see the bountye of pristine ages"; but this is less important than the accuracy of Norden's observations which is revealed to us in the accompanying illustrations. Norden was applying to ancient buildings and field-monuments a method of record that the naturalist and the herald now understood, but the usefulness of which the antiquary scarcely appreciated. It is sufficient to say that Norden's picture of the "Doniert" stone (Pl. IX, a) is in its carefully attempted accuracy an archæological innovation

---

[1] B.M. MS. *Harley* 6252. Norden refers in the dedication to Prince Henry (d. 1612) as "Duke of Cornwall"; in the text he refers to Camden as Clarencieux, Carew's Survey (1602), and to "her late Majesty"; but the survey seems to be based on at least two visits to Cornwall (cf. the reference to the visit of Don Antonio of Portugal in 1589). Norden's *Description of Cornwall* was published in London in 1728.

of importance (cf. Figs. 3 and 4), and of no less value are pictures such as that of Dunheved Castle (Pl. IX, b) and "Arthur's Hall" near St. Breward, and the Trethevy Quoit.

How these illustrations would have fared if translated into contemporary book-illustrations, we need not inquire; nor does it lessen our admiration, that his castle drawings, such as that of Tintagel and Dunheved, had no more express antiquarian pur-

FIG. 4

Camden's illustration of the Doniert stone, 1607.

pose than his huge and magnificent bird's-eye-view of Windsor Castle[1] and Holt Castle.[2]   Norden was concerned simply with the problem of recording, and he included antiquities in his ideal survey, just as he included park-boundaries, rivers, and roads.   Thus in his survey of Middlesex, published in 1593, he announced that it seemed to him a useful practice to record the inscriptions and coats of arms on funeral monuments, which

[1] B.M. MS. *Harley* 3749, taken in 1607.
[2] B.M. MS. *Harley* 3696, taken in 1620.

he did in places such as Edmonton, Ealing, Finchley, Hampstead, and Hackney, and his printed text is illustrated by cuts of the arms, again showing his vision and originality, for this kind of record had hitherto been confined to the manuscript collections of the heralds. He was not consistent, needless to say, in these and other antiquarian matters. His *Hertfordshire* contains little that is important in our present context, and his *Essex* nothing; his *Northamptonshire* has only the Eleanor Cross and the Danish Camp near Daventry; but it is in these works, particularly in the *Northamptonshire*, that Norden shows such learning and sense in his understanding of English placenames that on this count alone he should rank as an antiquary of note.

The regional topographical enterprises of the late sixteenth and early seventeenth century have for our present purpose been sufficiently described, but the names of two antiquaries of practical importance in connection with a more general progress in antiquarian knowledge have not yet been mentioned in this chapter. The first is John Speed (1552–1629), our second tailor-antiquary of London, whose signal service in determining the probable real appearance of an ancient Briton has already been recorded (p. 124). Of his sagacity in the matter of the British History there is no possible doubt. "I am of yesterday, and know nothing," he said of fabled origins, and he meant by that that he was not prepared to make history of anything but the records of credible historians who were in a position to inform him of facts actually within their knowledge; but with the main content of Speed's huge *History of Great Britaine* (1611) we are not now concerned. As a contributor to the ideal *Britannia*, however, Speed comes before us as an outstanding personality in topographical research, not because of his own field-work, but because of his leadership in method. His principal contribution to British topography was the use he made of maps, especially county maps. The *Theatre of the Empire of Great Britaine* (1611) contained over fifty of these maps, some prepared by Speed himself and some depending on Norden and Saxton, and these were issued in an atlas, in which each map is accompanied by a written description supplementing the information in the map, so that together maps and texts in Speed's hand became a new method of describing England. His texts are brief, much shorter than Norden's descriptions of the counties he surveyed, and they contain no original material of importance; but Speed had shown how to summarize topographical knowledge in picture and word. He also showed how to make an intelligent pictorial use of coins; naturally, there are mistaken identifications and faulty representations; but Speed spaced them out deliberately and emphatically as illustrations of his history, embedding them, as it were, in his narrative as evidence of the archæological reality of the rulers of each period. He made yet a third contribution towards the clarification of the *Britannia* material, for, as an expert in ancient Biblical genealogies, he greatly improved his account of Saxon England by displaying the family-trees of the principal royal houses; though here, be it noted, he proved more indulgent to Saxon legends than to those of the poor Britons, for his tables began by showing that the first royalties of all the Saxon houses were descended from Woden and Frea; but Speed was at any rate producing a welcome and visible order out of material not easily to be studied in other works, and his genius for system was also evident in his treatment of the fabulous heraldry of these Saxon kings.

The second antiquary, Sir Robert Bruce Cotton (1571–1631), nineteen years younger than Camden and Speed, was a wealthy man, distantly connected with the Scottish royal family of Bruce. As a boy he was at Westminster School, where he met Camden, and he then went to Cambridge; afterwards he returned to Westminster where he had a house near Old Palace Yard, and before he was thirty he was a Fellow of the Society of Antiquaries and famous for his already valuable collection of manuscripts and coins and British antiquities of all kinds. Cotton, however, is important not just because he was a rich and generous collector; but because he was a truly learned man and a diligent student of his famous books, and an acknowledged authority on British history. He understood how, in the light of the new and more practical scholarship, research into the British past ought to be conducted, and, indeed, he deliberately formed his great library, one of the principal foundation-collections of the British Museum, in such a way that it might be generally useful to antiquaries. There can be little doubt that his influence on his former schoolmaster resulted in Camden's increased interest in numismatics and probably also in Romano-British inscriptions, and we can be sure that the *Britannia* is archæologically very much the better for the tour Cotton and Camden made together in northern England in 1599.[1]

Collecting, except of manuscripts and coins, was not yet an archæological enterprise of significant importance; but John Twyne of Canterbury collected Romano-British antiquities of all kinds, and William Harrison collected coins; and no doubt there were others with similar cabinets of curios, for example, Rene Wolfe, a friend of John Stow, who had preserved a number of antiquities found in London.[2] It is also true, moreover, that sixteenth century learning had produced, in addition to Sir Robert Cotton, two collectors on the grand scale. One was Lord Burghley (1520–98), to the glory of whose library and coins, and to whose antiquarian knowledge, the youthful Camden paid a tribute when writing to Ortelius in 1577,[3] and the other was Henry Herbert, Earl of Pembroke, 1534–1601, who collected, in addition to manuscripts, ancient sculpture, coins, gems, and medals. The existence of such private museums is at least a reminder to us of a wholesome widening of the range of antiquarian interests that would inevitably help towards a more just assessment of mere British antiquities, and the great collectors of the next age must have been in some measure men of importance even for our narrow subject here. Of these the best known are another Earl of Pembroke, William Herbert, 1580–1630, Henry Howard, Earl of Arundel, 1586–1646, George Villiers, Duke of Buckingham, 1592–1628, and Henry, Prince of Wales, 1594–1612. The arrival of the Parian Marble in this country in 1627, and John Selden's publication of this and the other Arundel marbles in 1628, must, though indirectly, have had some effect on the study of Romano-British antiquities, and it is certainly a reflection of the school of thought of the dilettanti, and not a result of the enterprise of a practising British antiquary, that deliberately inquisitive excavations were made at Stonehenge in the reign of James I.[4]

[1] For this date see Haverfield, *Trans. Cumb. & West. Arch. Soc.* NS. XI (1911), p. 349.
[2] Stow, *Survey of London*, ed. Kingsford, I, pp. 293, 330, 349.
[3] Hessels, *Ecclesiae Londino-Batavae Archivum*. I, no. 71.
[4] John Webb, *Vindication of Stone-Heng Restored*. London, 1665, p. 127.

With William Burton's *Description of Leicestershire* (1622), and John Weever's *Funerall Monuments* (1631) we come to the end of our present study, for these two books belong to a new antiquarian age. Before the middle of the century the four antiquaries of the Surrenden Society, Edward Dering, Wm. Dugdale, Christopher Hatton, and Thomas Shirley, had pledged themselves[1] to the kind of research that can be fairly described as modern in its method, and Roger Dodsworth was laying the foundation of the renowned *Monasticon Anglicanum*. Already the fogs of mediveal antiquarian thought are seen to be lingering only in rapidly thinning wisps and patches, and in the clearer light of the Great Age of the Heralds, as the middle and later seventeenth century may fittingly be called by antiquaries, the topographical work of the Age of Camden is to be crowned by the publication of some of Britain's finest antiquarian books. Indeed, the expectant youthful antiquary of the new age was soon to have in his hands a volume that seemed to contain between its covers all the antiquarian virtues, and in 1656 it was thus greeted by Anthony Wood, then aged twenty-four, in his diary:

"This summer came to Oxford *The Antiquities of Warwickshire* written by William Dugdale, and adorned with many cuts. This being accounted the best work of its kind that hitherto was made extant, my pen cannot enough describe how A. Wood's tender affections and insatiable desire of knowledge were ravish'd and melted downe by the reading of that book".[2]

[1] *Archæologia Cantiana* I (1858), p. 55.
[2] *Life and Times of Anthony Wood*, I, p. 209.

Index

Agard, Arthur, 100
Albina, 24
Albion, name for England, 71, 100
Alfred of Beverley, 12
Andrew of Wyntoun, 78
Annius of Viterbo, 66, 71
Antiphilarchia, 46, 49, 116
Antiquaries, Society of, 100, 114
Archers, Society of, 38
Arms, Royal, fictitious, 35
Arthur, King, 8, 13, 14, 17, 36ff, 68, 93ff,
    109, 110, 111, 129
Arthur, Prince, 36, 106
Arthur, Duke of Brittany, 14
Arthur's Oon, 67, 68

Bacon, Francis, 37, 115
Bainbrigg, Reginald, 146, 147
Bale, Bishop John, 69ff
Baronius, Cardinal, 73, 113
Bochart, Samuel, 132
Boece, Hector, 65ff
Boston, John, 30, 57
Britain, name of, 40, 91, 92, 107, 108, 109
Brooke, Ralph, 60, 152ff
Broughton, Richard, 111
Bry, Theodore de, 124, 125
Buchanan, George, 84, 85, 99
Budé, Wm., 46, 115
Burghley, Wm. Cecil, Lord, 43, 166
Burton, Wm., 83, 167

Caius, John, 49, 72, 76, 77
Caius, Thomas, 77
Centuriators, 112, 115
Cambridge, see Universities
Camden, William, 76, 108–9, 119–20,
    143ff, 158, 160, 165–6
Cantilupe, Nicholas, 26, 52
Capgrave, John, 35
Carew, Richard, 61, 160–1
Caxton, William, 39, 95
Charles, Nicholas, 156, 157
Chaucer, Geoffrey, 60, 118, 119
Chester, Robert, 103
Churchill, Sir Winston, 102
Churchyard, Thomas, 40, 43, 158
Clain, J. T., 110
Clapham, John, 109, 113

Cooke, Robert, 156
Cooper, Bishop Thomas, 41, 129
Cotton, Sir Robert, 146, 165

Daniel, Samuel, 110
Davies, Dr. John, 101
Dee, Dr. John, 37, 43
Dering, Sir Edward, 167
Dodsworth, Roger, 167
Drayton, Michael, 75, 103, 109
Dugdale, Sir Wm., 19, 126, 167

Elyot, Sir Thomas, 42, 71, 91
Enderbey, Percy, 101
Enyas, Sir, 23
Erdeswicke, Sampson, 158

Fabyan, Robert, 39, 41
Faerie Queene, 126ff
Filmer, Sir Robert, 76
Foche, Abbot John, 106
Fordun, John, 66, 78
Fuller, Thomas, 58, 112
Fulke, Wm., 135

Geoffrey of Monmouth, 4ff, 89ff, 101ff
Gildas, 13, 38, 83, 93, 94, 116
Giovio, Paolo, 41
Giraldus Cambriensis, 12, 89, 134
Glastonbury, 15–17, 50–1, 87, 96–8, 112
Glover, Robert, 156
Godet's Chronicle, 120
Gordon, George, 10, 111
Goscelin of Therouanne, 30
Grafton, Richard, 39
Greek language, 89, 91, 101, 108–9
Greeks, in Britain, 91
Guy of Warwick, 22, 23
Guy's Cliff, 19, 22, 23, 148–9

Habington, Thomas, 158
Hakluyt, Richard, 43
Hall, Edward, 37
Hardyng, John, 24, 35, 39
Harington, Sir John, 43
Harrison, William, 39, 73, 141, 149, 166

Harvey, Richard, 99, 116
Hastings, Sir John, 111
Hatton, Sir Christopher, 167
Heere, Lucas de, 124
Henry, Prince of Wales, 166
Herbert, Henry, Earl of Pembroke, 166
Herbert, William, Earl of Pembroke, 166
Heywood, Thomas, 103
Holinshed, Ralph, 39, 73
Holland, Joseph, 101
Honnecourt, Villard de, 156
Hooker, John, 157
Howes, Edmund, 100
Higden, Ralph, 13, 39, 134
Higgins, John, 40
Humphrey, Duke of Gloucester, 34, 62

Indians, American, 122ff

John of Tynemouth, 30
Joscelin, John, 115

Kelton, Arthur, 39, 86

Lambarde, William, 43, 73, 99, 113, 116, 139–40
Langhorne, Daniel, 101, 125
Languet, Thomas, 41
Leland, John, 32, 42, 45ff, 85ff, 137–8, 142, 145
Lewis, John, 74, 100
Ley, James, Earl of Marlborough, 101
Lhuyd, Humphrey, 44, 69, 87, 136
Lily, George, 41
Lucius, King, 8, 112, 113, 159
Lyte, Henry, 100

Magnus, Olaus, 141
Major, John, 65, 78
Malmesbury, 15
Meigle, 68
Milton, John, 58, 126
Montaigne, Michel de, 122, 123
More, John, 110

Nasmith, James, 31
Nicolson, Bp. William, 111
Norden, John, 35, 161–4
Nowell, Lawrence, 116

Oldisworth, Arnold, 101
Ortelius, Abraham, 115, 118, 121, 136, 143, 166

Owen, George, 160
Oxford, *see* Universities

Parker, Dr. John, 114
Parker, Archbp. Matthew, 111, 114, 115
Parsons, Father, 111
Philipot, John, 155, 157
Phoenicians, 107, 132
Pole, Sir Wm., 157
Price, Sir John, 88
Prideaux, Matthias, 110
Prynne, William, 113

Raleigh, Sir Walter, 109, 123, 128–9
Rastell, John, 41, 109
Risden, Tristram, 157
Rogers, Daniel, 136
Rowland, R., *see* Verstegan
Rous, John, 19ff, 126
Ross, John, 100
Rudbourne, Thomas, 13, 35

Sammes, Aylett, 76, 133
Samothes, 71ff
Saxton, Christopher, 164
St. George, Sir Henry, 157
St. George, Sir Richard, 157
St. Helen, 58
St. Joseph of Arimathea, 15, 36, 52, 84, 111–2
St. Patrick, Charter of, 50, 91
Scaliger, Joseph, 118
Scota, 66, 69, 79
Seal, King Arthur's, 41, 42, 95
Selden, John, 76, 109, 166
Sheringham, Robert, 101
Shirley, Thomas, 167
Shakespeare, William, 132
Sidney, Sir Philip, 44, 128, 129
Slatyer, William, 74
Smith, William, 157
Speed, John, 76, 121, 124–5, 164–5
Spelman, Sir Henry, 112, 158
Spenser, Edmund, 118, 123, 126
Stillingfleet, Bp. Edward, 66, 112, 126
Stow, John, 39, 76, 158–9, 166
Strangman, James, 158

Talbot, Robert, 135–6
Temple, Sir Wm., 111
Thompson, Aaron, 102
Threlkeld, Dr. E., 142
Thynne, Francis, 156
Tiptoft, John, Earl of Worcester, 27
Trevisa, John, 14
Twyne, Bryan, 77

Twyne, John, 13, 37, 41, 68–9, 105ff, 121, 166
Twyne, Thomas, 69, 87, 105, 106
Tyrell, James, 111

Universities, antiquity of, 25, 38, 76
Ussher, Archbp. James, 112, 113

Vergil, Polydore, 13, 38, 41–2, 48, 68–70, 78, 79ff
Verstegan, Richard, 116ff
Villiers, George, Duke of Buckingham, 166.
Vincent, Augustine, 155, 157
Virunnius, Ponticus, 57, 58
Vitruvius, 121
Vowell, *see* Hooker, John

Warner, William, 40, 44
Watson, Christopher, 116
Weever, John, 167
Wedale, 91
Westcote, Thomas, 157
Whear, Digory, 110
Whethamstede, Abbot John, 34
White, John, 123
White, Richard, 73ff
Whitelock, Sir Bulstrode, 101
William of Malmesbury, 15, 16, 134
William of Newburgh, 12, 87, 134, 136
William of Worcester, 29ff, 54
Windsor, carvings and glass, 22
Wyat, Sir Thomas, 59, 61
Wynne, William, 157
Wolfe, Rene, 166
Wotton, Nicholas, 106
Wood, Anthony, 167